When the Skies Rained Freedom

A Novel

ANNETTE OPPENLANDER

First published by Annette Oppenlander, 2023
Averesch 93, 48683 Ahaus, Germany
First Edition
Visit the author's website at: www.annetteoppenlander.com
Text copyright: Annette Oppenlander 2023
ISBN: 978-3-948100-45-2 eBook
ISBN: 978-3-948100-46-9 Paperback

Editing: Cecily Blench, The History Quill
Design: http://www.fiverr.com/akira007

DEDICATION

To the people of Berlin, who showed resilience beyond words, who continued to believe in freedom when all hope seemed to be lost. And to the brave men and women of the airlift, who set out to do the impossible—and succeeded.

ALSO BY ANNETTE OPPENLANDER

English
A Different Truth (Historical Mystery, Vietnam War Era)
Escape From the Past Trilogy (Time-travel Adventure)
47 Days: How Two Teen Boys Defied the Third Reich (Novelette)
Everything We Lose: A Civil War Novel of Hope, Courage and
Redemption
Surviving the Fatherland (WWII Biographical Novel)
Where the Night Never Ends: A Prohibition Era Novel
Boys No More (WWII Collection)
When They Made Us Leave (WWII Historical Novel)
A Lightness in My Soul: Inspired by a True Story (WWII Novella)
The Scent of a Storm (WWII Historical Novel)
So Close to Heaven (Napoleon Wars Biographical Novel)

German
Vaterland, wo bist Du? Roman nach einer wahren Geschichte (2.
Weltkrieg biografischer
Roman)
Erzwungene Wege: Historischer Roman (2. Weltkrieg
Kinderlandverschickung)
47 Tage (2. Weltkrieg Novelle)
Immer der Fremdling: Die Rache des Grafen (Zeitreise Mittelalter)
Bis uns nichts mehr bleibt (Amerikanischer Bürgerkrieg)
Erfolgreich(e) historische Romane schreiben: Wie man Leser in die
Vergangenheit entführt
Leicht wie meine Seele (2. Weltkrieg Novelle)
Als Deutschlands Jungen ihre Jugend verloren (Sammlung)
Endlos ist die Nacht (amerikanische Prohibition)
Ewig währt der Sturm (2. Weltkrieg Flucht und Vertreibung)
Das Kreuz des Himmels (Napoleon Kriege biografischer Roman)
Zwei Handvoll Freiheit (2. Weltkrieg/Berliner Luftbrücke)

ACKNOWLEDGMENTS

In the summer of 2022, I attended a weeklong health retreat. Next to me at the group table sat an older lady, Loni Tiemann, who despite her advanced age was very lively. It turned out that she'd not only endured World War II and its aftermath in Berlin, she'd also witnessed the airlift as a fourteen-year-old girl. In later years, she'd met Gail Halvorsen, the famous Candy Bomber, also called *Uncle Wiggly Wings*, who'd shared two gum sticks with a bunch of German children, and thus kicked off a huge goodwill campaign, dropping chocolate and gum via small parachutes to Berlin's kids. Loni not only graciously agreed to share her vast collection of books and documents about the airlift, she also shared her sometimes painful memories.
Thank you!

"People of the world, look upon this city!" Ernst Reuter, Mayor of Berlin, September 9, 1948

"Today...a new chapter in the varied history of our people commences: Today, after the signing and declaration of the Basic Law, the Federal Republic of Germany will enter history." Konrad Adenauer, May 23, 1949

INTRODUCTION

When Germany surrendered on May 8, 1945, ending World War II in Europe, Berlin lay in ruins. As the capital and the site of Hitler's headquarters, the city had experienced more than three hundred air attacks, more than any other German town. British and American planes had dropped mines and bombs, creating a moonscape of eleven square miles. Russia's Red Army spent the month of April 1945 finishing off what was left. In street, door-to-door and room-to-room fights, another 190,000 people died, many of them civilians. British pilots flying over the city commented that it was unthinkable that anybody *down there*—in the field of ruins and rubble—survived.

But they did. While the four Allies—the US, Britain, France and the Soviet Union—divided up Germany and Berlin into four parts, nearly three million Berliners crept around basements and broken-apart buildings, scraping for food and firewood. Since Berlin lay like an island in the middle of the Stalin-governed eastern portion, the city, divided into four parts (sectors) as well, also hosted three western Allies.

When these western Allies introduced the new German currency, the Deutsche Mark (DM) on June 20, 1948, Stalin grew so incensed, he decided to take all of Berlin for himself, planning to annex the remainder of Germany at a convenient time later. On June 24, 1948, all rail, water, and road access to West Berlin was cut off.

Because the Soviets had confirmed only the three air corridors into Berlin's western sectors in writing—all other access agreements had been verbal—those air corridors were the only way to connect these sectors with the western world. Even before the blockade began, most West Germans and many western countries did not believe it would be possible to maintain a western presence in Berlin.

It was just a matter of time before Stalin would take over and force two million West Berliners under his rule…

LOTTE

How fragile life is. Snuffed out in an instant, erased by the millions—the essence of war. Oh, how I hate it, that faceless, cruel war that has taken everything I hold dear. And yet, in its aftermath, when it was finally over, I rose from the rubble along with my fellow Berliners, to live and fight another hour, another day—a lifetime.

Berlin, September 1948
I look up as the sky darkens with another low-flying plane. American cargo planes, large and seemingly too heavy to remain in the air, colossal hunks of steel, are here to save us. They carry everything from sugar to dried potatoes to oil and coal, everything to supply the three western-occupied sectors of Berlin.

The air is balmy, a mild day with lots of sunshine, a last remnant of summer, yet the droning sounds above send shivers up my back like icy gusts in winter. It has been nearly three and a half years since Berlin saw its last bomb attacks—attacks that lasted for years and many of us survived only by a miracle, hiding in basements among the wreckage.

The air vibrates as another plane passes overhead. My hand slides into the pocket of my dress to find the brass button, wrapped in my father's handkerchief. I run a forefinger over its surface and though I cannot see it, I could draw the eagle's wings in the dark. *Maybe he is up there right now, flying overhead.* Would I know, would the button I'm carrying somehow submit a signal, some invisible wave? *Nonsense,* I scold myself. *Why do I bother?*

I remember my task and continue toward the reopened grocery store on Felix Street to pick up rations. For nine years now we have been receiving food with ration cards. First it was Hitler who forced us to abandon normal life and threw us into an abyss of destruction and shame. Once the war ended, the Russians, then the Americans continued with the ration system.

Since Stalin blocked all roads and railways three months ago, Berlin is in the middle of a new crisis. Stalin wants to starve us out and force the Allies to leave the city, so he can take over all of Berlin, another dictator to bend us under his will.

But the Americans, British and French are putting up a fight— for us. They have vowed to support us from the air, feed two million Berliners by flying everything in. I doubt it can be done. Already the little we have is getting sparser.

Mountains of rubble line the path, where houses and homes of millions used to be. Mile after mile there is nothing but ruins, burned-out cars, lying on their side like giant insects, bomb craters and incinerated trees, stretching their blackened limbs into the sky. Even now, three years after the war ended, the air is filled with dust and a faint burnt smell. Remnants of walls, with gaping holes where windows used to be, rise up like broken teeth. How can this city ever recover?

My feet hurt when I return to our place. My shoes are worn, my big toes have poked holes into the tips, the soles so thin, I feel every stone underneath.

The bag I carry is far too light to contain enough food for ten days.

"Mama, I'm back." Several pairs of eyes look at me as I enter— three families share one room—only Mama seems too busy to register my appearance. She hums as she hunches over a torn shirt that used to belong to my father. "Will you help me cook dinner?"

I gently take the shirt from my mother's hands and show her the contents of my bag. "Here, look, we've got flour and canned meat."

Mama looks at me as if I've been away for weeks, her eyes carry that familiar mix of fear and anxiety. "Where have you been? I didn't know, I thought—"

I grab Mama's hands. "It's all right. Will you help me make a soup?"

"You work too much, Lotte, your father should be back any

moment. He'll know what to do." Her gaze flits to Oma Tilly, who shares our space with her granddaughter Margo. Tilly hardly reaches to my shoulder and must be in her late sixties, but she is full of energy. On the other side of the blanket separating us from our neighbors lives Albert, a former baker, who lost his right hand from a misguided grenade and now mostly sits, staring out the only window, and his thirteen-year-old son, Karl, who does his best to take care of him.

We share a single stove/oven for cooking and heat, and I try to ignore the sounds and conversations that so easily filter through the room.

Where families with parents and children, brothers, grandparents, aunts and uncles used to live, we now consist of remnants and broken pieces that refuse to be mended.

Worse than having to share is the fact that Stalin has also cut Berlin's water and power lines. Isn't it enough that we hardly have anything to continue living? Isn't it enough that Hitler sent away my father and robbed Fritz of his brain, must Stalin take what little is left?

Suddenly, I can't breathe. Mama looks up, confused, as I pull on my shoes and hang the canvas bag over my shoulder. I never leave without it because occasionally I come across something to take home or trade on the black market. The rubble still holds many surprises, a dented pot without a lid, a piece of wood to burn— maybe a leg from a former chair, floorboard, or shelf.

With a "I'll be back soon," I rush past Oma Tilly, who throws me a concerned glance, through the grimy corridor that gapes open at the end, down the stairs, some of them crumbling and uneven.

Only when I feel the wind on my damp forehead do I slow. Despite the late hour, the streets are filled with people: two women in their best dresses, likely the only ones they own, arms linked, whispering to each other, three boys no older than ten, their faces smudged, their knees stained from searching the ruins, an old man with permanently bent shoulders, clutching a cloth bag as if it contained a treasure.

I wander past, caught in my own world, trapped. On Volkmar Street, I pass by a wall plastered with notices, organized in lost and found, searching for rooms, searching for men, women and children. That last section is the largest—millions of people are still missing. I stand there, scanning the desperate calls: *Who has seen Willibald Schulz?*

… I'm searching for Maria Frank, last seen on March 21, 1945 in Berlin Kreuzberg. Some notices have black and white photos, now faded and shadowy, showing men in uniform, children in Sunday dresses. The words blur and dance.

Only when I hear the excited voices of two girls do I look up. They can't be more than fifteen, both in pigtails and skirts that are too short. I am about to pass them, when I notice the US flag printed on a piece of paper the girls are studying.

"Help wanted," it says in bold black letters. "Adult men and women, interested in working for the airlift, may report to Tempelhof Airport. Payment in Deutsche Marks, one warm meal. US commandant, American Sector."

Just north of here, American planes land every few minutes to deliver lifesaving supplies. *He may be there*, the voice in my head whispers. As if to mock me, my hand slides into the pocket, squeezes the rounded metal of the button. Normally, it calms me, but now it feels hot, as if it's been dropped into the fire.

Book I: May 1945 – February 1946

CHAPTER ONE

Berlin, May 1945

It is over. Finally, this insanity of a war has come to an end—Berlin has surrendered. Mama smiles at me and then gives me a rare hug. Through the blouse I feel her shoulder bones, as pronounced as mine.

Both of us have tears in our eyes, just like the two older sisters who we are sharing a coal cellar with. We all look at each other, at once relieved the bombs have finally stopped, at the same time unsure of what comes next.

"Maybe we should look for a better place to stay," I offer, keeping to myself that I'm also hoping to find more food.

"But we have a bed here." Mama nods at the cot we share. "It may be worse somewhere else."

"Then I'll head out to scrounge." Scrounging is a general term that encompasses everything from stumbling upon a shredded wool blanket, a kitchen utensil or piece of wood to stealing outright. If it's of any value and not nailed down, if nobody is looking, I'm taking it. That is the way everyone lives now. If you don't, you will likely perish.

"Be careful," Mama says. Even the old sisters mumble a warning.

We can't stay hidden forever, I want to say, but all I do is nod and move through the broken door of our hideout up a few crumbling stairs, half buried under bricks, to the outside.

The air is mild this morning as I take off toward the south. There is no road, just a dusty path across ruins and rubble, which forces me to move slowly and watch every step. Stray a little and I may break through a hole and land in some basement, may be buried forever. Still, I cherish the quiet… no planes, no sounds of falling bombs, just human voices here and there—people going about their business.

It does feel like Zero Hour, what the world coined as the end of the war and the beginning of something new. What exactly I don't know, yet I can't deny the inkling of hope.

A few hundred yards south, I come across a fresh bombsite; the chances of finding things are higher here, but it is also more dangerous to climb around the shifting rocks and mortar. Bizarrely twisted wood threatens with splinters, glass shards cut hands, or worse… a body or what is left of it lies beneath.

After the final battle for Berlin last month, when nearly 200,000 people lost their lives, there are corpses everywhere. Many are buried and likely will remain in their stony graves for years. Countless times I have walked past lined-up bodies, hastily covered in bits of bedding or towels, or sometimes just with a pillowcase over their heads, my hand firmly clasping Mama's, although at twenty, I'm far too old for such a childish display.

I have just begun to pick up rocks to search underneath, when from the corner of one eye, I see two women hurry past. Everyone knows to be careful, but these two are stumbling along as quickly as they can muster. That's when I hear it: men yelling, the rat-tat of gun shots, rough laughter—Russian soldiers. Drunk on vodka and victory, they have been swarming the city in search of entertainment. Women. Rumor has it, the Red Army isn't too selective, they take women of all ages.

Adrenaline rushes through me, weakens my knees as I crouch low. But there is no place to hide on this mountain of debris. I scramble higher, aware that the ground beneath can shift at any moment, not only to bury me, but to give me away.

The men shout again, deep voices, threatening even in laughter. They likely have their eyes on their prey. I continue climbing, my focus on a still standing chimney.

Faster, I must move faster.

Another shot rings out. Somewhere beyond the broken walls, a woman cries out. "No, please, no."

Any second the men will pass by below. If they look up and to the left, they'll see me.

In a last effort, I grab the rough edges of the chimney, hoist myself up behind it. Palms bleeding, I crouch and breathe shallowly, while I listen, my heart beating in my neck. Heavy boots stomp past, more shots are fired. I peek around the chimney, see that one of the two women has stumbled and fallen.

The men have caught up to her, hoist her to her feet and take her behind a half-wall. Even without seeing it, I know what is happening. It is strangely quiet now and I wonder if the woman is still alive. Maybe it would be better to die than live with the shame.

I think of Mama in the cellar and hope she'll stay well hidden.

I don't know when I arrive home. It's much later than I planned, but the Russians frightened me so deeply, I remained behind that chimney for an hour. Worse is that they crisscross the city in hordes, and it is impossible to know where they will show up next.

"We should move south," I say as soon as I drop the three pieces of salvaged floor planks to the ground. I also found two cans without labels, a clump of dandelions and two onions that grew behind the walls of a former garden. Surely it belonged to someone, but I have grown a thicker skin when it comes to stealing.

"Why are you so late?" Mama asks as if she hasn't heard me. "I was worried."

"Had to hide." In my mind, I see the young women running, hear the men hollering. I force a smile. "I'm here now. Let's see what's inside these cans. I'll make a fire."

The chimney in the corner has a hole in it and is luckily unclogged, so we use it for cooking and heating. Mama fixes meals in an old cook pot without handles. Cans are another matter. We don't have knives or can openers. In the fall of 1944, we hid in a bunker during one of the air raids and by the time we emerged, our apartment had evaporated with everything inside.

I use a nail and a piece of brick to poke holes into the top of the first can. After ten minutes we pour the contents, green peas, into the pot to join the onions. Mama, always afraid we will run out of food, has hidden the second can.

"Where are the sisters?" I ask as we sit down.

"They left to look for a cousin in Neukölln, hoping they can move in. If not, they want to return here."

I take a deep breath. "We need to move as well, Mama. It's unsafe. The Russians are roaming."

"But we are in the American sector."

"Except the Americans aren't here. At least not yet."

"Where would we go?"

"South, Mama, just a bit farther, away from downtown. Hopefully, we'll find a better place." *Away from the Russians*, I want to say, but all I do is smile.

"I was just hoping to stay near our home, you know, in case your father returns." Mama's eyes glitter as she takes a spoonful from the pot. We are careful to eat slowly and one at a time to stretch out our meal.

"We'll leave a note on a wall nearby, for when he returns." I keep my voice light, for Mama's sake, but also for mine. My father has been gone for five years, my fiancé Fritz for two. The last field post we received from Papa was in October of last year, shortly before we lost our apartment. He'd been in Courland near the Baltic Sea. Who knows where he is now? If he is even alive? I don't know where Fritz is either. His last note arrived last August.

By the time we leave, it is late afternoon. Each of us carries a bundle with a few kitchen tools we have organized along the way and a dented zinc bucket, inside of which nestles the pot with the remaining can, one shriveled carrot and a tiny jar of face cream. We won't eat again tonight, though my stomach already snarls. I have gotten fairly good at ignoring the rumbles—to a point. The main thing when looking for a new place, aside from a suitable roof, ideally with a door, is the availability of water. After the winter and spring bombings, even half-way intact apartments have neither electricity nor water. The only places we find water are at the street pumps sprinkled throughout the city. Usually, they are easy to spot because lines of people snake in front of them at all hours.

I catch myself looking over my shoulder, scanning the people clambering through the wreckage. Most of them don't look up, intent on keeping their footing, their thoughts probably on the task of finding another meal. They are like us, lost souls trying to make sense of their lives that are no longer. Yet I am also relieved about the silence. I tell myself that I have nothing to fear, even if this new reality carries its own danger.

Suddenly, there is movement on the street. A girl comes running our way, gesticulating. "Ivan is coming."

Sure enough, several men in Russian uniform are walking toward us. It's hard to know if they're searching for German soldiers or Hitler Youth boys, anyone with a uniform or a good time with the next woman who takes their fancy.

I pull Mama by the sleeve and together, we follow the girl into a street, clamber across the rubble that slips beneath our feet.

"Over here," she says, waving, as she disappears into an opening in a former villa. The hole is near the ground, some kind of basement. We follow as fast we can, scrape our knees and find ourselves in an empty coal cellar, where several children and a mother and baby have also taken cover.

Outside shots are fired… moving closer. Rough voices holler *uraeh*, *uraeh*, glass shatters when they throw away empty vodka bottles. I sense the other women's terror, feel Mama tremble next to me. What will these men do to us, if they find us?

Steps crunch outside as we press ourselves to the ground. There is no escape now, we are trapped like mice in a cage. The steps grow louder. They must've seen our weak attempt to try to escape.

The room darkens as a Russian pokes his rifle through the opening, yells, "Nazis outside now!" in bad German.

Surely he can see there aren't any. He climbs inside, shouts at the top of his lungs as he towers over us, weapon pointed at our heads. I feel Mama and the girl from earlier next to me as the breath I draw rattles the air. Is this our last moment, is he going to throw a grenade or just execute us? I no longer feel my body or the icy floor that reeks of coal dust. My entire being consists of ears only, trying to guess what the man will do.

In the corner next to us, a little girl whimpers. That is obviously too much for Mama, because she clambers to her knees, then stands up and embraces the children, pulls me to her side, mumbling, "I'm not dying on the ground." That's how we stand and stare at the Russian man, who can't be much older than eighteen. He doesn't even have beard hairs and his eyes are the light blue of the sky outside.

How long we stand there, I don't know. Only that at some point, Mama shouts, "Why don't you shoot, then? Shoot!"

He doesn't, just watches us and finally lowers his rifle. Maybe he thinks we've lost our minds, maybe we have.

I don't know what will happen to the children, the other girl, or the mother with the baby. That's what this war has gotten to. We just barely have enough energy to keep ourselves going. After the man leaves, we crawl back outside and continue on our way. Several times, I look at Mama, who keeps her eyes straight. Today, I've seen a new side of her.

Holding hands, we continue south. Even if there are no glass windows left, more buildings are somewhat intact the farther we come, which gives me hope. But from the looks of them, all are occupied. What are the chances of finding an empty apartment anywhere in Berlin? Maybe Mama was right. At least we had the cellar, knew our way around. We pass by a butcher shop with an open truck parked in front. Three men are carrying half sides of beef inside, the air is filled with the odor of smoked meat on the verge of spoiling and clouds of swirling black flies, their buzz loud in my ears. They follow the men into the shop as if it's the most natural thing in the world. Posters on a house wall warn of dysentery, urge us to boil our water and cook our meat thoroughly, to bury our waste deep. *How deep*, I want to ask. Not deep enough for the millions of rats crawling through the rubble.

"Wait here," I say every so often, before I take off, checking a building. Each time I return. By now I'm ready to go back to our hole, but it is too late to get there during daylight. It is way too dangerous to be out in the dark.

"Let's ask over there," Mama says. She points at the dozens of women and children waiting by a water pump.

While Mama gets in line, I address the first woman I see. "Do you know of a place to stay?"

She simply shakes her head, her eyes empty, her face powdered with dust. I continue down the line, repeating my question over and over. Most of the women don't even look up.

"We need a place to stay," I try again. The girl I'm addressing has to be my age, she looks a bit cleaner than the rest and carries two buckets. Gray eyes meet mine, not gray like the sky, but a light gray with a tinge of blue. In them lies a glint of something, a tiny spark ready to ignite.

"Who is *we*?" Her voice is surprisingly deep, almost manly, and in stark contrast to her delicate shape, the small hips and hazelnut-colored hair, swept upward into a shawl. She appears quite clean, even her hands are free of dirt. Unlike me; I look like I crawled from a dank hole. My palms are black and sticky with coal dust, my clothes stained.

"My mother and me." It comes out too fast, almost defiant, but the girl doesn't seem to be offended. She looks at me, apparently waiting for more. "We're in a broken-apart cellar… too dangerous with all the Russian soldiers."

To my surprise, the girl nods. "Get your water, I will wait for you."

"Did you find a place?" Mama asks when I join her in the line.

I shrug. "Not sure." To her credit, Mama remains silent and when we fill our bucket fifteen minutes later, I almost expect not to see the girl. But there she is, perky nose and all. And utterly unexpectedly, I smile when our eyes meet. She gives me a tiny nod, swivels on her heels and heads down the street.

"Where are we going?" Mama pants. She's been holed up so long, even walking tires her.

I say nothing, just keep my gaze on the back of the girl. She picks her way carefully, lightly, more like a dancer, past a broken-down Wehrmacht truck and a Russian tank that lie there like colossal hunks of steel.

Abruptly she comes to a halt and says, "Over there, the brown building."

Again, she takes off, faster now despite the buckets of water, as we are struggling to keep up. All the while I keep staring at the apartment building that appears somewhat unscathed among the ruins. Next door the walls are broken open to reveal a dining table, two chairs, a tub and a torn-apart bed. The floors above consist of rubble. Above that hangs a leaden sky.

At the main door, its former glass inserts are covered by a patchwork of wood and tarpaper, the girl waits once more. She carefully unlocks the door and lets us enter. I shake my head. When have I last been in a building that had real doors?

We are heading to the second floor, where the girl once again unlocks a door. A measured woof greets us and the next moment Mama and I are being sniffed by a white and beige mutt that reminds me of a hairdo gone wrong. It is covered in curls and fuzz, and I want to hug it on the spot.

"This is Hugo," the girl says. "I'm Margret, Meg."

We introduce ourselves while I try to figure out Meg's motive in taking us home. Meanwhile she opens the door to the kitchen where she sets down her buckets, then a sitting room, each of them looking like no war has ever reached inside: a couch, two stuffed chairs, a table and sideboard, each neatly placed and free of dust—only the windows are boarded up, no house in Berlin has glass—before she stops at a third door.

"This is your room, if you want it. Provided you help me find food, collect water for us and take Hugo on occasional walks. Money or cigarettes are good, of course, but I doubt you have either."

"Whatever you need, thank you," I hurry.

"Where are your parents?" Mama asks.

Meg throws her a quick glance, then looks away while her fingers get tangled in Hugo's coat. "Both dead. Father fell in Stalingrad. Mother got into a bomb blast during an excursion." When she looks up, her eyes shine. "Where is your father?"

I shrug. "We don't know where Papa is, or Fritz… my fiancé."

Meg says nothing. There is nothing to say. Most of us are waiting and wondering about the men who left years ago—whether they'll return and in what state. But in the end what matters most is to find the next meal and survive another day.

I'm in heaven. Last night I slept in a real bed with pillows and a comforter. It's a tiny room with an even smaller window, the bed just large enough for two adults sleeping sideways. Yet it is a place above ground, clean and away from prying Russian soldiers. Still in awe, I traipse into the kitchen, where Meg heats water on a stove.

"I've got a bit of wood," I say. "Thank you for the bed."

Meg turns to me, her expression grim. "Don't thank me constantly."

"I just thought—"

"Look, I picked you off the street because you needed a place. We've got to take in people anyway. But that doesn't make us friends." She rushes past me, while I stand there open-mouthed.

Deep in thought, I place the wood I'd collected yesterday next to the stove.

"What a nice bed," Mama says, entering the kitchen. She looks better than in days. Last night, we washed and hung up our clothes to dry. What an amazing feeling to have clean skin and a dress that is no longer coated with filth.

"Just don't tell Meg. She's mad I thanked her again." Now that I think about it, I'm angry.

Mama wraps an arm around my shoulder. "Give it time. You never know what she's going through. Hopefully, she'll let us stay for a while." She smiles at me. "Just think, no Russians."

So true. Up here in this apartment, we are away from any threats roaming around outside. I return Mama's smile. She is right, Meg can be grumpy all she wants, the main thing is we're safe.

CHAPTER TWO

Nearly two months have passed. Thousands of women, including the three of us, have been ordered to help clear Berlin's streets of rubble. It has become a lot easier to travel because we can now walk again normally while Russian trucks and tanks pass by us at all hours. Next to the cleared roads, though, the nightmare continues, the magnitude of this destruction is indescribable, impossible to ever rebuild. At the same time, I am anxious to do whatever it takes to forge a new life. After all, I don't have to fear bombs or the next crazy order from a dictator. Rumor has it American troops will arrive soon to take over their sector, and I wonder if that will change anything.

After cleaning and stacking bricks all day in exchange for a loaf of bread, Meg, Mama and I take off to search for additional supplies, and wood or anything else worth trading. Some days, I find nothing, on others I am lucky. Like today, when I find a copper sculpture of a horse and rider in a crevice beneath a floorboard. Heavy and beautiful, the statue fits easily into the crook of my elbow. I wrap an old rag around it and hurry home, intending to show it to Mama and Meg. Most of all, I look forward to washing off the grime from the hot summer day.

An American jeep passes me, then another, followed by several trucks. A couple of times I hear whistles, but I keep my head low. First the Russians, now the Americans. I hurry faster, hope to leave those men behind me.

But along the road near Meg's home, three more jeeps park.

Americans in uniform are on foot, climbing across the rubble. Compared to the Russian soldiers, these men are clean and well dressed, and their eyes focused. What in the world are they looking for?

Intent on avoiding trouble, I rush past them toward Meg's place.

"You, Fräulein. Wait." The voice of the man is deep and energetic, carries authority despite its youth, the voice of the enemy who won the war.

I stop in my tracks and slowly turn. A man in a khaki-brown uniform, no older than twenty-five, clean-shaven, with a square chin and a bit of chocolate-brown hair showing under the cap, marches towards me. He smiles ever so slightly, before he tips his hat.

"You live here?" he asks in bad German.

What's it to you, I want to say. Instead, I nod.

"Please show me."

"Show you what?" This time our eyes meet and though his are shadowed beneath the cap, I know they're the bluish gray of Lake Constance, where Papa took us on a vacation a hundred years ago… When life had been constant, with a full pantry and routines of school and home life I'd considered boring.

"Your home, I need to see it," the soldier says, pulling me back to the present.

I want to ask why, but all of a sudden, I'm afraid. Will he drag me into a dark corner, ask his friends to join him. But the man seems all business and, despite his request, polite.

I dig among the rubble to find the spot with the hidden key and when I open the door, he follows me inside.

After redepositing the key, I climb the stairs, open the inside door with another key that sits beneath a loose floor tile.

The man just follows me inside, marches from room to room while I stand there in the hallway, the statue still in my arm. Why aren't Mama and Meg home yet? I longingly stare at the entry door while the stranger inspects every corner.

"You live here alone?"

I study the tall figure, the clean uniform and black shoes that have retained their shine despite the dust that blankets Berlin.

"This is my friend's place, my mother and I are guests."

He nods, massages his forehead with immaculate fingers. "It's nice." There is the smile but again it fades immediately.

"We will need to take over your apartment."

As the words *take over* and *apartment* whirl through my head, searing heat knots my throat. This man is going to steal our home? It wasn't enough that they destroyed everything, now they want what is left. The knot bursts as I shout and cry at the same time. "You can't do that."

"I am sorry," he says, avoiding my gaze. "We don't have enough places to stay. Shouldn't be for long."

"So you just march in and take the little we have left?" My voice sounds all shrill and ugly. I don't care.

"What is going on?" Meg asks as Hugo woofs and sniffs around the soldier's legs. She and Mama stand in the entry door, each of them carrying a bag.

"They're confiscating your apartment," I shout.

Ignoring the dog, the American turns toward Meg. "Lieutenant Mitch Cameron. Sorry, miss, the US army is in need of additional housing."

"So you help yourself to ours," Meg says coldly. I admire her for her self-control.

Mama rushes to take the man's hand. "Surely there is something you can do."

"Where are we supposed to go?" I sob, hating myself for crying.

Lieutenant Cameron looks at me and, for an instant, his detached manner seems to disappear. He seems genuinely concerned, as he focuses on me. "I'm really sorry, it's an order from above. You're reasonably close to Tempelhof Airport."

"Can't you find someplace else?" Meg asks.

Lieutenant Cameron shrugs. "I wish I could." He pulls out pen and notebook. "Now give me your names and the address. I'll try to get you some compensation."

"How long do we have?" I say quietly as I see us walking the streets in search of another place.

"A couple of hours, no more."

The three of us scramble into the kitchen, where Meg rips open every cupboard. "Collect everything, I'll be damned if we leave our things to them."

Mama sighs. "We can't possibly carry all this. What about our comforters?"

Meg closes the door and takes our hands. "It'll be fine. I've got an idea."

Two hours later, we are settled once more. Not like before, not happily like a human being should live. No, we are back in the cellar—Meg's cellar. It's nearly pitch black down here, the air smells musty. We are burning one of the precious candles to see anything. The room, lined with empty shelves, is at the back of the house. The others are full of debris, the coal cellar filthy.

"I used to hide here during bomb alarms," Meg had said when we climbed down.

I look at Mama, who appears outwardly calm, except her eyes dart around the narrow space. Once we lay down our blankets, there won't be room to walk.

It takes us five trips to move Meg's possessions down… plates, silverware, cooking vessels, two buckets, assorted towels and blankets, clothes, pillows and framed photographs.

The Americans have arrived and are moving boxes and suitcases into the apartment. Lieutenant Cameron is one of them. Undoubtedly, he is making himself at home on Mama's and my bed.

I fight down the anger and help Meg carry a box with her mother's tablecloths. It is our last trip before she hands over the keys. "I'd rather burn them before I leave them for the Americans to soil," she says under her breath. "I've got to clear a space in front of the basement window, so we can see something. We don't have enough candles to last."

"Let me help," I say.

Like most of Berlin, the building's former garden is buried under rubble from the adjacent houses, including the basement window. We clamber to the back of the house, where bricks and mortar are piled at least six feet high.

"The window should be down here somewhere," Meg says. Already her hands and legs are covered in dust.

I grit my teeth and wrap the cloth strips tighter around my hands. "Then we'd better get to work."

CHAPTER THREE

We work all afternoon, picking up rocks and throwing them a few feet to the side. Progress is painfully slow. Because the rags keep slipping, the skin on my palms is shredded from the sharp edges of the rocks. Mama has supplied us with water and soup cooked from potato skins the Americans discarded, but by evening I am famished, my shoulders burn and my lower back throbs with the occasional sharp twinge traveling up my spine.

"It will take at least a week, maybe longer, we should ask that lieutenant for candles," I say, following Meg across the rocks.

"Too bad he doesn't help. Doesn't want to dirty his fancy uniform."

"We could mention it."

Meg stops and faces me. "What, the uniform?"

I laugh, a strange sound I haven't heard in a long time. The next moment, the ground beneath me gives and I slip into a crack. Searing pain shoots up my leg as it hits something beneath.

Worse, I'm stuck. Half of me is buried beneath the rubble. Around me, the ground shifts.

Meg, who is only a few feet away, cries, "Damn!"

I lift a hand that is caked with bloodied dust. "Don't come closer."

Meg swallows, then nods. "I'll be right back."

I try to fight down my terror. Something down there is terribly wrong. My leg screams and something warm runs into my shoes. More blood, no doubt. Strangely, I can't feel any ground beneath my feet. Twice I try to push up, but each time more rocks slide past me into the hole. If I don't watch, I'll fall in farther, maybe disappear. The memory of the coal cellar where the Russian held us at gunpoint returns. My throat tightens as I try to get air into my lungs. I can't be down in a hole.

Above me the evening sky burns orange in glorious brightness. *Think of something else*, my mind urges. *Anything but the throbbing pain beneath, and the gaping void wanting to swallow me.*

Before my closed eyes appears Lieutenant Cameron. How clean he is, how put together. I wonder what he does for the army.

And then he really *is* there. Cameron and two other soldiers are following Meg across the rubble. One of them calls for a rope, the lieutenant puts a hand on Meg's forearm to make her wait.

"Fräulein, Lotte, try not to move. We are getting you out."

As I nod numbly and try not to cry again, the back of my mind registers that he remembers my name. The second soldier hands Lieutenant Cameron a five-foot metal rod which he uses to poke the soil in front of him. Slowly, he edges closer.

I try to be still, but the pain in my leg is not only excruciating, it's radiating upward farther and farther, through the hip into my ribcage. I seem to consist of nothing but nerves. Nerves that are on fire with hot and angry tentacles. Worse is how helpless I feel and embarrassed to be pinned down like a slaughtered pig.

"Almost there," the lieutenant says. I no longer see the others, just the hulking figure of the American. "I'm Mitch, by the way." He catches a rope from somewhere and slowly lowers himself to his knees. "Can you lift one arm, just one?"

Again, I nod. No words form in my head, it's a balloon full of air. I lift my right arm as Mitch forms a lasso and throws it in a quick move over my head and arm.

"Now take down that arm and see if you can lift the other through the rope." I do as I'm told, pieces of mortar slide toward me and disappear.

Mitch smiles encouragingly. "Very good. I'm going to tighten the rope, so you won't slide any further."

I watch his immaculate hands grip the rope tightly, feel it close around my ribs. "I'll move backwards now, just relax, okay?"

"Okay."

As Mitch straightens, I notice four or five other soldiers behind him. Meg and Mama are also there. He calls some command and two of the men grip the rope.

Together they pull while Mitch tries to direct the rope upward. That's the last I see because the pain in my leg explodes once more. It is all I can think of. Mortar and brick pieces slide past me as I'm lifted from the void.

I don't want to look, but I have to know what is going on with my leg. My shoes and socks are soaked with slimy red, but the real problem is the area beneath my knee. My entire shin is a bloody oozing mess. I can't tell what is what, because of all the filth caking everything, only that the pain is cutting like razor blades.

"Lotte, look at me." Mitch's face swims above me. "We are going to lift you onto a stretcher now, okay?"

I eye the man who took my home and is saving me. How can he be my enemy and savior at the same time? A giggle rises from my throat, escapes into the evening. The sky darkens, turns black.

Mitch's face comes into focus as he hands me a bottle filled with a dark-brown liquid and two pills. "Take these with the Coke. It'll do you good." We are back in Meg's kitchen, where I lie on the floor by the boarded-up window, my leg elevated on a footstool. Everything below the knee is covered with a white bandage. Apparently, I was lucky because whatever cut me barely missed the artery. I've got several deep slashes along the shinbone and calf. Somehow the Americans have organized a doctor, who cleaned and sewed up the leg while I was passed out.

Cool sweetness enters my mouth, bubbles fizz on my tongue. "Thank you."

"What were you thinking? Don't you know how dangerous this rubble is?"

I look at the man who is sipping a yellowish liquid from a tin cup. Doesn't he realize that without searching the rubble for edibles, valuables or firewood, half of Berlin would be starving to death? "We were going to clear space in front of the basement window to have light down there. Candles are hard to find, and it's nearly pitch black in the cellar."

Mitch takes a sip, shakes his head. "It's our fault, you wouldn't have gone there had we not taken over your place."

"Maybe." Despite the Coke, I feel sleepy. "I'd better go. Mama and Meg will—"

Mitch rises and extends an arm. "Since I can't have you sleep up here, I will at least help you down."

As I put weight on my foot, a groan escapes me. The pounding increases, the pillow on the stool dances. Mitch slings an arm around my waist and helps me to the door.

Showing the way with a flashlight, we descend the stairs one by one. The cellar is silent—it must be late. Hugo growls softly while Meg and Mama stir in their beds, pale faces in the semi-darkness.

In the shuffle of getting comfortable, I forget to thank Mitch for his help.

The next morning, Meg heads out with Hugo to scrounge while Mama stays with me. On the shelf rest three boxes of candles. Also magically, a piece of hard cheese, two loaves of bread and a bottle of bourbon whiskey sit next to a bottle of aspirin.

Mama serves me breakfast as I balance on the only stool. The bone deep inside my leg hammers and radiates to my hip and toes. The little room's walls are shrinking as I groan. "Let's go out," I say to distract myself.

Mama appears to be glad and helps me navigate the stairs. It's a beautiful day, so we decide to find a spot in the sun. I slump onto what is left of a wall across from the apartment building, leg stretched out, waiting for the hammering inside the bandage to fade. At least the air is fresher outside.

All morning, US soldiers come and go. As the sun creeps higher in the sky, I become uncomfortably hot. My leg aches and itches under the thick bandages.

"I need shade," I say to Mama, thinking longingly of the comfortable bed and couch we had at Meg's.

Mama wipes the sweat from her forehead with a pink handkerchief she's owned as long as I remember. "Let me take you back inside."

As we cross the street, a truck arrives. A dozen civilian men with axes, shovels and buckets exit and disappear behind the house.

Mama and I look at each other, then follow them.

But we don't get very far. One of the Americans who helped Mitch yesterday steps into our way. "Sorry, too dangerous."

I peek past him, hoping to catch a glimpse of Mitch. "The doctor will stop by this evening. Come up around six," the man says.

I nod, suddenly looking forward to visiting the apartment.

Meg, who returns in the afternoon with additional bread and a can of mystery fat, helps me upstairs.

Dr. Rupert, as clean-shaven and businesslike as the rest of the men, asks me into the kitchen, where he undoes the bandage and inspects my leg. He is nearly bald, with golden spectacles which he now lowers to within five inches of my skin. At last, he wraps my leg with clean bandages and hands me a box of pills.

"Sulfonamide, take two a day with lots of water. Will keep the infection out."

Without another word, he leaves. I hobble to the hallway and peek into the living room, where two servicemen are reading papers and drinking whiskey.

"Excuse me, I'm looking for Mitch," I say in bad English.

One of the men looks up, dark eyes scrutinize me from top to bottom, his gaze like a slimy insect on my skin. He takes a sip from his glass and grins. "He's returned to Frankfurt."

My instinct tells me to leave, instead I hear myself ask, "What's in Frankfurt?"

"*US airbase, dear,*" he shouts as if I'm deaf. "Mitch is flying cargo." The man jumps from the couch and approaches. "You're welcome to stay, we could use a little entertainment," he says, standing so close, I smell the drink on his lips. His friend chuckles and says something I can't understand. "I'm Greg, by the way." He extends a hand which I reluctantly shake.

Again, my gut sends a warning. "I'd better go."

With a mumbled, "Bye," I turn away, relieved Greg returns to the couch. From the middle of my chest rises a feeling of unrest. Is it disappointment? Nonsense. Why should he tell me about his job or even say goodbye when I didn't even thank him last night?

CHAPTER FOUR

Meg, Mama, and I are struggling to fit into the cellar. Even if the men have cleared the debris from the back window, so that daylight filters through the metal rods and we get fresh air, the mustiness of the stone walls and the tiny space are closing in on me. There is no access to a chimney, which means we can't cook or heat. Any fire has to be made outside. All we can hope for is to find a different room before winter or that the Americans vacate.

Both are unlikely, because the Allies are now governing Berlin and the rest of Germany. Churchill, Stalin and Truman are meeting less than twenty miles from here in Potsdam to decide about the fate of our country. In a way, I'm thankful they're here because what Hitler left, that pile of smoking rubble that used to be an orderly country, needs all the help it can get. We're rudderless now, hoping to be saved despite the horror of what Germans and the Third Reich did to the world, to Jews and minorities, the infirm and disabled. I'm not sure we deserve it.

My leg is healing slowly, making walking a chore. Most days, I sit outside, watching the street, watching the coming and going of the Americans. Against my better judgment, I focus on every arriving car, try to guess who is sitting inside. Greg emerges, squints against the sun, then sneers at me when he sees me staring.

"How's the leg?" he shouts from across the street.

"Fine."

Please don't come over here. But the man obviously doesn't care about my scowl because he strides across the dusty road and stops in front of me. "Really? You look like three days of rain."

None of your business. "I'm fine," I say aloud, trying to peek past the man who stands too close. He's even more muscular than I realized, the shirt of his uniform stretched tight across his chest.

"Say, if you like, we can go out sometime. The Brits have a club." My English isn't too firm, but I think he's asking me out. When I don't answer, he continues. "When you feel better, of course."

Trying not to show my distaste, I force a smile. "Once I'm better, I'll be busy helping my mother and friend."

"That skinny girl with the perpetual pout?"

"Yes, Meg. She's got a right to be upset, it's her place you're staying at, in case you forgot."

I don't know if he understands me, but he leans even closer, his expression a mix of glee and hostility. "I've got news for you, girl, you lost the war."

Don't I know. If I'd not be so clumsy, I'd walk off. But even getting on my feet takes time, and I'm not running from anybody for a while. Greg is obviously not done, pointing a forefinger at my chest. "You're going to do what *we* want. No more hiding behind a strong man."

"I'm not hiding, I'm glad it's over. He was a monster."

"With lots of helpers."

I push myself up with the stick Meg organized for me, trying to keep my gaze on him. "I didn't and neither did my mother, but I get what you're saying." We're at eye level now, his face close. "That doesn't give you the right to harass me."

Greg laughs and raises both hands, palms out. "Aren't you a sensitive one." He swivels on his heels and marches toward our house as I hobble after him. Somehow, I know I haven't seen the last of him. Mitch would never say such things.

After a week, Dr. Rupert returns to take another look. Reluctantly, I meet him upstairs in the kitchen. From the living area, a mix of voices can be heard, accompanied by Frank Sinatra crowing "Embraceable You." Rupert yanks open the window, it's stifling hot and reeks of leftover food and alcohol.

"Let's see what we've got." Rupert carefully unwraps the filthy bandage. No matter how I try, I can't keep anything clean in this dusty town. He bends low once more, sniffs and clucks. I risk a look, afraid of what I'll see. My leg looks like something from a butcher, pink and crusted over in places.

"Will it heal?" I ask, though I'm afraid of the answer.

Keeping his focus on my leg, Rupert grumbles, then nods. "Just keep taking those pills." He pulls off his glasses for a moment and faces me. "Won't be pretty like the other, you'll have scars." He readjusts his glasses and rewraps the wound with clean bandages.

"Look who's back." Greg appears next to us, a glass of brownish liquid in his hand.

"I'm going then." Rupert, bag in hand, nods curtly and disappears while I scramble up from my chair, intent on hurrying after him.

But Greg is faster. A hand lands on my shoulder, just barely missing my breast. "Why so fast? Come and join us."

"I've got to help with dinner," I say, taking a step backwards to get away from his slimy fingers. The way to the door is cut off. "Why don't you leave me alone?" I don't even recognize the voice that bellows at the American, it's loud and forceful.

Greg seems surprised and, to my relief, steps aside. "Never mind, missy. You're in quite a mood tonight."

I slip past him, let out a deep breath. Only when I'm in the hall do I begin to tremble. Unless the doctor needs to take care of my leg, I vow not to return.

As the angry wounds of my leg turn into scars, I accompany the others to look for treasure. My success rate is rather low. I'm afraid to climb through the rubble—Rupert has warned me to stay far away—and after an hour on my feet, pain and weakness force me to take a break.

Yet I realize I've been lucky. To escape the war unscathed, to have Mama with me. And there is Mitch, who helped me when I needed it most.

If this horror of a war has taught me one thing, it is to appreciate the smallest things. A cup of *hot* tea, a smile from Mama, the blue sky free of threatening planes, the feeling of fullness after a meal, the simple quiet when walking the streets, and lying down, knowing that there won't be any more bombs.

At the same time, sharing the tiny basement is driving me crazy. When we all lie down, there is no more room to walk, hardly enough to breathe. Worst is Meg's mood. She was never very talkative, but ever since she had to move down here, she's hardly saying a word.

In the afternoon, Mama and I are heading to our former

apartment, the one we used to live in when the bombs hit, the one Fritz and Papa know as our last address.

Secretly, I wonder if they'll return and when and in what shape. I know Mama has similar thoughts, but neither of us utters a word. It's as if saying things aloud would summon some negative force.

These days I have trouble remembering Fritz's face. I remember parts of it, his long, slightly too large nose, the square forehead, his hair, brown like mine, but not the color of chestnuts, more like aged oak. When he was on leave in the summer of 1943, he asked me to marry him. At barely eighteen, I'd felt special to draw the attention of a man, especially one who seemed so grown up. As long as I can remember he'd lived across the street. But he never looked at me much other than to say hello or give a friendly nod. That is until that summer, when he returned from France.

Being away had changed him, the easy smile he'd carried had vanished, replaced by a kind of wariness. He'd just showed up at my parents' apartment and asked me to take a walk with him. And I went, half curious, half worried that I would make a fool of myself.

He'd not said much about the war, only that it was dirty, and he'd craved privacy. During the next two weeks, we walked together every day. I'd expected him to kiss me, after all, a few of the boys in school had expressed interest years ago. But Fritz never did. He seemed content to hold my hand and exchange the occasional word. Most of the time, he stared straight ahead while I racked my brain to come up with some interesting topic.

Except for school, I hadn't experienced much, so I told him about my friend, Ruth, who'd disappeared the year before, how we used to visit each other.

Every day, I asked myself if he'd return and every day, he did. After two weeks, we'd spoken little and never about things that matter. He didn't ask me to accompany him to the station, just squeezed my hand, pecked a kiss on my cheek and promised to return as soon as he got leave.

The second time he returned, the cloud surrounding him had extended to his shoulders. He walked slower, his gaze toward the ground.

"I'm back," was all he said the following summer, when one morning, he stood at the door.

I threw my arms around his neck, and that's the first time he softened a bit. He hugged me as well, even smiled. The evening before he had to return, we exchanged our first kiss. Wet and awkward, I didn't know what to think or feel. "Will you marry me, when I return?"

I'd looked into his eyes and nodded. "Of course."

Now I am not so sure. I hardly knew him, didn't understand what I felt. Is it obligation or longing? Then there is Papa, who'd been drafted in May of 1940. Initially, we'd expected him back within months, if not a year. Like Fritz, he did return, and like Fritz, he left again after a week or two.

Nowadays, all we do is wonder about their whereabouts. Some men have started appearing in the streets, often wearing the remnants of German Wehrmacht uniforms, often disfigured by scars or an eyepatch or walking with crutches because they're missing a limb.

When we search the remaining walls and nearby notice boards for signs of Fritz and Papa, we find no trace. There are pieces of paper, bits of cardboard, notices written with chalk. Our message is still there, albeit faded.

Leni and Lotte Berger alive, new address Richardstr. 19.

We add *basement* and spend another half hour reading every notice nearby. Of course, we aren't alone. All of Berlin seems to search and wait for the men in their lives.

"Where have you been?" Meg yells as soon as we enter the basement. "I've been worried, I thought you ran into trouble, got hurt."

"I thought we mentioned we'd visit our old apartment to check for messages," says Mama mildly. Judging by her reddened cheeks, she's exhausted from the dusty heat.

"You didn't say it to *me*." Meg focuses on me, her eyes still blazing. "It's your turn to make dinner."

"Fine." I abruptly turn to the water bucket, which is empty. "Maybe you could fetch water?"

Meg crosses her arms in front of her chest. "Why should I? I've been running around all day, looking for food while you hardly do a thing. It's always about your leg. It hurts, you have to rest, blah, blah. But you aren't too tired to walk to your old place."

"First of all, it took us almost all day."

"Why did you go then? It's useless anyway. All those men are long dead."

My eyes blur. "Thanks a lot for your optimism."

Mama sighs. "We are alive, girls. Nobody is bombing, nobody is shooting. If we lose hope, we may as well lie down and give up. It's what makes us human. To hope for change, cling to it, if we must."

Meg stares at Mama, then grabs the water bucket and wordlessly hurries outside.

"What has gotten into her?" I ask.

Mama gets up and puts an arm around me. "She is lonely and sad. She sees us and is reminded of her loss. Give her time."

While Mama opens a can of corned beef and cubes an onion, I shave wood slivers from a clunky piece of oak, likely the remainder of a table, for a fire starter. With the potato flakes we got from the Americans yesterday, it'll be a decent meal—if we can get the fire started and lit for long enough. It's always a guess how much wood it takes to cook a meal. We can't waste any.

I stash wood shavings and larger pieces in a bucket and climb the stairs to the front door of our house, when I collide with a man pushing open the door. My bucket clatters to the ground, wood spills across the tiles.

"Why don't you watch your step," I yell.

"My goodness, Lotte?" Mitch says, momentarily he seems to have forgotten his German. He bends low, returning the mess into the bucket.

"Hello," I say, taking in the perfect haircut and uniform that is as usual spotless—unlike my dress and shoes, which he is no doubt seeing up close. All of a sudden, I feel as grimy as I surely look.

A small smile slides over his face, then disappears. "How is your leg?"

The bandage on my leg is nearly as gray as the rubble around us, but I have no access to clean bandages. Embarrassed, I move my leg behind the other good one. "Pretty well."

Mitch has taken off his cap and holds it between his hands. "Maybe the doctor should take another look. I could call for him?"

"No need, thank you, I've caused enough trouble."

The smile is back. "No trouble."

"What about the anti-fraternization law… mixing with the locals?" Why can't I stop pushing the man's buttons?

He sighs, then nods. "It's stupid. The war is over. You've got enough to deal with." A glint of curiosity appears in his expression. "How are you managing downstairs?"

"Not too well. Meg is angry all the time. We're dreading the next winter."

Mitch looks past me to the clear blue sky, a blue so intense it almost hurts the eyes, making the utter destruction around us even more stark. "We'll hopefully be out of here by then."

And if you're not, I want to say. Instead, I pick up my bucket. "I'd better go, we need to make dinner."

Mitch tips his hat and easily, lightly, climbs the stairs, while I fight the urge to inspect his backside. I don't know why I can't ask him some smart questions or at least sound half-way intelligent. He must think I'm an imbecile, and thankless to boot. Oh, why do I even care?

With a huff, I hurry outside.

CHAPTER FIVE

After dinner I am anxious to return to the street. Not just because I hate our tight quarters, I need time to think. It's a beautiful windless evening; the dreaded dust that makes everything gritty, creeps into my mouth and onto my skin, and removes the color from your life is lying motionless.

The streets are busy—like me, Berliners are escaping their holes for a moment of bliss. If that is possible, considering that clouds of black flies have descended on certain areas and rats have multiplied. We all know what it means, yet none of us talk about it or even acknowledge the fact that there are still many bodies buried beneath the rubble.

Since my calf aches, I sit across from our house to watch the activity. Down the street a handful of boys play soccer with an empty can. Their high voices express excitement, even joy. How is it possible to feel joyful in the middle of Armageddon? And yet I feel myself smile, wishing to be back in time when my parents and I lived in a comfortable apartment, when the biggest worry I had was to finish homework or get along with my teachers.

"I have asked the doctor to stop by tomorrow morning." Cap under one arm, Mitch is crossing the street toward me.

I attempt to straighten, fail and sink back onto the rock. "Thank you." From down here, the American is impossibly tall. As if he's heard me, he lowers himself onto the ledge next to me. I turn toward him. "I never properly thanked you for rescuing me from that hole and getting the doctor."

"No need." He pauses. Up the street, boys scream with delight. "Life is tough enough. Truth is, I feel guilty for stealing your home." He looks at me, his jaw tight. "They tell us to have no mercy. Germans are the enemy and may pull out rockets at any moment." He scoffs. "While we sip whiskey upstairs, all I see are people struggling to survive on close to nothing."

"Hitler waged war on the world, killed millions. Many cheered him on, did his crimes for him."

Mitch faces me. "Did you… cheer him on?"

"I liked the camaraderie of the girls' camps, exercising and singing. I didn't comprehend the big picture, that he wanted to take over the world, kill people that didn't fit the German ideal."

A memory rises in front of me, visiting my friend Ruth, how her father always handed me a treat, a piece of licorice or fizzy powder, a cookie or, on Saturdays, a slice of raisin bread. Until the day the SS destroyed his store, tore it apart and broke the windows. Ruth had come to me crying while Mama fixed hot cocoa.

"…your father."

I stare at the immaculate man next to me. "I'm sorry, I didn't…"

"That much is obvious. I asked where your father is?"

I shrug. "I'd better go inside."

"I'm sorry, I shouldn't have asked." Mitch rises abruptly and offers me a hand. "It must be incredibly hard not to know."

As I grasp his hand, I feel self-conscious. He pulls me up, waits until I stand firmly before he lets go. Together we cross the street toward the house.

To my surprise, he clears his throat before he says, "I wonder if you'd like to go out with me. I hear they have opened cafés on the Ku'damm." I stare at the American, so cool and collected. What does he see except for a street urchin subsisting in a basement hole? I haven't even asked him about his family or how he became a pilot. He must misunderstand my hesitation and shakes his head. "Never mind. I better go."

He is already at the door when I call after him. "I'd go out with you."

He turns then and there is that half-smile again. "Tomorrow afternoon around three?"

I nod.

But as soon as he disappears, I realize I made a mistake. How can I go anywhere, looking like this? A dress coming apart at the seams, filthy with dust and thin from months of wear.

I've got to ask Meg.

"You're doing what?" Meg stares at me, open-mouthed. "How can you walk around with the enemy? Thieves who took my home." She rushes over to me, places both hands on my shoulders. "Didn't you say they're pilots? For all I know he threw his bombs right on our heads."

I bite my lip as I imagine Mitch sitting up there in the sky, dropping mines over Berlin. How can he ask me out, when he tried to destroy us all? *Maybe he didn't participate*, the voice in my head whispers. And if he did? Didn't Germany bring it upon itself? Maybe I should tell him to go to hell. Oh, I don't know what to do.

I'd intended to ask Meg for a dress. I know she owns three—now hanging neatly in the corner of our cellar—because, unlike us, she didn't lose her wardrobe.

Mama puts an arm around my shoulder. "Are you sure? You don't even know him."

"He is nice," I say simply.

"Nice, right." Out of Meg's mouth it sounds venomous.

"He got a doctor."

Meg clucks. "If he hadn't stolen our place, you wouldn't have needed one."

"Can I borrow a dress?"

Meg huffs something unintelligible before she begins to rummage through the garments hanging in the corner. Without a word, she flings something red in my direction, grabs the nearly empty water bucket and disappears.

The stains haven't come out, but I washed my dress, which is now draped over a shelf. As it dries, I wipe myself down and then put on Meg's dress. She has been conspicuously absent all morning, only appeared for a bit of lunch, crackers and some mystery meat from a can, before she took off again.

Wanting to avoid Mitch showing up downstairs, I hurry outside long before three. The new bandage the doctor gave me this morning is still white. Meg's dress, red as poppies, looks gaudy against the gray wreckage. I rub my sweaty palms and take deep breaths. I don't even know what I look like because we've got no mirrors.

I didn't sleep much last night and, until an hour ago, wanted to cancel. But somehow, I never made it upstairs, likely he wouldn't have been there anyway. I wander back and forth, watch the women lugging water buckets, wood scraps and bundles of household goods past me. A woman with a headscarf drags a cart piled high with a comforter, suitcases and pillows, likely in search of a new home. Everyone keeps their eyes on the ground in front of them, and if one looks at me, lips purse in a sign of contempt. I have no right to walk around in a clean dress, being idle while everyone is scraping. If they knew I was about to go out with the enemy, they'd spit at me.

I'm about to return to the basement, when a jeep arrives, honks once, before Mitch jumps out. "I'm sorry I'm late." He stops in front of me, a bit breathless, yet grinning. It's the first real smile I've seen. "Let me help you into the car."

The jeep takes off with a lurch. I've never even sat in a car and now I'm riding next to a stranger. He drives carefully, slowly, circumvents pedestrians who crisscross the street, men, women and children dragging carts and lugging wood or other treasure, other cars and horse carriages and the first trams. The closer we get to downtown and the Ku'damm, the more people crowd the streets. Alongside, mountains of rubble, ruins and pockmarked façades slide by.

Everywhere people are working, stacking stones, shoveling and carrying buckets. Considering the square miles of destruction, it seems ludicrous to even try.

I notice my fingers cramping each other. A weight sits on my chest, makes it impossible to speak. What would I say anyway? The man next to me is silent too, appears to concentrate on the road.

When we arrive on Ku'damm, I can't believe my eyes. There, in front of the broken buildings, sit men and women around tables. They are drinking, eating and talking as if nothing had happened.

"I'm astounded how many people are about," Mitch says. "I saw film footage taken from the air. You wouldn't expect that anybody lives in this town." He climbs out and opens the door for me. "But this is Berlin and I have the feeling Berliners are fighters."

"The war nearly destroyed us all. I think we've developed the uncanny ability to enjoy the tiniest silver lining." I scan the crowd, sitting in the sun, apparently hungry for life, hungry for a new beginning. As I am standing there next to the American, I feel a fresh sense of being alive myself. A giggle rises from my throat, which catches the attention of an older woman pulling a cart past us. She stares at me with hateful eyes.

"Traitor," she hisses.

As if he hasn't heard her, Mitch takes my elbow and guides me toward the tables. "Let's sit and talk."

I nod numbly, watching the ragged woman disappear in the crowd. "Many people don't understand that we are even talking to you." I think about Meg's incredulous expression when I told her about going out. Her words echo through my head. "Did you… fly, I mean, did you drop bombs here?"

Mitch sighs. "Not here, but… I wish I could tell you I didn't fly missions. But I did farther west. The war made us do things."

I try imagining Mitch in a bomber as he pushes buttons, as he releases deadly loads over some other German city. My mouth is bitter. Next to me a woman laughs. She is sitting next to two British soldiers in army uniform. Everything feels twisted, confusing, a world of opposites. "Why did you become a pilot?"

Mitch sets his cap on the table and folds his hands. "I've wanted to fly since I was six years old, so when I turned eighteen, I joined the Air Force." His voice trembles a bit as he avoids my gaze and I have the feeling that there is something he isn't telling. "That was in '38."

A waitress appears. "*Bitte schön.* What would you like?"

I've waited for this moment. For years I imagined sitting in a restaurant, participating in a normal life. "Coffee, please, if you have it."

"Make it two."

The girl nods. "Very well."

I look at the man in front of me, who seems to be lost in thought. "Where did you learn German?"

"Grandpa came from a little town near Hamburg and he sometimes spoke to me in German. After the war started, he grew quiet. But I took German in the military." He throws me a wistful glance. "I suppose it came pretty easy."

I want to ask him why he invited me here, but I can't bring myself to say it.

The coffee arrives, there is even milk and sugar. In that moment, as the aroma of the coffee enters my nose, the world rights itself, it is a normal day, when two people go out for a drink in the sun. In that moment, all the grayness of our desolate lives falls away. As I load my cup just to taste the sweetness, I sense Mitch's gaze on me.

"What were your dreams? Did you have plans?"

I look at the man across from me, think about my former life that evaporated years ago. "In school, I wanted to design clothes, even had a sewing machine and tried lots of things."

"You could do it again."

"What, go to school?"

"Why not?"

I huff. "We lost everything in the bombing, got barely anything to eat, just the rations the Allies are bringing in. Don't get me wrong, I'm thankful for receiving anything. But it isn't enough, every day is a struggle. We dwell in the cellar."

"With time, things will become better."

"Time has little meaning right now." I throw him a glance, know it's defiant, even angry. His expression is full of concern, even a little pity. "Is that why you asked me here, because you feel sorry for me?"

Mitch sighs. "I did in the beginning, but I asked you because I wanted to get to know you better."

Next to me the woman laughs again. All of a sudden, I feel annoyed. To distract myself, I take a sip, likely a brew of coffee beans and chicory, but sweet and hot. It touches my tongue, travels down my throat, spreads in the middle of my belly. Amazing. "Thank you for the coffee."

For a while, neither of us speaks. Strangely, it isn't awkward, just new. My mood lifts as I watch the people around us, the struggling conversations between occupiers and German Fräuleins, the chats between girlfriends and couples. The sun shines hot and bright, ignorant of the state of this place.

On the sidewalk, an unending stream of refugees creeps past, their eyes hollow, their skin gray with dust. They drag suitcases and carts, pull children and old women along. They've come from the east, Silesia, Prussia and parts of Russia. They are not allowed to remain, because there is no room and not enough food. Supposedly, they're moving on into camps farther west.

What right do I have to be upset when all those people have nothing, not even a home to return to?

Mitch eyes his wristwatch, some fancy model with a brown leather band. "We'd better leave soon. I've got to report to duty tonight."

I drain my cup, study the lines on Mitch's face. I want to know more about his family, about what he likes, but maybe this is too forward, too nosy.

In front of the house, he helps me out of the car, his grip firm on my forearm. "Take care of yourself."

I try a smile, fail and just nod. "Thank you," I say in English.

He tips his hat and hurries upstairs, just as Greg comes down. Even in the gloom I notice an ugly scowl. "Too busy, eh?"

Wordlessly, I turn toward the cellar stairs, intent on getting away as quickly as my bad leg allows. The door above smacks shut and I sigh with relief.

Mama is resting on her blanket while Meg is cutting up the ragged remains of a cabbage into a pot of water.

"How was it, fraternizing with the enemy?" Meg asks.

Lots of women do it, I want to say. *What's so wrong about wanting some normalcy?* Yet I feel like a cheater as the image of Fritz in his Wehrmacht uniform rises in my mind.

I take off Meg's dress and hang it carefully on the hanger. Why did I even bother? Mitch must be utterly bored with me.

On Ku'damm, a man waves from afar. I know it is Fritz, even though I can't make out his face. He runs towards me, but the closer he gets, the less recognizable he becomes. Half his face is covered in burn scars, pinkish white cords of mangled flesh, his hair has turned gray. As the distance between us melts away, he no longer walks, he is sitting in a wheelchair. A blanket covers his lap and there is nothing but air where his knees and feet should be. He throws his arms around me, icy skin touches my neck.

I awake with a whimper, bathed in sweat. In the darkness, the air around me is still as a black cocoon—the world has stopped. I don't even hear Meg or Mama breathe.

What would I do if Fritz were an invalid? Or Papa? Many of the returning soldiers out there have injuries, some are obvious, others hidden. Only their eyes provide a window into their shattered souls that try to deal with the unmentionable they have done and seen. Wouldn't it be better if they didn't return at all, are they already lying in some unnamed grave?

CHAPTER SIX

On August 4, Meg storms into the basement, waving a newspaper.

"I was passing a kiosk and there were dozens of people lined up. Look what happened." She smacks the paper on the tiny table in the corner and shouts. "Stalin, Churchill and Truman decided to annex everything east of the Oder/Neisse rivers. No more Eastern Prussia or Silesia. It belongs to the Russians now. And the Poles."

"What does it mean?" Mama asks.

"It means all those refugees who are passing through can't ever go home."

"How could they do that?" I whisper.

Ignoring me, Meg slowly unpacks her bag… flour, bread and potatoes, three tablespoons of sugar, a scrape of some red paste that is supposed to be strawberry jam. "How can we survive on these rations?"

I stare at the food and our empty shelves. How indeed? The powers may have decided what to do with Germany, but we've got more important things to deal with. Our category V ration cards are nicknamed *graveyard* cards for a reason. What Meg brought home for us—she's been collecting our rations as well—is supposed to last ten days. By the looks of it, we'll have eaten everything in less than half the time. That's despite the fact that every few days, we find some sort of "gift" in front of our cellar door: a couple of cans of corned beef, a box of powdered milk, even three bars of Nestlé milk chocolate. Chocolate, when have I last enjoyed such a delight? Even if Mitch hasn't uttered a word, I know it's his doing.

"I could ask Mitch to help us." It's out before I have time to think.

"I'd rather swallow my tongue," Meg shouts.

"Why are you so damn proud, Meg?" I shoot back. "We lost the war, remember?"

"Easy, girls," Mama says.

Ignoring her, Meg faces me. "He's the *enemy*, Lotte. Without him and his friends, we'd still live upstairs, have a bed to sleep in and things to trade on the black market."

I bite my lower lip and turn away. Meg is right, of course.

She reminds me of my friend Ruth, who was just as headstrong. That day when she and her mom disappeared, I searched their place for a note, some kind of sign that she'd left for me. There was none, just emptiness. I ran through the house, screaming her name, returned several more times until one day, another family moved in. Just like that, as if Ruth and her parents had never existed.

By now, I know the SS must've taken her, stuffed her into one of those death camps because she was Jewish, like they'd taken Ruth's dad two years earlier after they'd destroyed his store.

I swallow to push away the bitterness. Where are my principles, my morals?

Mitch hasn't been home in eight days. *He may not return*, the voice in my head comments. *Even if he does, why should he help or take you out again? And why would you want him to? Why don't you just quit thinking about him?*

"I'm going to scrounge," I say aloud. "Mama, will you join me?"

Tired of finding little, we are heading east—*you are leaving the American sector*, beneath some Russian gibberish. Main water pipes function as paths, sometimes we have to turn back. So far, the Russian-occupied part of Berlin looks just the same except for the images of Stalin and propaganda messages I can't decipher.

A couple of women are cutting limbs from a birch tree with old hatchets, a handful of kids, the youngest no older than six or seven, are wandering with packs on their bags, eyes huge in their skinny faces. Many children have lost their parents and are searching for remaining family to take them in.

Red flags, swastikas cut away, hang from buildings, a greeting to the Russian occupiers. Wherever we go, they are removing the last signs of Hitler's reign, swastikas are chiseled from buildings, monuments toppled. As if it were that easy to erase the past.

I'm afraid what Hitler did, what the German people allowed to happen—by complacency or participation—will stick to us for generations like some invisible stench. I ask myself why nobody noticed it early enough. Surely there must've been signs when Hitler rose to power. Why are we so blind to these men… their insane lust for power?

I am thankful, my leg is feeling better. The angry scars have faded a bit. Faded as I feel. Insignificant as an ant in the desert sands. Not only has Berlin crumbled into nothing, the rest of Germany has as well. It is being governed by strangers, cut into pieces and sold to the highest bidder. Where do we fit in, where do we go from here? A terrible urge rises inside me. I want to escape, leave this place behind.

"Over here, Lotte. Help me."

I haven't noticed that Mama has left my side. She is attempting to lift a wooden beam that is stuck beneath a partial house wall.

"It's too large, Mama," I yell. "We can't carry it back."

"We can use the wood to cook."

Reluctantly, I clamber across the rocks to join her. I cannot afford to fall again. Most of the beam appears to be buried and when we pull, it doesn't budge. "Let's try a few cellars, maybe we'll find leftover coal."

Mama follows me back to the path. "I knew we should've brought Meg's hatchet."

"We could return together, bring Meg to help."

We are on some street that used to be lined with trees. Now only the stumps remain. Houses here are smaller, though as broken as the rest.

I point at one. "Try over there. I'll take the next one. We'll meet on the street in a while."

I hurry on, frustrated about our lack of progress. The next place is so broken, the entire first floor is buried. The one after that looks more promising. I clamber around the side and find stairs leading into the basement.

"Hello," I shout. The last thing I want is to surprise people squatting here. But there is no sound, nothing.

The outer door is missing, so I creep inside. "Hello?"

Nothing, just the musty smell of stale air and the faint scent of coal. I take a careful step, then another. With it, the light fades. I've got neither matches, nor a lighter or candles. I stop in front of a door. Knock and listen. Still nothing.

Pushing it open, I wait for my eyes to adjust. In the gloom, I make out a few empty shelves, wooden boxes and under the stairs a handful of briquettes. When I emerge minutes later, my nose full of coal dust, my pack is filled.

I remember Mama and hurry down the street. The cellar two houses down is empty. I rush back outside, turn 360 degrees, trying to guess which house Mama may have visited. It'd make the most sense to wait right here. Surely she'll be back any moment. How much time has passed?

People hurry by, most ignore me. They carry that typical stare, a mix of exhaustion, hunger and purpose. Some of them also carry a glint of hope. Those are the ones who lift their heads to look at me, some even nod. Not smiling, no, that would take too much energy, but a recognition of another human who is experiencing similar hardship.

"Mama, where are you?" I whisper. My pack, full of briquettes, no longer matters. Nor the gnawing in my middle, my constant companion. My entire focus lies on the street and its inhabitants. Minutes pass, surely an hour has gone since we parted. Maybe longer. Worry creeps up inside me, an icy feeling, though without shade, the August heat is stifling.

The little voice in my head is back, nagging me to do something. I pick up my pack and move down the street, try another basement. This one is occupied by women and children. I call from the entry, ask if they've seen a middle-aged woman in a gray-striped dress.

They haven't and I hurry outside, try the next one and the next. Either the places are empty, buried or have inhabitants. Nobody has seen Mama. The worry inside me expands to slimy tentacles that choke me. Down the street, an army truck with a red star is parked— Russians. Remembering the women running in the streets in early May, I shudder. I know we've been lucky. Judging by the stories told waiting in line for water and food, tens of thousands of women have been assaulted.

Please, Mama, be safe.

As I approach, three soldiers appear in the entrance of a building, whose first floor has somehow escaped destruction. They head toward their vehicle, whistling. I pretend to inspect a rock and crouch low—no need to draw attention—breathe deeply as the truck sputters to life and rattles past. I straighten and continue down the street when, from the corner of my eye, I see a figure emerge from the building the Russians just left.

Mama. At least I think it's her. Except she hobbles like Grandpa used to in his garden in Potsdam.

"Mama?" I don't know how I get to her, only that I take in her expression, her eyes wide and shiny, strands of hair loose under the headscarf, her dress full of dust and her legs and shoes caked with dirt. I grab my throat, the choking feeling is back. Blood smears her calves and knees, some stains her shoes.

She doesn't seem to notice me, weaves left and right like a sleepwalker. I grip her hand, pull her close. "Mama, I'm here."

"I think I lost my bag." She looks at me, the smile on her face reminds me of a child.

What happened, I want to scream. But I know, of course, I know. I saw those men, saw their gleeful expressions speaking of another conquest. Another German woman put in her place, the spoils of a victor.

"Mama, are you hurt?"

She lowers her head, not quick enough because I see her chin tremble. I remove her scarf, shake it out, fix her hair and wipe some of the blood from her legs. She says nothing, just stands there and lets me remove some of the unmentionable. Disgusted, I toss the scarf and drape an arm around her. Together, we hobble down the street like two invalids.

How I loathe this place, the filth, the lack of water or safety. It takes us forever to get home because Mama has trouble walking. She is clearly in pain, but no sound comes across her lips. Anger, no, white-hot fury, has replaced my worry. I want to scream, want to kick something. Yet all I can do is lead Mama back into the American sector, back into our basement hole as the voice in my head repeats: you did this, it was your idea to visit the Russian sector, it was your idea to split up and search for coal.

CHAPTER SEVEN

Meg and I help Mama wash and clean her clothes. Meg never says a word, just goes twice to fetch new water, shares the last bit of soap and an extra dress. At some point, when Mama has fallen asleep in the corner, she comes over to me and places a hand on my forearm.

That's when I break down. As I sob and dampen Meg's shoulder, she holds me like a baby.

No words are exchanged, but Meg's presence soothes my soul— at least a bit. As I lie in bed and Mama sighs and mumbles, sleep refuses to come. Again and again the scene from this afternoon repeats, the Russian soldiers, Mama stumbling out of the building, her expression of bewilderment and shock—her silence on the way home.

It must be after midnight when I decide to get up. The room is pushing in on me and the smell of the briquettes makes my stomach queasy. I need air, lots of air.

The road outside is dark and silent. I sink onto a stack of bricks. Upstairs, lights flicker through the cracks of the boarded-up windows—the Americans are still awake.

Time loses all meaning as I stare into the darkness. We are supposed to have peace, Mama has made it through the entire war.

I realize this is an illusion. What we have now is a different type of war. The rules have changed, but the war is still on. The Allies are running the country. Us.

The urge to walk away and disappear returns. I'd leave Europe, go someplace without ruins and starvation, a place where I can study and work, eat at a table and sleep in a bed.

A sigh followed by a sob rises into the night. I'll never go because I've got Mama to take care of, Papa and Fritz to wait for.

Suddenly, I feel bone tired. My limbs are filled with rubble, my eyes grow heavy. But the thought of returning downstairs keeps me from getting up. I just sit there, in a daze, feel my head sink forward, jerk awake again and again, until I finally drift off.

"Lotte? What are you doing out here?" Mitch's face swims above me. A whiff of aftershave mixed with sweat hits my nose. I look around, try to get my bearings.

It is early morning, the sun is bathing the street in the first light. Except I'm shivering. Memories of yesterday return, the attack, the terrible march home.

"Lotte?"

I focus on Mitch, take in his appearance, the brown jumpsuit, the lines beneath his eyes. He's been up too. "I couldn't go inside," I say, as if that makes any sense.

"Why not?"

I just shake my head, rise from my rock bed. My calf pulses as I dust myself off. It's useless, of course, but I'm ashamed of the way I look in front of this put-together man. "I'd better go."

Mitch walks with me and I'm thankful for his silence. Inside the door, he hesitates, opens his mouth, closes it. With a nod, he climbs upstairs as my fingers cramp around the railing. Already the air has left my lungs, is too thin to breathe. "Get a grip!" I mumble. "You've been living in basements for a year, you can do it now." A tremble rises from my legs, climbs into my hips, up my spine. I squeeze the railing harder, gulp air, take a step, then another. I can do this. Must do this. For Mama.

I open the cellar door and rush to the window, take deep breaths. Only then do I have the strength to face the room. Mama is lying on her back, eyes wide open, while Meg is rummaging through our supplies. This morning, we've got a slice of bread each, a scrape of margarine and the red mystery jam on the menu.

"I'm going out to heat tea water," Meg says, throwing me a curious glance. Thankful she's not commenting on my absence during the night nor the way I must surely look, I hand her the stash of peppermint leaves I collected in an abandoned garden. "Maybe you can cut the bread?"

It is clear to us both that Mama won't be helping anytime soon.

In fact, I'm unsure if we can leave her alone, which would severely reduce our ability to scrounge.

"Mama?" I whisper as soon as Meg has left. "How are you?" Mama is still staring at the ceiling, her gaze inward despite her open eyes. I gently touch the back of her hand, which cramps around the blanket's edge. "Can you hear me, Mama?"

Very slowly, Mama turns her head. A smile brightens her expression. "Lotte, I think I'm hungry. Will you set the table? I think I'm in the mood for omelet this morning."

"Sounds delicious, how about I help you get up?"

Again, Mama smiles and then grips my outstretched fingers. I settle her on the old footstool while I carefully cut the rye bread. Each slice must be exactly the same and not too thick. I try to ignore the rumbling in my middle, I could eat the entire loaf by myself, even if rumor has it that the bakeries add sawdust and ground acorns to stretch the flour.

"It isn't very clean in here," Mama comments from the stool.

"I know, Mama. I will dust later."

Meg sweeps into the room, carrying a steaming pot. "Tea is done. We need to look for wood again. Have only enough for another day or two."

"Who are you?" Mama carries that bewildered expression again.

I throw Meg a worried glance, but before I can say anything, she rushes over to Mama. "I'm Meg, I'm living here with you two."

"Oh, you are Lotte's friend."

Again, Meg and I exchange a glance before we both say, "Old friends."

Mama seems satisfied and dives into her bread slice, thinly covered with the whitish margarine and reddish paste. Suddenly, she makes a face. "I don't know about you, but that jam tastes strange. Why don't we get a jar of blackberry jam instead?"

It's true, Mama used to make dozens of jars from the berries we collected each summer in the woods. "I'm afraid we ate all the jam," I say aloud.

Meg thoughtfully sips from her mug. "I'm going to leave as soon as I've finished the tea." She eyes Hugo, who lies in the corner watching us. "I've got to find him some food, anything." I don't want to know what she's referring to, but it's hard enough to feed ourselves, keeping a dog is a luxury few people are willing to afford.

"Be careful," I say. "I'll take Mama outside, see if she can walk a bit.”

All morning Mama and I are on the street. We walk a few feet, then Mama rests. I think she is in pain from the assault. There is still blood and I worry the Russians have damaged her insides. Maybe it is a blessing that she has forgotten what happened.

While Mama rests, I scan the rubble for wood, pick out pieces of scrap metal to trade. My belly complains almost constantly, so I try to distract myself by watching the people. After a while I slip back downstairs to fetch water to drink. The sun boils above us today, the horizon hazy, the air above the road shimmies. Mama's cheeks burn, so I drape the remnants of a towel over her head.

Down the street the Americans come and go. I ignore them, concentrate on the wood and metal slowly piling up next to Mama's feet.

As the sun crests and the heat becomes unbearable, I take Mama back inside, place her on the bed for a nap. It takes all my concentration not to think about the tight space with its coal stench.

“I'm hungry,” she says with a small voice. This is how it has to be with a child. That's what she is right now, a child with a simple mind who has forgotten who she is. *At least she still knows you.*

Once she falls asleep, I climb back out. Filling my lungs with gulps of air, I walk around the side and sit in the shade of the house. At this point, I'm ravenous and lightheaded. All the water in the world can't take away the gnawing.

In front, a car door slams, voices drift across. American voices who sound strong and dominant. A man laughs, a second joins in. These men may be here, but they live on another planet. Their reality is that of winners who drink whiskey and eat three meals a day.

Above me, a window covering is removed.

“Lotte?”

I look up. Mitch leans across the windowsill. “Hello.”

“What are you doing down there?”

“Resting.” It's hot, I want to shout. My mother is sick and I'm starving. But it takes energy to be angry. Energy I don't have right now.

Moments later, Mitch walks around the building, a box tucked under his right arm. He's wearing a white T-shirt and brown army pants.

“Here, why don't you eat?”

I stare at the contents of the box he is setting at my feet… four apples, a bag of blue plums, cans of meat, dried milk powder, bread and two packs of Lucky Star cigarettes. Did he hear my thoughts?

Suddenly the food blurs and a sob rises between us.

With a sigh, Mitch settles next to me. "What is going on?"

I shake my head, just stare at the glorious food. With a shaky hand I take a plum, sniff it, before biting into it. Juice drips, sweetness explodes on my tongue. I close my eyes, chew and swallow.

I spit out the pit and collect it again. Maybe I can plant trees. A giggle rises as I imagine the pit growing into a tree. It'll be years before there are any plums. Still…

"Lotte, I'm worried about you."

Remembering the man next to me, I take a second plum and face him. "I'm sorry. Thank you for your help. It has been hard…"

"Something happened, didn't it?"

I nod as I scrape the plum's skin with my teeth. "Mama was attacked yesterday. We went to the Russian sector in hopes of finding coal. I left her… she…" The scene repeats, the soldiers leaving, Mama stumbling like a drunken teenager.

"She was raped?" Mitch's voice is matter-of-fact, but there is a trembling beneath it I have never heard.

I nod, my throat tight again, even too tight to eat the plum. I place it back in the box, the flesh a gory yellow where I pulled away the skin.

"Is she hurt, I mean other than…?"

"I don't know. She is still bleeding. I have thought about taking her to the hospital."

Mitch jumps up. "Where is she now?"

"Sleeping downstairs. Her mind isn't right." Again, I can't continue.

"Stay here, I'm calling the doctor, it can be dangerous."

Without waiting for an answer, Mitch hurries off, jumps easily across the rocks and disappears. Enemy or not, thankfulness fills my chest. I take a ragged breath and pick up the plum when I hear a wail. It is high-pitched and so forlorn that despite the heat, goosebumps spread on my forearms.

I rush downstairs, but not without grabbing our precious box of food, worried what I'll find.

"Mama."

She sits on her bed and hugs herself as if she's seeking comfort in her own arms. I embrace her and hold her still until the trembling subsides.

"I had a bad dream," she finally says against my shoulder.

I lean back, take a look at the woman who has turned from mother to child. "I'm sorry, I should've been here." Remembering Mitch's treats, I hand Mama a plum.

She closes her eyes as she eats. "Oh, we used to have a plum tree in my parents' garden." The walls of the cellar press on me as I wonder if Mama will ever recover.

"How about we'll go outside for a bit. It's not so hot anymore and we'll take one of those glorious apples with us."

Together we climb the stairs and return to the shady side of the house. I'm taking a blanket to sit on and if it weren't for the rubble, it'd almost feel like a picnic.

Sometime in the afternoon, a jeep with a red cross stops in front. Minutes later, Mitch returns with a man by his side. It isn't the doctor from last time, this one is younger and wears round silver spectacles.

"Dr. Fisher." Without preamble, the man kneels in front of Mama and holds out a hand. "It's good to meet you." His German is surprisingly good, too.

Mama begins to tremble while trying to stand. With the uneven ground, she wobbles and would've fallen had Mitch not caught her by the elbow. "Frau Berger, Dr. Fisher is here to help you," he says calmly. "You don't need to be afraid."

Dr. Fisher nods. "How about we go upstairs?"

"Lotte, what do these men want?"

I squeeze Mama's hand. "You are hurt and they are here to help you get better."

Mama seems to accept that answer, because she nods at the doctor. As we climb the stairs, Mitch mumbles to me, "Dr. Fisher is a family doctor. He'll know more about women's issues." I wonder if he'll place Mama on the kitchen table, but Mitch has already thought ahead. "You better use my bedroom," he says as soon as we enter Meg's former apartment, which smells of whiskey and stale food.

We follow Fisher into a room on the east side, its window open, letting in a breeze.

As Mama lies down on the bed, Mitch disappears again. I take her hand as the doctor examines her, try to concentrate on the fresh air and ignore Mama's whimpers. I'm glad I'm sitting near her head and don't see what the doctor is doing.

"I'm going to give you something to sleep," he says to Mama. "But first I need to speak with your daughter."

He waves me to him, his expression serious. "Your mother has internal injuries. I'll need to repair them, so the bleeding stops. I will ask Mitch to assist. Is that all right?"

I nod numbly, equally relieved Mama is getting help and worried about her recovery.

Mama wakes around six in the evening. We are alone in Mitch's room, men's voices trickle through the walls. My stomach aches with hunger again, but I don't want to leave Mama.

"How are you feeling?" I ask.

Mama wiggles her legs a bit. "What happened?"

"Dr. Fisher operated on you, so you can heal." I try to decide what to tell her, how to explain something so terrible. I know she remembers, but maybe her subconscious mind is too worried she may have a breakdown.

A knock on the door pulls me from my thoughts. "I brought you something to drink." Mitch waves two bottles of Coke. "The sugar will help."

"Can you help us move downstairs?" I ask.

Mitch hesitates, then shakes his head. "You better stay here tonight. I'll take the sofa in the living room."

"We can't, I—"

"Of course you can." He turns to leave. "I'm going to tell Meg and will organize dinner."

It's too much, I want to say, but the door is already closed.

<h1 style="text-align: center">CHAPTER EIGHT</h1>

Once Mama is asleep, I slip into the hall. I need air and want to check on Meg.

Male voices come from the living room, which I'm hoping to pass undetected. No such luck.

"Hey, missy," one of them calls. "Where are you going?" His voice slurs and he is speaking English, but I recognize the tone anywhere—it's Greg, the stocky American. Going faster, I reach the entry door, open it and am almost through when Mitch hurries after me.

"Sorry about that," he says. "Idiots are drinking too much." He eyes me curiously. "Going for a walk?"

I nod.

"Would you like company?"

In the background the soldiers are hollering.

"What will they think?"

Mitch throws me a crooked smile and shrugs. "Who cares?"

He follows me down the stairs, using a flashlight to light the steps. Dusk bathes the street in gray tones.

"I apologize for my buddies," Mitch says as soon as we reach the street. "They're celebrating…" He frowns, then continues. "We bombed Hiroshima and Nagasaki… with atom bombs. Everyone is expecting that the war ends soon."

I'd forgotten that the US and Japan are still at war. "Atom bombs?"

"This scientist, Oppenheimer, developed them in Los Alamos,

thinking we'd use them against Hitler." He hesitates. "I'm very glad it didn't come to that. They're much more deadly than expected."

"How deadly?"

"They estimate that more than a hundred thousand people died."

I shudder. "From two bombs?" The sound of whistling, falling bombs, followed by earsplitting explosions reverberates in my mind. How often did Mama and I sit in some basement or bunker listening to the devastation outside? On just one day in the middle of March, more than a thousand planes dropped more than three thousand tons of bombs. Despite it all, despite those planes coming more than three hundred times, dropping tens of thousands of air mines, phosphor burning bombs and bombs of all sizes that rattled the city like a never-ending earthquake, not nearly as many people died. Whatever Oppenheimer invented changed everything. I put a hand to my mouth to keep from crying out.

Mitch is obviously concerned because he watches me carefully. "Are you okay?"

Still unable to speak, I shake my head.

"I hope we'll never use another, though I suspect, now that they have them, they'll produce more."

"And the Soviets?"

"They will, too."

I push away the image of bombs dropping and wiping out entire cities. It is too much. The American seems impossibly tall tonight. "I so appreciate your help, though I don't understand. You didn't have to do this. None of it. We lost the war and—"

Mitch takes my hand. "Hush, now. Don't you think you're dealing with enough? It's no hardship for me to sleep on the couch. I can't imagine you and your mother deserve starving in that hole beneath us."

"But Hitler killed all those people, murdered millions of Jews."

"So, by extension, you should suffer some more?"

"Maybe." I look up at the man whose heart is larger than most Germans'. "Maybe we have to atone for Hitler's sins and for supporting him all those years."

"I can't imagine Germany would've supported him, had they known where he was leading them."

I scoff. "In hindsight, we are all smarter." All of a sudden, tears press. "You know, I had a Jewish friend, Ruth. Her father owned a tiny grocery store on our street." Mitch remains silent, but he still holds my hand. Waiting. "After the SS destroyed his store, he was arrested. And one day a few years later, Ruth and her mother disappeared." I take a breath, remember the horrific morning when I found her sitting among the remnants of her father's store, glass shards covering everything.

"Maybe she is safely living in Boston, or she moved to England."

Mitch blurs as the tears demand release. "I'll never know. All I can think of is that I did nothing, didn't even connect the role of the government with my friend. Just continued in the Hitler Youth like nothing had happened."

"How old were you?"

"Thirteen."

"I don't know about you, but when I was thirteen, I was riding horses or going fishing, I certainly wasn't thinking what President Roosevelt was up to. Besides, I'm not condoning throwing atom bombs on Japanese cities and killing a hundred thousand civilians instantly and who knows how many more over time."

When I sniff in response, Mitch produces a handkerchief.

Without another word, we begin to walk. I take deep breaths, try to think of something happy or smart to say. The air smells of rain, the wind has picked up. Thunder rumbles over downtown, followed by a sharp flash. "I'm sorry, I'm burdening you with all this."

"No burden, but we should probably head back."

Despite his words, we continue walking. "Will you tell me about your family?"

A sharp crack rips open the sky, followed by a mighty rumble. I involuntarily freeze while my mind tries to determine whether there is another bomb attack.

"Lotte?" Bending low, Mitch is studying me. "It's just a thunderstorm."

A rushing sound erupts as sudden raindrops hit my face. Rain, of course. I lift my face, meet Mitch's gaze. He is smiling.

And I feel myself smile back. Just like that.

"I like you, Lotte. Despite what you might think, you are a tough young woman who has to deal with way too much." Serious again, he wipes a raindrop from my nose, his touch gentle on my skin. It is almost dark now, and his eyes are obscure pools. Around us the wind blows, warm droplets wash away the dust.

And then his hand cradles my cheek, soft… comforting. I look at this man who I hardly know, who comes from a foreign place and used to be Germany's enemy. But this man is no enemy, he has a good heart and is willing to help, when he surely could turn his back like the others.

My hand comes up on its own, touches his temple. And then his lips meet mine, soft and knowing at the same time. As our kiss lengthens, we draw closer together, our bodies meeting each other for the first time, my left hand on his shoulder, my right in his hair. His nose is a bit too large for his face, but you forget that when you look into his eyes that sparkle like a summer day in the country. There we stand on the street, rain pounding on us, cleansing the air and washing away the dust. My dress is soaked through in seconds. What does it matter when all I feel is this man in front of me, his kindness and strength?

I am having trouble breathing, a tiny storm spins faster and faster inside my stomach and chest.

Above us, a flash crackles, followed by thunder. "We'd better head back," he says near my ear.

Holding hands, we run, my focus on the flashlight's path Mitch is illuminating for us. Only when we reach the entry do we stop. I'm dripping wet, water fills my shoes. I think of the basement, that I forgot to visit Meg and that I have no spare clothes. But I need to return to Mama.

The rain has cooled the air and I'm suddenly shivering. "Let's go up, I'll loan you a spare shirt."

I say nothing, wondering if he is expecting to share my bed tonight. As if he's heard me, he says, "No worries, I'm on the couch. You take care of your mother."

I squeeze his hand as a thank you, but we let go as we enter the apartment. Thankfully, Greg is gone, one soldier is sitting in the living room, reading by the light of a lantern. He eyes me curiously, but says nothing.

We rush past and, as promised, Mitch hands me a shirt before he kisses my nose and disappears.

I hang up my wet clothes and put on Mitch's shirt. It feels like he is right here and despite my mother, who is sleeping peacefully, my skin tingles as if he's touching me. Outside, soft rain murmurs like tiny voices, cool air fills the room.

As I lie there, I marvel at the strangeness of life. One moment, everything is black and hopeless. The next, I feel alive again.

I smile in the dark and nod off.

I awake to a sound next to me. Mama is sitting up in bed, mumbling. "…what will I cook for breakfast? I have to buy eggs and butter…"

"Mama?" I climb out of bed, remembering too late that I'm wearing Mitch's shirt.

Mama stares. "What are you wearing, dear?"

"My clothes got wet last night, so Mitch loaned me a shirt."

"Who is Mitch?"

"The nice man who got a doctor for you. Remember, the doctor helped you?"

Mama looks lost for a moment. Then her expression changes into a half-smile. "You'd better hurry to the stores. I want to have breakfast ready, when your father returns from his shift."

I turn my back for a moment, buying time. I don't know if it's better to tell Mama that there hasn't been butter in three years and that Papa's last field post arrived last fall, or to play along.

As I change back into my nearly dry dress, I say, "The doctor said that you'll need to rest. So let me worry about breakfast, all right?"

Mama nods and leans against the pillow. "Is this our bed? I don't remember…"

"Mitch is letting us sleep here until you're better. Now let me get you some tea and bread, just promise me to stay put."

Again, Mama nods.

Closing the door behind me, I tiptoe through the hallway. In the living room, Mitch is curled up under a blanket. Relieved that nobody is stirring yet, I hurry to the basement.

Meg is up, fixing herself a slice of bread from Mitch's gift. "I suppose that's from the American?" she says. "And you had a nice night in his bed, I presume."

Fighting down anger, I say, "I'm thankful because he got Mama a doctor. It was pretty bad. He had to operate and repair the damage. Mitch offered us his bedroom until Mama is better."

Meg bites her lip. "Sorry, how is she?"

"I think she is feeling better, but her mind is still confused. She doesn't remember that Papa is gone."

"I guess I'll be by myself for a while."

I sit down next to Meg. "Not long, just until Mama is better."

"I'll be out again later. Found a few pieces to trade." She points at a cloth with two long knives and an intact ceramic pot.

"You take the cigarettes Mitch gave us. Unless you want me to come with you."

Meg sighs. "I'd prefer it if we went together. I don't trust some of those fellows."

"I'll join you after breakfast." With that, I carry two slices of bread, two apples and a few chunks of Spam upstairs.

The black market by the Brandenburg Gate is crowded with mingling and mumbling men, women and youths, dressed in everything from tatters to suits and Allied uniforms. Black markets are forbidden, the Allies have placed signs all around, but that doesn't seem to stop anyone from coming here.

Mitch warned me to be careful, but he had to report for duty at the army headquarters in Dahlem. All I can hope is that Mama stays put in bed.

Meg cradles the knives that are a bit dull and nicked, while I carry the pot with the cigarettes inside. The rain has passed, leaving puddles Hugo seeks out for a quick drink. The air is cleaner, yet thick with humidity. My dress clings to my skin and I'm thirsty, wishing to be back at the house.

We look at each other before Meg places a hand on my back. "Let's go. We can do this."

Together we join the fray, walk this way and that, Hugo always near Meg's leg. Many people have placed their goods on the ground for inspection: writing paper, bottles of wine without labels, a woolen hat and mittens, a fur coat, assorted pairs of reading glasses, leather boots, sandals made from tires, a grandfather clock…

In one area, a few farmers seem to have congregated, offering eggs, bread, cabbage, potatoes and beets. Judging by the crowds waiting their turn, they're doing a steady business. I zero in on the egg seller, a woman of Mama's age, while Meg pulls me toward the cabbages and potatoes.

"We can do a lot more with the vegetables," she whispers.

"I'd just like to make Mama an omelet."

"Let's see what they want first. Then we decide."

Meg offers her knives to the vegetable seller, but he shakes his head. "Only cigarettes."

Meg squints at him. "How many for that cabbage and twenty potatoes?"

"Thirty."

"Fifteen."

"Twenty-five."

"It's too much," I whisper.

Meg ignores me and eyes the woman. "Eighteen, last offer." She nods down the aisle, where more cabbages and potatoes are displayed.

The woman seems to weigh her options and finally nods. "Deal."

Meg fishes the cigarettes from the pot and hands all but two to the woman while I carefully store our purchases in my pack.

"Now let's get you some eggs." Meg is already five steps ahead and by the time I catch up, she's addressing the egg seller, a boy of maybe sixteen. "How much for two?"

"Fifteen cigarettes."

Meg huffs. "Too much. I've got two cigarettes left and these two knives." She opens the cloth rag and shows the boy the knives.

"I only take cigs."

My heart sinks, Mama will have to do without an omelet.

As we turn away, a woman pulls me aside. "If you have access to stubs, you know, when the soldiers throw out their butts, collect them. You'll get your eggs, twenty-five stubs for one." She winks at me before melting into the crowd.

By the time we get home, I'm soaked in sweat, but reasonably happy. In the end we traded the knives and remaining cigarettes for a loaf of bread and a bundle of beets. And I've got a new goal. Several of the Americans smoke. All I need to do now is raid the ashtrays.

CHAPTER NINE

After storing our goods on the basement shelf, I carry two plums and the ceramic pot we didn't trade upstairs. Meg plans to fix cabbage and potato soup, but first needs to collect more wood for the kitchen fire.

"Let's go outside for a bit," I say, entering Mitch's room.

The bed is empty, Mama's shoes are missing. In an instant, worry grabs me. An icy, slimy thing that makes me short of breath, as if I'd jumped into a frozen pond.

I rush into the corridor, yelling, "Mama?"

An American, eating his ration kit in the kitchen, eyes me curiously.

"Have you seen my mother?"

He shrugs and returns his attention to the food.

I check the living area, the bathroom, which reeks of urine and worse—so far none of Berlin's utilities are back on and the men use buckets for their business that are emptied into a pit in the back of the former garden.

"Please, Mama, where did you go?" I whisper.

I rush downstairs. Luckily, Meg hasn't left yet and promises to help search.

On the street, we run in opposite directions. I stop off and on, ask a passerby if they have seen a woman with blonde hair in her forties. Lots of people fit that picture, but I've got no photograph.

An hour passes, maybe more. I've found no trace and decide to return to the house to regroup. I need more help. Maybe Mitch will be back soon, and he can drive the jeep to look for her. Meg has not returned yet, so I run upstairs again to check. There is no sign of Mama. For all I know she may have tried to return to our old apartment, the one we lived in as long as I remember. Before the bombs hit.

In my mind I see her wandering around Berlin, lost and hot, thirsty and desperate. I may have to contact the police, Berlin's newly appointed German men who wear the old uniforms of the Prussian state to put as much distance as possible between their appearance and that of Hitler's Reich. But what am I going to say? A blonde woman is missing in a city of nearly three million people plus thousands of traveling refugees?

She may fall and hurt herself or wander into the Russian sector before I find her. Panic fills me and the world around me shimmies. I realize I haven't had any water since we left for the market this morning. The fabric of my dress is drenched from my neck down to my hips, my tongue feels twice the size and it's hard to swallow. Fanning myself, I take water from a bucket in the kitchen. Let the American complain, I just need a minute to rest.

And I need to find another dress to change into, maybe ask at the ration office for a replacement. I could sew something from rags, but there are no needles or thread. I contemplate wearing Mitch's shirt, but it isn't proper in public, so I wipe down my face and am about to return to the street when I hear singing outside.

Maikäfer, flieg.
Der Vater ist im Krieg.
Die Mutter ist in Pommerland,
Pommerland ist abgebrannt.
Maikäfer, flieg.

I recognize the song, but more importantly, I recognize Mama's voice. She's right outside. As I race downstairs, I wonder why she is singing a children's song of the May beetle that rhymes with the father being in the war, the mother in burned-down Pomerania. It's such a strange, sad song of loss.

I want to yell at Mama for wandering off, but when I see her sitting in the shade at the side of our house, singing and humming the song in an endless loop, my heart swells. Relief is a beautiful sensation, a feeling that fills me with warmth, not the heat of this sticky summer day, but the comfortable warmth of a woodfire in winter.

"Mama," is all I can muster. She looks at me, her eyes wet with tears.

"I missed you, Lotte," she says simply, as if I've been away for years.

"I missed you, too." I embrace my mother and so we sit until Meg and Hugo appear by our side.

Meg fans herself and sinks next to me. "Thank goodness, I've been searching half of Berlin."

Our eyes meet. "She was right here."

"I'm exhausted. I'll get our cookpot. Maybe you can help me with the soup?"

I grab Meg's hand. "Thank you for today."

Meg's eyes sparkle a bit too bright, before she shakes her head and rises anew. "Better get busy. I could eat a horse."

I giggle as the image of Meg taking a knife and fork to a horse rises in front of me. Meg breaks into a smile and soon we are both laughing.

"What's so funny?" Mama asks.

"We're just happy to be alive." As I say it, I realize it's true. Not only that, nothing is more important than being with the people you love.

As the sun cools, Meg, Mama and I are slurping cabbage and potato soup. It contains neither salt nor spices, but it is the best thing I've eaten in a while. More importantly, the hollow sensation I carry most days has left for the moment—a cozy warmth fills me.

Afterwards I take Mama back upstairs, help her wash and get into bed. Her sadness has been replaced by quiet content.

Only then do I realize how exhausted I am. In the hallway I run into Mitch, regretting it instantly, because I know I'm looking like a mess. My dress is drenched, and I must carry the dust of Berlin on my skin.

"How is she?" he asks, not commenting on my dilapidated state.

"Fine, I think." I can tell he is tired as well, so I say, "Would you mind if I slipped away for a bit?"

He smiles. "Just promise to return later?"

I nod before hurrying for the exit. Hopefully, Meg has enough water left for a decent rub down.

"Oh, I almost forgot," Mitch calls after me, "I've got something for you." He rummages through a stack of boxes and hands me a package, wrapped in brown paper. "It might come in handy."

"Thanks." I press the gift to my chest and marvel once more how I could've gotten so lucky.

After the heat of the day, it feels almost comfortable in the cellar. Meg sits near the window, reading from a tattered copy of Agatha Christie's *Appointment with Death* some British soldier gave her.

I inspect the water bucket and get my towel, but first I must know what's in the package. I pick it up, sniff it, but it tells me nothing. I loosen the cord, unwrap the paper.

Inside lies a carefully folded dress, cream colored, with a tiny print of pink roses. I shake it out, study it like a foreign object. It looks new and I've got no idea where Mitch could've organized it.

"Are you going to try it on or what?" Meg has put down her book and watches me.

I meet her gaze, try to read her expression. Is that a smirk on her face?

The truth is I'm afraid to try it on, afraid to ruin it in five minutes. Everything is so filthy, the basement, the streets, my hair and skin. It takes massive quantities of water to wash hair and without decent soap, it almost feels futile. Not to mention that we've been asked to use water sparingly, for drinking and cooking only.

"I'll get water in the morning," I say while slipping into the dress. Unlike most dresses that people are sewing these days, simple shifts, that take as little fabric as possible and still do the job, this one has a full wide skirt and, as I turn, swishes this way and that. I'm afraid to stain it and, not for the last time, I miss a decent mirror.

Meg just sits there silently, her expression unreadable. "You look very pretty." She gets up and rearranges the strands of my hair, steps back and inspects me once more. "Good."

"Does that mean you approve of me seeing the American?"

She scoffs and turns back to her book. "You don't need my approval."

"But you're my friend."

"Maybe I'm just envious of the attention you're getting. Besides, he's helping your mother and that's as good an argument as any."

I rush to her side and embrace her. At first, she's all rigid, but then I feel her arms soften around my shoulder. After a moment, I let go.

Meg's eyes are a bit glazed again, but there is a tiny smile on her lips. "Be good."

After I check on Mama—she is sleeping soundly—I'm about to look for Mitch, when he appears in the door.

"You are beautiful."

"Thanks to you."

"Nonsense, that's just the outside." When I don't answer, he continues, "The way you take care of your mother, deal with all this."

I think about my dream of running away, of leaving Germany behind. But Mama isn't the only one I can't abandon. Papa is out there, so is Fritz. Why don't I tell Mitch about them? I'm engaged, after all. "What choice do I have?" I say aloud.

With a sigh, Mitch extends a hand. "Care for a walk?"

The streets are filled with people this evening, but I only relish the sound of the swishing fabric around my knees and the feeling of having somebody solid walking next to me. Mitch has let go of my hand and I wonder if I've said something wrong.

"Will you tell me about your family?"

Mitch proceeds to talk about his parents, who are in their fifties, his father a doctor and his mother an elementary school teacher. He describes the house he grew up in, some two-story white home with a huge garden, chickens, and horses.

"What about siblings?"

Mitch hesitates, then shakes his head. "Where's your father?" he hurries.

"Papa is missing."

"I'm sorry."

Do you have a girlfriend, I want to ask. But I don't because what we have here wandering on these ruin-lined, dust-covered streets in the south of Berlin feels too fragile to survive such a question.

Nor does he ask about a man in my life. Instead, we speak about safe things. I tell him about our visit to the black market, about the search for Mama.

As a couple of women pass, one of them hisses, "Yank sweetheart," in my direction. They throw me the same hateful glance as the woman on Ku'damm, when Mitch took me to the café.

Mitch reclaims my hand and brings me to a stop. "You think you can get used to that?"

I say nothing, just look at the man who is making me feel protected… and special. In the settling dusk, his hair appears dark as chocolate, only his eyes retain the warm gray of a jackdaw.

"I have no right," he continues. "I just like you… a lot." He sighs.

"They told us to hate Germans, ignore you all, just do our thing and watch out for attacks. All I see are a beaten-down people who struggle for every breath."

"Aren't you afraid to be reprimanded?"

Mitch grins. "Let them try." He pulls me behind a wall and embraces me. To my surprise, a swarm of bees whirls through my middle. As if they have a mind of their own, my arms lift to Mitch's shoulders.

Our kiss is soft and warm, the bees hum louder. I touch his hair, feel his hand on the small of my back, his chest and belly press against me. We explore each other's mouths, our breaths quicken. Time is no longer important, nothing counts but the man in front of me, who seems genuine and kind. Is that what love feels like? Or am I just glad somebody is helping Mama and me? All I know is that I never felt anything like this with Fritz. Back then, it was curiosity and newness, what seemed to be the right thing to do.

When we finally stop, it is dark. In earlier years, Berlin was always radiant. Restaurants and pubs stayed open until morning, street lanterns shone—a sparkle lay across Berlin. All of that grew muted during the war, when we used black-out shutters to hide the city from night bombers.

Now, we have no lanterns, no light bulbs and no restaurants. Even if we did, we have no electricity, at least not in this neighborhood.

Mitch fumbles in his pocket and produces a flashlight. His arm wrapped tightly around my shoulder, we pick our way back to the apartment.

"I really like sleeping in your shirt," I whisper as he kisses me in the entry.

He chuckles. "I'm glad, but I'll keep my eyes open for a decent nightshirt. Now we better head upstairs. I'm off for a couple of days, should be back Thursday."

I want to ask where he is going, but I know he wouldn't tell me about his missions, so all I say is, "Be careful."

The next morning, I'm in the apartment's kitchen to fetch water for Mama and me, when Greg enters. He reeks of stale whiskey and his eyes are red-rimmed, but his uniform is spotless, the creases of his shirt still visible.

"Still sleeping in Mitch's room?" he asks. "I thought you lived in the basement." Arms crossed over his chest, he watches me like a snake about to strike a mouse.

"We'll be going back very soon," I hurry, too shocked to say something snappy. "It's just... Mama was sick."

"Taking up with the Russians."

Heat rises to my throat as I face the American. "*Raped* is more like it."

He shrugs as the corners of his mouth lift into a cynical smile. "War spoils, remember, you lost. Well-deserved as far as I'm concerned."

I want to smack the man in his arrogant face, but I just grab our water cups. Greg still blocks the doorframe, so I face him defiantly. His eyes are the gray of cement dust and just as caustic. He steps aside, leaving barely enough room for me to pass. My hands shake and some of the water dribbles on the floor as I hurry to Mitch's room. Mama is sitting in bed, looking much better. My heart aches to pull her out of her comfort.

"Let me help you dress, we need to move back to the basement."

Mama eyes me curiously. "You look upset."

I chew on my lower lip and collect the few items we possess, assist Mama.

As we enter the hallway, I worry about Greg lurking and yelling at us, but there is no sign of him. I lead Mama to the basement, each step like an increasing strangle hold on my throat.

CHAPTER TEN

"What are you already doing here?" Like most mornings, Meg is prepping bread slices with mystery jam. "I was going to deliver breakfast upstairs."

"Mitch is gone and… there is this fellow… Greg." The man's face rises in front of me, the sneer and arrogance. I swallow, unable to repeat what he said about Mama. "Anyway, he was nasty."

"I want to go back to bed," Mama says. "I'm just upset that your father isn't home. I expected him hours ago."

Meg rearranges Mama's blankets in the back corner. "I'll help you." Our eyes meet over Mama, who is crawling onto her bedstead. "I'm sure he has his reasons."

To her credit, Mama neither complains as she settles down nor comments about Papa. I hand her the bread, which she eats silently. I think about the last time he came to visit during the war. He looked so strange and distant in that uniform, the skin around his eyes and mouth carried new folds. We never talked about the war or what he was doing in it. Time was precious and the ugliness of that other life wasn't allowed into our home. At that time, we still had our apartment, even if we spent more and more time in the cellar or, when time allowed, in the official bomb shelter. I wonder what he is doing now, if he is a prisoner somewhere and if we'll ever find out.

To push away my thoughts, I busy myself with the sorting of our shelves. A bag of flour, a precious one with sugar, some cans, a tiny jar of mystery jam and a few cans of meat. My gaze longingly wanders to the metal-framed window. The tightness of our space becomes even more obvious. I hate it here. The air appears too thin to breathe and just the thought of spending a winter here makes my skin crawl.

Mama has just gone to sleep when the doctor appears. Meg has gone out for the daily scrounging while I'm struggling through the first pages of her Agatha Christie novel.

"Hello?" In the doorframe hovers the doctor.

I jump up, embarrassed about our room, but he nods a greeting and throws a glance at Mama on the ground. "How is she doing?"

"Pretty well, I think. I mean her injury seems to heal, the bleeding has stopped. It's just her head, she seems to have forgotten what happened. She seems to have forgotten a lot of things."

"That can happen with trauma. Give her time. You'll have to be patient." He sighs as he takes in our hovel. "Surely this is only temporary."

"I wish. We lived upstairs until…"

"We took your home." The doctor looks puzzled. "But didn't Lieutenant Cameron give you his room, especially now while he is absent?"

"He did. I…" Again, the nasty American's face rises in front of me. "Somebody else did not want us there."

The doctor studies me. "Who?"

I shake my head.

"I understand. I'm sorry. Some men are still very angry."

I'm angry, too. No, I'm furious about having to deal with this. I manage a half-smile and say, "I very much appreciate your support. I know many women are not getting the help they need. The hospitals are supposed to be terribly crowded." It's true, the daily water line serves as a news channel. While we wait, all sorts of information travels up and down. Right now, America's atomic bombs are the main subject.

After a nap, I take Mama back outside. We fetch two buckets of water and I fix peppermint tea in the shade of the house.

Finally, I allow myself to think about Mitch. Behind my closed eyes, I feel his lips on mine, his firm embrace. As soon as I do, the bees are back. I take a deep breath as heat rises from my middle. I realize I miss him, though it has only been a few hours. I never missed Fritz like this.

It's wrong, my mind comments. "I can't help it," I whisper.

"What is the matter, child?" Mama watches me, her eyes full of concern.

I throw her a smile. "Everything is fine."

We spend the day outside, Meg and I taking turns watching Mama while American jeeps and trucks come and go out front. They have also confiscated the apartment on the main floor, men's foreign voices rising through the open windows. Only one voice is absent.

In the evening we are preparing a feast. Today's rations included an allotment of 150g of margarine, real coffee and sugar. In the pan sizzle potatoes, their aroma filling my senses. For dessert we'll have sweetened coffee.

By the following day, Mitch has not returned. I'm afraid to ask about his whereabouts, so I stay with Meg and Mama. All evening, I wait, listen for steps on the basement staircase. The hope that has accompanied me for the past two days wavers. Some of the struggling women have become prostitutes to earn extra food and clothes. Just the thought turns my stomach.

I sleep uneasy, dream about the old apartment, how we used to listen to the radio together, eating the butter crumble cake Mama fixed every Sunday.

And then he is back. I'm about to drain our bathroom bucket, a horrible affair I can't get used to, when he walks up from his jeep.

I set down the bucket and scramble toward him. "You're late."

"And you're up early." The smile he gives me erases any doubts I had. He takes my hand and pulls it to his chest. "I'm filthy and tired, but I'll see you in a bit?"

"Your bed is available."

"Oh?"

Greg's comments return, but I shake my head to make them go away. "We're downstairs or outside, when you're ready."

Mitch studies me, then says, "The war is over, you know. Hirohito has surrendered."

I think about the devastation of Oppenheimer's bombs, wiping out a hundred thousand Japanese, likely all civilians. "That was the price they paid," I mumble.

"A terrible price, but this dreaded war has finally ended."

As I hurry to return to my nasty task, I think about the senselessness of it all. How powerful people crave more power, how they ensnare their followers to support them. Until it is too late.

When I head outside a few minutes later to fetch water, Mitch appears next to me, carrying two buckets himself. "Will you tell me what happened?"

"It's just better if we stay downstairs."

"Why?"

I throw him a glance. "Not everyone likes us."

Mitch pulls me to a stop. "Something did happen. Tell me."

I force a smile. "Everything is fine."

A wrinkle appears between Mitch's brows. "It's Greg, isn't it?"

Just the name makes me cringe. "No."

"You are such a bad liar."

"Mitch, let me do that." A girl of maybe eighteen, with most of her blonde hair hidden under a scarf, stops by our side. She's cute with an upturned nose and the light-blue eyes of an early spring day. Ignoring me, she continues, "It's Andi, remember, you fellows hired me to do the housework?" She has maneuvered herself within a foot of Mitch and gazes up at him with a smile.

Mitch grins back and sets down the buckets. "By all means, go ahead." He takes my elbow, steering me down the street. "Lotte and I will walk together."

If she understands his rebuff, she doesn't let on. "I could come along. Still have a lot of questions about your place. I want to make sure I do everything right."

Mitch's hand has found mine. "Just do the things you do for the others. And while I'm gone, you can skip my room."

Andi's mouth pulls into a pout while she throws me a side glance. It's no more than a split second, but enough to know that she wants Mitch for far more than cleaning. She touches Mitch's forearm and says, "I'll do whatever you need. I'm just so thankful for the job." Then she picks up the buckets and hurries off toward the street pump.

Mitch lets go of my hand, picks up my buckets and resumes to walk. "Where were we?"

"Would you prefer to accompany her?" I ask, hurrying after him.

He laughs.

"What's so funny?"

"You are."

"She seems quite interested in you."

"Nonsense, she's simple. I need a girl who broods and carries the world on her shoulders."

"That's what you think of me?"

Mitch stops anew. Sighs. "Come here."

"I'm right here." I know I'm acting stupid and jealous. Like an idiot.

He moves closer and pulls me into his arms. "I'm sorry, that was a bad joke. I like you for many things, so hush."

At that moment I want to kiss him badly, I don't even care that we are standing on the street in broad daylight. All I know is that he makes me feel safe—and special. I listen to his breathing, feel the firmness of his chest.

"We should be careful, for your sake," he whispers.

I touch his cheek and nod. "We'd better get that water before Meg and Mama begin to worry."

Waiting at the pump, the blonde girl manages to wave enthusiastically at Mitch while ignoring me once more. "See you soon," she cries, causing some of the women around her to comment, "Yank-lover… what's wrong with you…" The girl doesn't seem to care as she watches us pass and line up ten feet behind.

"Maybe you should go," I say, but Mitch shakes his head. "I'm going to help you carry."

"I can do it."

"I know you can do it. But I want to help. I'd help my sister or mother, too."

"What about your girlfriend?" It's out before I have to time to think. Mitch looks at me as the question hovers between us like a poisonous cloud.

He hesitates and finally says, "It's complicated."

I bite my lip. Of course he has a girlfriend, he is smart and good-looking. I'm plain stupid to expect otherwise. What does that even mean, complicated? "Maybe you should head home," I say quietly. "I need some time alone right now."

He looks at me, opens his mouth, closes it. Then he tips his cap and walks off while I stand there like an idiot. Why did I ask? Why could I not just enjoy his help and attention? Live in the moment and enjoy a bit of fun while it lasts?

The blonde girl is gone by the time I head back. I'm taking much longer than necessary, trying to decide what to do when I see Mitch again. I half expect him to wait for me in front of the house, but he isn't there.

Climbing downstairs, the air squeezes my lungs as the scent of briquettes grows stronger. The image of Mama, stumbling through the rubble, returns. *Come on, go,* my mind urges. And slowly, step by step, I descend into the cellar, out of breath as if I'd climbed the Alps.

As soon as I put my water buckets down, Meg is grabbing her bag. "Your mother has been sleeping. What took you so long?" She's about to leave, when she stops and looks at me. "What happened? You look like a storm is about to hit."

I just shake my head as tears clog my throat, spill out accompanied by a giant sob. "He has a girlfriend, in the States."

Meg puts down her bag and pulls me down next to her on the bench. "Did you really expect all those men are unattached? They are away from home a long time, of course they want some fun."

"He could've told me."

"He obviously just did and that went over well."

I bite my lip. Meg is right, of course. Not only that, I'm a hypocrite. Mitch doesn't know I'm engaged to Fritz. Even if it was a spur-of-the-moment thing and I don't love him, I promised to get married. Even if Fritz lies in some forgotten grave, I should've mentioned it.

Meg rises and picks up her bag again. "Come on, go upstairs and tell him you're sorry."

I stare at her. Is that the same Meg who'd been pissed about me talking to the Americans? "I thought you didn't like them."

Meg grins. "I don't, but I think Mitch is all right."

After confirming that Mama is still asleep, I climb to the second floor. After I knock and nobody answers, I slip inside, the door hasn't been locked most of the time. The hallway is empty, so is the living room. In the kitchen a girl is singing. As I hurry past, I recognize Andi's voice, hoping she won't see me.

I throw a quick glance inside, just as she looks up from mopping the floor.

"Hey, what are you doing here?" she cries, as if I'm some common thief. Ignoring her, I rush to Mitch's door and knock. The yelling behind me continues. "Wait, stop."

Just as Andi rushes me from behind, shouting, "I asked you what you're doing here," the door opens. I notice the rings under Mitch's eyes, the slumped shoulders. How did I not see how tired he is?

The next moment, I'm on the floor, the girl above me. "You shouldn't be here," she pants, holding down my arms with surprising strength.

"I suggest you let go this instant," Mitch says from some place above. Anger colors his voice, something I've not heard before.

Andi releases me. "I just thought…"

"You thought wrong. Now go and do your stuff."

Mitch's hand appears in my vision and I grab it. "I'm sorry," I say, but before I can say more, he pulls me inside, throws shut the door, and kisses me. It's a different kiss altogether, this one is demanding and so exciting I begin to tremble.

When we come up for air, he takes a deep breath. "Damn, woman. I didn't want this, I meant to do my service, hang out with the other pilots."

"I'm sorry," I whisper, though I'm not sure what I'm sorry for.

He pulls me into his arms again. "You've got nothing to apologize for. I should've told you. But I didn't know… not until you asked… that there may be a problem." He rakes a hand through his hair and looks at me so seriously, I have to smile.

"I'm the problem?"

With a sigh, he lets me go and motions me to sit in the only chair across from the bed. "You're not the problem, it's me. It turns out that I like you a lot more than I realized. Until you asked about Helen."

"Your girlfriend."

He nods. "Well, we were high school sweethearts and things are sort of routine. It was easy and convenient, though I suspect she's been seeing somebody else." He sits down on the bed across from me and takes my hand. "Here you come along, and I realize I want to spend way more time with you than I ever did with her." He rubs a finger along my palm, which is distracting and delicious at the same time. "I wasn't really sure how you feel about me." A slight grin brightens his expression. "Thanks to Andi, I know."

"I behaved terribly," I whisper, hardly able to process the information Mitch has laid out. Despite his stature and strength, he appears vulnerable.

"Oh, come here." I don't need to be asked twice and climb onto his lap. "I thought about you the entire time I was in the air."

I offer him my mouth and for a while, life retracts. Outside, Andi no longer sings, but I don't care, all I want is to be with this man, this strange American who has entered my heart.

"Will you lie down with me?" he asks after a while. "I mean, just to sleep. I'm beat and need to catch some rest before I report this afternoon."

And so, without much ado, we lie down together, he behind me, a protective arm around my waist. As he sleeps, I just listen to his even breathing, feel the warmth of his body on my back. His hand is relaxed, clean with short oval fingernails, despite the filth we deal with. I want to touch it, run a fingertip along the skin, but I'm afraid I'll wake him.

For the first time in years, I am happy.

With a pang I remember Mama. How much time has passed? Mitch is still sleeping and I decide to sneak downstairs to check on her.

Mama is sitting on the bench, eating bread. Even from the entrance I see that she's taken way more than her ration.

I rush up to her and gently take the loaf out of her hands. "Mama, please have Meg or me give you food."

"I was hungry."

"I know." How can I scold her when the gnawing in my own middle accompanies most of my days? "Let's get some air, all right?"

We walk up and down the street, the air superheated on this August day, my thoughts on the man upstairs and what he will think when he wakes up. I guess, amazingly, we are a couple now, a German girl of twenty and an American pilot.

I smile.

CHAPTER ELEVEN

Earlier, Meg marched off to the black market with three packs of cigarettes Mitch has gifted us. He doesn't smoke and handed them to us along with meat cans, powdered milk and potatoes. We also have gum, milk chocolate and a bottle of whiskey on the shelf. We'll use the whiskey to trade for something special.

Mitch and I are taking walks whenever possible, that is, whenever Meg is there to take care of Mama and whenever Mitch is available between shifts. I long to be alone with him, kiss him in private instead of sneaking around and embracing behind the wall of some ruin.

We have been out to another café on Ku'damm and I'm learning to ignore the glances of others. Some are disapproving, but not all, some carry envy when they see me in my new dress next to a good-looking man in uniform. In the end, it doesn't matter. What matters is that our time together, our talks, no longer awkward, whether funny or serious, are always interesting.

Tonight, Mitch is taking me to a dance. What?

I stared at him when he told me that there are parties all over Berlin. How is that possible when the likes of us are squatting in basements?

We stop at the officers' club Harnack-Haus in Dahlem, a sprawling building with a park in the back. Mitch hurries around the jeep and helps me climb out. "It's still pretty rough, Russians were here before us."

I don't mind rough, I want to say. Though I wear the new dress, my heart hammers in my throat.

As we walk toward the building, the first thing I notice is electric lights. Wonderous shafts of brightness send glittering fingers into the night. As we enter, I'm immediately swallowed by the noise, not only the voices of hundreds of men and women, but the sound of music, some kind of jazz. I have left earth and landed on an unfamiliar planet. The only thing that keeps me grounded is Mitch's forearm, firmly attached to mine.

He leads me to a counter, behind which a man is pouring drinks. Whiskeys and vodkas, red and white wine line the mirrored shelves. I'm just staring as the bartender addresses us. I'm afraid to drink, especially strong liquor I've not even seen in years. Here it seems to flow like water. Already, the air is saturated with alcohol fumes mixed with aftershave and women's perfume.

"How about a glass of champagne?" Mitch asks. "It's pretty light."

I nod numbly while I try to take in the scene. Women in elegant dresses with perfect hair dance with men in uniform. They wear makeup and high heels. I also wear different shoes, sensible black pumps, slightly scuffed. Meg found them on the black market and picked them up for me. I thought they were perfect until now. Because this here is glamor. Some women even have gold necklaces whose sparkle competes with their glowing lipstick. I want to shrink and hide in the shadows, especially when a few of them throw me measured glances. I can just imagine what they're thinking: ugly duckling has joined the party.

Fighting down my discomfort, I ask, "How is this possible?"

Mitch hands me a glass with a pale bubbly liquid. "Some of the cargo I fly goes straight here." He lifts his whiskey glass and for the first time in my life, I'm drinking real champagne. Mitch is right, it is light—tart and sweet at the same time. Bubbles tickle my throat. It's even ice cold.

I nod, but that's not what I mean. I want to know how all these people can look so perfect, how they can wear jewels and smell of expensive perfume.

As the band begins a slow waltz, Mitch squeezes my hand. "Shall we dance?"

I'll try, I want to say, but I'm still in shock. Again, I nod and follow Mitch to the dance floor. I feel as if everyone is staring at me… us, until I feel Mitch's hand firmly on the small of my back. "It's okay, just follow my lead," he whispers into my ear.

So, we dance, a couple in the middle of party mayhem, an island of two. Despite my unrest, I breathe in Mitch's scent, citrus aftershave and lavender soap, feel the smooth fabric of his uniform. His hand holding mine is warm.

A few times, men address Mitch, pat his back or call a greeting. One of them wears a British uniform and smiles at me as he talks to Mitch.

"Frank Evans is a buddy of mine," Mitch explains. "His mother is American, but he chose to fly for the RAF."

"My father wanted us to live in England," Frank says in my direction.

Internally, I cringe. The Royal Air Force is responsible for most of Germany's destruction. Men like Frank rained millions of bombs onto our cities. *Right or wrong, Germany started the war*, the little voice in my head comments.

I excuse myself and search for the restroom. Already, my cheeks feel hot and I wonder if my hair is showing its stubbornness. It likes to curl this way and that, no matter my attempts at taming it. That's fine when you wear a scarf most of the time, not here where perfection is expected.

Several women chat excitedly and seem to know each other as they powder their noses and reapply lipstick. I hurry into a stall, glad to hide from the crowd. Nobody will believe what is happening here, heck, I wouldn't have believed it myself.

I realize that the sewer system is also working and I flush as if it's a normal day in Berlin. Since I don't own lipstick, I just wash my hands and check my hair, try in vain to adjust some of the stubborn locks. I frown at myself and am about to leave when a young woman steps next to me. Her hair lies around her shoulders in waves and reminds me of burning flames.

She throws me a smile and says in German, "It'll pass. The first time I visited I nearly fainted." Without waiting for a reply, she hands me a gold tube. "Here, put that on, it'll bring out those beautiful mahogany tones in your hair."

Whispering, "Thank you," I take the lipstick and apply it. The woman is right, my entire face lights up.

"Ask your lover to get you one," the woman says. "And stay away from that hard liquor." She pats me on the shoulder and floats out of the room. I just sit there and stare at the figure in the mirror, a whole mirror without cracks. I didn't realize Berlin had any intact glass or mirrors left. Obviously, I was wrong.

As I hurry back, a man stumbles out of a side door and about bowls me over. "Sorry," he slurs, before catching himself. Then he laughs and takes a step toward me. "Well, if it isn't the cellar rat."

With a pang I recognize Greg, Mitch's roommate, and produce a curt nod.

"Why so tightlipped?" He steps closer still. "I sure don't get what Mitchy sees in you." His gaze wanders over my breast down to my shoes in a way that makes me feel naked and ashamed. "I suppose you do look pretty fine under that." His hand lands on my forearm as he leans in. A cloud of whiskey fogs my vision as he whispers, "We could have a go next time, when Mitchy is away. You German Fräuleins don't mind spreading your legs for us Americans, do you?"

I rip free my arm and hurry off. The last I hear is his laugh, loud and wet and somehow threatening.

"What's wrong?" Mitch says, when I join him at the table. Frank has apparently returned to his friends.

"Nothing, maybe we should go."

"I ordered you another champagne." Mitch points at our glasses, his filled with more whiskey, mine sparkling pale yellow.

I scan the room, worried Greg will approach me and make a scene. But there is no sign of him, so I smile and take a sip. "I think I'd better eat something."

Mitch jumps up. "Of course, I'm sorry, you must be starving." He offers me his arm and though I want to crawl into his embrace and hide there forever, I follow him to the buffet. I know that the human body revolts if it's provided with rich food after a long period of sparse nourishment. But the tables, clad in white cloths, are bent under an assortment of delicacies: dried sausages, cheeses, breads, sardines, tiny black globes—caviar, as Mitch explains, traded with the Russians, eggs, various salads and, and… I load my plate and though I tell myself to eat slowly and enjoy every bite, I'm way too distracted and uncomfortable.

As soon as I've finished, I know it was a mistake. My middle rumbles and stretches as if I'd eaten a watermelon.

"I need to go outside." Without waiting for a reply, I hurry toward the backdoors that stand open and let in a breeze.

Mitch catches up to me on the lawn, though all I want is to retch in peace. Instead, I feel his arm wrap around my shoulders.

"I need… to," is the last I get out before the entire dinner reappears. Mitch holds me by the hips as wave after wave empties me. At last, I come up for air. My eyes are blurry from the strain and my mouth tastes bitter.

Wordlessly, Mitch hands me a handkerchief. I feel utterly empty and bone tired. Worse, I'm embarrassed to act like this in front of Mitch.

"I'm sorry."

Mitch leads me to a stand of trees that have miraculously survived until now. "Don't be. It's my fault. I should've explained this place beforehand. I was just afraid you may not want to come."

My knees feel wobbly, so I lean into his chest. "I wouldn't have."

"Let me get you a soda and dry bread. Then I'll take you home."

I nod, thankful and also worried I may have ruined everything. After all that misery, the bombings and burned bodies, I seem to be unable to enjoy this kind of decadence. When I think about Mama and Meg, it feels downright wrong.

Mitch returns with a large box, a glass and two slices of bread. "I had them pack us a picnic."

I sip gratefully, smooth my sore throat. "How did you manage that?"

He laughs. "Sometimes I organize a few extras for the kitchen staff. They're grateful and I get a favor."

As we sink onto a bench, I nibble the bread, chew slowly, enjoy the flavor in my mouth. It's nearly dark out here, the air cool now, voices and music muted. "I don't know how you put up with me, when you could have half the glamorous women inside."

Mitch places a hand on my back. "I don't want glamorous, I want real." He sighs. "Look, I don't care about all those fancy clothes, the makeup and lipstick. I'm interested in what's underneath, the real person. You."

"But I feel totally out of place."

"Because you're real and true." Mitch takes my hand and squeezes it. "Most of them are interested in status and looks. I don't mean just the German women. A lot of the guests here are from the US, some from Britain. They're here because they won and want to enjoy this phenomenon of Berlin, the broken city—*Schadenfreude*. They're sightseeing Hitler's places, the Reichstag, his offices, the bunker. It's great entertainment for them."

Wordlessly I lean against Mitch and so we sit peacefully. By the time we slip out of the club, it's late and the noise inside has swelled so much, it feels as if thousands are inside. The music can hardly compete, deep voices, cackling ones, laughter and screams are mixing to a crescendo. Alcohol vapors fill my nose as we hurry past couples squeezed together in the shadows.

I should be tired but by the time we arrive at the house, I'm wide awake. In the entry, Mitch hesitates. I listen to his breathing as he pulls me close. "I'm sorry about tonight."

"I should apologize," I say, leaning against his chest. "It feels thankless."

Instead of an answer, Mitch's mouth finds mine. My body turns to rubber, soft and yielding and no longer mine.

"Let me walk you downstairs," he says after a while. We're both out of breath and I feel giddy with joy and excitement.

"I could come up for a bit." It's out before I have time to check myself. Maybe some of that champagne made it into my head, but I'm ready for more.

Mitch slings an arm around my shoulder and leads me upstairs, using a flashlight to help us navigate.

I'm relieved the living room is empty, I don't want anybody seeing me, especially not Greg.

In the darkness of his room, Mitch finds me again. I help him take off his jacket and unbutton his shirt.

"You sure about this?" Mitch's voice is strangely hoarse and even deeper than usual.

"I want to enjoy life," I whisper. "Everyone earlier seemed to have fun. Everything seemed so easy and light, as if no war has happened."

I feel Mitch's mouth slide down my neck, which makes me shiver. We undress each other and though it is dark, my hands, mouth and skin see everything. It is equally delicious and exciting, and I want to cry with joy.

I fall asleep in his arms, tired and happy.

CHAPTER TWELVE

I awake with a start. It's morning and through the windows comes the soft pitter patter of rain. I keep my eyes closed, just listen to Mitch's even breathing. My limbs feel pliable and relaxed—nourished. Not in my wildest dreams had I known what my body was capable of and how amazing it felt. Before Fritz left, he and I spent a few stolen hours in the shed of his parents' garden. It was exciting to hide and explore together. But even after this one time with Mitch, I know this is different. There are layers of pleasure I didn't know before. Already, I'm aching to touch him again, climb into his arms to feel utterly safe.

I watch him sleep, his lips slightly opened, his expression relaxed, his short hair reminds me of the rich soil in the woods after a rain. His face is tanned, the straight nose speaks of strength and determination. One hand is stretched toward me as if he's trying to find me while he is sleeping. Something warm and soft grips my heart.

Trying not to disturb him, I quietly climb out of bed, dress quickly and hurry downstairs, the picnic box firmly tucked under my arm.

"It must've been good," Meg says dryly, looking up from her tea mug. Luckily, Mama is inspecting her blanket and seems to take my late appearance in stride.

I can't suppress a grin, realizing I feel ravenous. "Here, let's eat."

As Mama and Meg cry out with each new item they discover inside the box, I change into my old dress and tuck away the shoes.

As we savor potato salad and a can of sardines, Meg eyes me curiously. "Are you going to tell us anything or is it a secret?" By her expression, I know exactly that she knows.

I proceed to tell them about the club, not about the jewel-clad women in search of entertainment, not about Greg, not my getting sick, but the music and our dance, the glittering bar and loaded buffet.

"It sounds like a dream," Mama says. "I used to go dancing with Papa. I wonder why he is staying out so long. I want to dance with him through the night, too."

Meg and I exchange a glance. In the following silence, voices erupt upstairs. A man is yelling something while another tries to calm him. I can't make out the words and am about to dismiss it, when I notice that Meg has turned white as bleached flour.

She rips open the door and flies upstairs. I follow and by the time I reach the hall entry, Meg is standing in front of a stranger. Except he doesn't seem to be a stranger to her, because they are embracing while tears spill down their cheeks. The man is wearing a tattered uniform and now I notice the empty sleeve stuffed uselessly into the side pocket.

Two Americans are leaving through the front door, yet the couple stands unmoving. Meg's eyes are closed, the man's wide open. If he notices me on the steps, he gives no sign.

I consider checking on Mitch, but there is Mama, so I silently return to the cellar. Mama is rummaging through the picnic box and with a happy cry takes hold of an apple, bites into it with closed eyes.

I say nothing, just watch her joyful expression. A drop of juice rolls down her chin, while my mind is on the scene in the hall upstairs. Meg never mentioned a man. She'd said that her family was dead, at least that's what I assumed. In addition, many millions are missing, mostly men who have not returned from the war—like Fritz and Papa.

When the door opens, I move next to Mama, Hugo howls and hurls himself at the stranger who bends low to awkwardly pet the dog with his left hand. Meg's reddened cheeks glow in the low light. "This is Hans." After she introduces us, we stand there, eyeing each other.

"Your boyfriend?" Mama asks.

Meg throws me a weary glance while Hans produces a grin that looks more like a grimace. "I'm Meg's husband."

"You're married?" I cry.

Meg nods and looks away. "I couldn't bring myself to talk about him. It's not like any of us do these days."

She's right. We may be waiting, and a portion of our day may be filled with thoughts of the people we are missing, but talking about them takes too much energy. I'm also afraid of my imagination. So many things could've happened, all of them bad. Yet isn't Meg my friend? Are we not sharing the most intimate space?

Suddenly, I'm mad, so mad, I huff and storm out… up the stairs outside. All this time, Meg never breathed a word, let us believe she was utterly alone. I feel betrayed. We live together, help each other. I stop in my tracks, take a deep breath. The sun has pushed away the rain, it's a beautiful morning in September, the air hazy above the dusty road—fall is coming.

The fact that Hans is back complicates everything. The cellar room is already tight, now it'll be impossible. There is no privacy. Mama and I will have to move, which means I'll either have to leave her by herself or take her along on excursions.

Worse is that we'll have to find a new space, a room with a roof. Winter will be here before we know it and every square inch of housing appears to be taken. And what will happen with Mitch? He's been nearby, has helped and kept a protecting hand over us.

"Sorry."

I turn on my heels and am face to face with Meg, who looks guilty and happy at the same time.

"I thought we were friends."

"We are."

"You could've told me. You said your family had died."

Meg chews on her lower lip. "It's true my parents were killed in the bombings. I thought he was… gone, too."

"So this apartment belonged to Hans?"

"His family." Meg places a hand on my forearm. "Please don't be mad. I didn't want to be disappointed. It was easier to think of him dead than to hope and worry every living minute. I thought if I expected him, I'd tempt fate."

In a way I understand. I haven't told her much about Fritz, though if I'm honest, it's because I feared her disapproval. Engaged woman has affair with foreign enemy. "I'll start looking for another place today."

"I'll help you as soon as I get Hans settled. He needs to register, so he can get ration cards."

My thoughts return to the Americans upstairs. Why can't they just disappear? Oh, what am I saying? Even now, every fiber of my body longs for the man upstairs.

All day I search. In vain. Every cellar and livable space with a few walls and a roof is occupied. Progress is slow because I've taken Mama along, so Meg and Hans have privacy.

New doubts have returned. What if Fritz returns, what if *he's* missing an arm… or worse? At the same time, my body aches to be with Mitch. In fact, it's all I think about while we search the notes plastered on walls, buildings and fences. Most of them are offers to trade or missing persons.

A couple are looking for roommates in exchange for food rations, but both are already taken when we visit.

I'm hot and exhausted when we return. Mama is dragging behind and hasn't uttered a word all afternoon. I read it in her eyes that she's upset, even she knows we can't stay.

Meg and Hans are sitting on the bench, holding hands. She points at the pot, sitting on the shelf. "We already ate, I made soup and there's bread from yesterday."

She doesn't ask about our day, it's too obvious.

While Mama and I eat, there's a knock. Meg opens it and Mitch's tall figure fills out the doorframe.

Tipping his cap, he addresses me. "I was looking for you."

I swallow the last bread and rush toward him. "Let's go."

Outside, Mitch takes my hand. "I've got to move," I whisper. "Meg's husband has returned. Apparently, the apartment was his family's. There isn't room for the four of us down here."

Mitch squeezes my hand and pulls me to a stop. "I'll ask around."

But I'm too upset to return his smile. "We've searched all day. There's nothing."

We end up in his room, his mouth on mine as soon as the door closes. I lose myself in his body, the sensations his hands evoke, the feeling of closeness and warmth.

I want to remain in that state even though I know it's an illusion.

"You can stay here," he mumbles, placing a kiss on my bare shoulder. I think of the three people downstairs, the crowded space.

"Just for a while."

I awake in the morning. Mitch is already up, wearing his uniform.

"I'll be back this afternoon." He points at a hunk of bread and several small packs. "There's even honey," he says. "Take your time."

After he leaves, I remain in bed, eating the food Mitch left me. I chew slowly to savor the sweetness of the strawberry jam and honey. I can't remember the last time I ate real jam or real honey.

Glad the hallway is quiet, I return to the cellar. While Meg and Hans are rolling up their bed, Mama throws me a reproachful glance. "You were gone."

"It's too crowded," I say, avoiding everyone's gaze. I know this isn't acceptable and certainly no long-term solution.

"Breakfast is on the shelf." Meg points at the bread slice and sliver of fat. They tell us it's margarine, but it tastes like mineral oil. I don't have the heart to tell them I already ate, so I stuff the slice of bread into my mouth and chew furiously.

Neither of us says anything as I help Mama dress.

Drizzling rain greets us as we step into the street. The dust that coats the city turns into mud. I take a deep breath and take Mama by the hand.

Please let us find a place today.

CHAPTER THIRTEEN

Mitch has been away for ten days. In his absence, I don't dare sleep in his room, afraid Greg will approach me, afraid somebody will turn me in. But sleeping downstairs like sardines is unbearable. Even if Meg and Hans say nothing, I know they're waiting for us to leave.

Twice Mama and I returned to the old apartment, looking for signs of Papa or Fritz. But the old markings are still on the building and there is no sign anybody has been there. Though Mama is much better physically, her mind is still fragile. She is often mute for hours as we trudge down streets, ask people if they know of any living space, study the notes and knock on doors.

The temperatures have dropped to the low fifties, and I am wearing my only coat that is way too light for winter.

A woman on the street has told us about a place near one of the neighborhood water pumps.

We keep asking until we reach a building whose roof is half missing. Beneath the other half, the walls appear sturdy, and though its windows are boarded up, it looks occupied. We're about to enter when an older woman, her white hair tied into a ponytail, appears, lugging two bundles of wood tied with string. Behind her trails a girl of no more than ten and though her dress is worn and too short, it is as clean as the girl's little face. She also carries a wood bundle, albeit much smaller.

"Excuse me, I'm looking for a place for my mother and me." The old woman hesitates, then hurries through the door. "My mama isn't well," I yell after her. "She was assaulted and is confused a lot."

That last bit brings the woman to a halt. She puts down the wood and for the first time makes eye contact. "What's wrong with her?"

Mama stands next to me, smiling at the girl. "What's your name?"

"Margo," the girl says.

"You're working hard, Margo." Mama moves a strand of sand-colored hair behind the girl's ear.

Margo watches the stranger earnestly and answers, "Oma says we need to work together."

While Mama talks to the girl, I approach the woman. "Ever since she was gangraped, she has withdrawn. This is the first time I've seen her interact with a stranger." When the woman remains silent, I hurry on. "We're living in a cellar, but my friend's husband returned and there is no more room for us."

A sigh rattles in the old woman's chest. She picks up the wood and says, "Better come with me then. Let's see if we can make this work. I'm Tilly."

The apartment is small, one bedroom, a kitchen and a small living room. Like Meg's place, this one has a bath and though there is no running water, it's a place to wash privately. And the most beautiful thing of all, there is a functioning oven we can cook on.

"Margo and I sleep in the bedroom, so you two will need to use the sofa."

"I'll sleep on the floor and I can help with whatever you need." I'm so relieved, I want to kiss Tilly's wrinkled cheeks, consider telling her about Mitch's care packages. *Better not mention him*, my mind comments. *Who knows what Tilly thinks about fraternizing with the enemy, who knows if Mitch will still want to see me now that I live ten blocks away?*

"Let's give it a month, then we'll reevaluate," she says, watching Mama help Margo undo the knot of her wood bundle.

My eyes blur as I squeeze Tilly's forearm. "Thank you."

Unsure if Mitch has returned, I knock on the door upstairs.

Greg opens. "You again." His gaze travels all the way to my toes and back.

"I'd like to see Mitch."

"Isn't here."

"Are you sure? He said he'd be back today."

Greg opens the door wide and makes a sweeping gesture with one arm. "Be my guest, check for yourself."

I hesitate. The little voice in my head nags. "It's all right. Will you tell him that I'll be back tomorrow evening?" The last thing I'm going to do is tell this creep about our new place. But then I imagine how Mitch will look for me and wonder why I left so suddenly. "You have any paper?"

Greg steps back to let me in. "Newspaper is in the living room." He follows and hands me a pencil.

Jotting down a couple of lines, I fold the note and hurry past Greg to Mitch's room, which feels empty without him. The pressure in my gut rears up. "I've got to go," I tell Greg, who is still hovering in the hall.

Greg's hand shoots forward and grabs my wrist. "Why so coy, let's have a little fun. Mitch won't be back for a while."

Like a reflex, I step on his foot and tear loose. Racing downstairs, I half expect him to give chase, but the only thing that follows me is his laugh that echoes through the staircase.

I consider waiting on the street, but it is already late, and I have to move our few belongings. Meg allows me to keep the blankets and a few kitchen things. I also collect a few cans of mystery meat, a packet of artificial honey, three potatoes and a handful of onions. Tomorrow is ration day, so we can stock up.

Lugging back bags and blankets, I find Mama, who I've left with Tilly, sleeping on the sofa. The old woman is mending Margo's dress by the shine of a candle.

"A young man was here," Tilly says as I add our supplies to the shelf. "Said he'll be back tomorrow."

I smile, thinking that Mitch must've found my note. "I'm sorry, I didn't mean…"

Tilly tucks away her sewing needle and straightens. "None of my business. Young women should be able to go out. God knows you need some enjoyment in your life."

Again, I want to hug Oma Tilly. Instead, I wish her a good night and stretch out next to Mama on the floor.

But sleep eludes me. Truth is, my skin tingles all over. Mitch has awakened my body to a point I didn't think possible. I turn on my back, remembering our time together, his gentle touches, the incredible feeling of closeness. I'm thankful for having him in my life, I'm thankful for having found Oma Tilly.

I'm up early, waiting in the water line. The air is crisp this morning, another sign that winter is on its way. I'm anxious for Mitch to drop by, hoping he'll return this morning.

"Lotte?"

I freeze and drop the bucket, but before I have time to turn, the man whose voice I haven't heard for more than a year and a half stands before me.

"Fritz," is all I muster before being enveloped in my fiancé's arms. He reeks of sweat and worse, his arms hard around my body. I think of Meg's husband and pull back, curious and afraid at the same time to find parts of him missing.

His face is so thin, his eyes seem twice as large over protruding cheekbones. But it's not the size of his eyes, it's the way they look at me, kind of flinty. Even without telling me, I know they have seen terrible things. The skin on his hands is gray with dirt. He wears the old Wehrmacht uniform with its emblems removed, his shoes held together with thread.

"I'm so glad I found you," he says.

I know it's his voice, but it sounds different, deeper, kind of gravelly, as if he's having a sore throat. I quickly scan his body, take both hands in mine. They're whole. He is whole.

I should feel happy, excited… elated. Instead, a lump like a clenched fist lies in the pit of my stomach. I don't know what I feel.

His gaze is still on me and I realize I haven't said anything. "I'm so glad to see you."

He pulls me close again, his mouth searching for mine. I quickly turn my head, so his lips brush against my cheek.

The people waiting in line are cheering. "Congratulations… you found each other," they say. Some have tears in their eyes.

I smile and nod as Fritz slings an arm around my shoulder.

And freeze.

Across the street, a jeep door opens and Mitch marches toward us. In that moment, everything decelerates. Every step Mitch takes happens in slow motion, I see it all, the immaculate uniform, the shirt and cap, but most of all, I see his face, the blue eyes that appear almost gray right now, the frown wrinkling between his brows, the searching look.

I don't feel my body, I'm weightless like a puffy cloud, except for Fritz's arm around my shoulder. I want him to let go, want to throw myself into Mitch's arms, but Fritz is happily chatting with the woman behind us.

Mitch comes to a stop a safe distance from the line and us, is staring at me in disbelief, his expression one of hurt and anger. "You could've told me."

I'm sorry, I want to say. *I don't love him, I love you.* But no words leave my mouth. When I say nothing, he tips his cap, turns his back, even his shoulders carry the hurt as he rushes away. The engine revs and he's gone.

"Who was that?"

I feel Fritz's gaze on me, but all I can do is watch the dust cloud that slowly settles across the street. Mitch is gone. He's come at the worst possible moment.

Fritz's hand on my shoulder clamps down. "Damn Yanks."

CHAPTER FOURTEEN

Fritz sits at the edge of Tilly's sofa and stares at me. I've brought him in reluctantly, don't want to upset Tilly.

"You never explained who the Yank was." Something aggressive lies in his eyes, darkens his voice. I can't remember ever seeing him like this.

"A friend."

"I see."

I walk to the window to avoid looking at Fritz. "He helped Mama and me with food."

"And?"

"Nothing." I shake my head, know exactly that I'm a terrible liar.

"Out of the goodness of his heart." Sarcasm drips from every word.

I turn toward him and try a smile, fail. "Why don't you tell me what happened? I heard nothing for so long, I thought…"

"You thought I was dead."

Tilly enters with Mama and Margo and immediately wrinkles her nose. It's true, the entire living room reeks, likely Fritz has lice too.

I jump up, worried Tilly will throw us out on the spot. "I'm sorry, this is Fritz, my fiancé."

Tilly scrutinizes Fritz, taps a forefinger against her lower lip. "Hello again."

"I was in Siberia, spent the last year in a gulag," Fritz says to no one in particular.

"You'd better take a bath," Tilly says. "Come with me."

At the door she turns around. "Lotte, stoke the fire and fetch more water. He needs a proper scrubbing."

An hour later, Fritz is in the tub. Tilly has found him a suit from the 1930s that belonged to her husband, who died of tuberculosis before the war started.

"You know," she says while we sit in the kitchen, waiting for Fritz to finish, "he can't stay. It's too crowded. I'm not doing that to Margo."

"I didn't know he…"

Tilly's wrinkled hand lands on mine. "Of course not, how could you? I'm surprised they let him go. My son, Margo's father, is still in some place over there."

Like Papa. Aloud I say, "Maybe he can stay with his parents or some other family." Somehow that idea makes me feel better.

After lunch, Fritz and I are taking a walk. The suit is a bit long, but clean. Shadows lie beneath his eyes, and I wonder if he's going to tell me about his ordeal.

He takes my hand, his fingers bony and unfamiliar. "I'm glad I found you, especially because that address you left at your old apartment building is wrong."

"We just moved in with Tilly. Haven't had time to change the message. Meg helped us, shared her place, but when her husband returned last week, we knew we had to move."

"Who's Meg?"

"The woman we stayed with until yesterday." I stop as something nags me. "Who told you where I live?"

"Some Yank. He seemed quite interested when I told him we were engaged, and I didn't have your last address. Short fellow with a broad chest."

"Greg," I whisper. "Of course."

"What do you mean?"

"Nothing." My heart aches as I think of the note I wrote for Mitch, listing my new address. Greg read it and when he heard that Fritz and I… My throat tightens as I imagine Greg telling Mitch that his lover is engaged to a German. The glee he felt watching Mitch's expression. Likely, Mitch hadn't believed him and had driven over to see me just when…

I clear my throat, try to push away the tears, as Fritz abruptly stops and pulls me close. He hasn't noticed a thing. "I'm sorry, I know you've had a hard time." He lets go, sweeps an arm through the air. "I can't make sense of it, the city… is gone." Defeat swings in his voice. "All that fighting and dying for nothing."

"We are alive," I croak.

"You live like rats."

What is the alternative? We don't have one, we are stuck. From what I hear, most cities in Germany are destroyed. "I'm sure the gulag was terrible, too."

Fritz flinches. "I'd better register and pick my ration cards." Without looking at me, he turns on his heels and takes off down the street.

I didn't even have a chance to ask him about his plans or where he'll stay. I look after him, a man who appears twenty years older than I remember—a stranger. Will he ever share what he went through so I can understand what changed him? My heart aches as I think about Mitch. I would've thought it hard to connect, coming from such different worlds, but I felt he understood me, genuinely cared for me. The new Fritz seems incapable of emotion.

Give it time, my head comments. *How much time*, I want to ask. All I want is to hurry back into Mitch's arms.

Fritz is back in the evening with two packs of cigarettes, a loaf of bread, potatoes, packages of sugar, dried milk and chicory coffee. The anger from earlier is gone and Tilly invites him to stay for a dinner of cabbage soup. To celebrate, we drink chicory coffee for dessert.

The later it gets, the more nervous I become. When Tilly and Mama do the wash in the kitchen, Margo has gone to bed, I address Fritz. "Tilly wants you to find another place to stay, it's too crowded here."

Fritz's gaze sweeps around the room. "I thought… there's plenty of room, I don't see why—"

"It's Tilly's place. Mama and I just arrived, and I don't want to be a nuisance."

Fritz says nothing, just glares at me, then Tilly, who is talking to Mama.

"Maybe you could find your parents or some other family?"

"You have seen the city?" The edge is back in Fritz's voice. "Even if I find them, if they're alive, I doubt they'll have room."

"But you lived with them before. I thought you searched for them already."

"I came looking for you. It took long enough. Good thing that American helped." Suspicion lies in his eyes. "You probably want free rein with that pilot. What happened, who is he?"

There is the dreaded question. I'm half-tempted to tell Fritz that I love Mitch. I know I do. It's the only thing I know for certain. But then what? I'm engaged to Fritz, he's a war veteran, sickly and discouraged. And Mitch will fly away any day and not return. All I'm left with then is Fritz. And I've got to think about Mama, who needs my help. Fritz could be a good friend, help us secure another place or additional supplies.

"Nobody important," I lie. "I tore open my leg in the ruins and he was kind enough to get a doctor."

"Kind enough," scoffs Fritz. "A few months ago, he was dropping bombs on your heads."

I bite my lower lip, say nothing more. Already Fritz's cheeks glow with anger.

"Tonight, you can stay here," Tilly says. I haven't heard her approach. "You'll have to sleep on the floor. I'll get you a blanket."

Fritz still stares at me as if he could extract the truth through my forehead.

I jump up and cry, "Thank you, Tilly, that's very generous. Mama and I will get ready for bed."

Fritz mumbles something before he rises. "I'm going for a smoke."

Wait, I want to say. *Don't smoke our currency.* But he is already gone. In the back of my mind, I ask myself where he got the cigarettes. They're not part of our rations.

The mood remains glum. After a breakfast of bread with scraped-on fake margarine, sprinkled with a tiny bit of sugar, Fritz takes off in search of his parents while I leave under the ruse of looking for firewood. I know Tilly is worried about heating and cooking this winter. There's still no coal and the search for wood propels people farther and farther into the countryside. It's forbidden to cut down trees, but they just disappear overnight. Cut apart with axes and knives, anything to find a way to cook or grab a bit of warmth.

Mama is staying with Margo, the two of them seem to be perfect for each other.

As soon as I'm outside, I head toward Meg's place. I've got to tell her about Fritz, but more importantly, I need to see Mitch.

Somehow, I need him to understand. My insides scream with longing, all I want is to crawl into his arms and make the last day disappear.

As I draw closer, my steps slow while my heart hammers in my throat. Several American jeeps and a truck are parked in front. It's anybody's guess if Mitch is home.

I descend to the cellar and find the door closed. A new lock is in place, likely Meg's husband has installed it to discourage thieves.

No more delays! My heart jumps around in my chest as I climb to the second floor. Inside, music is playing, some American tune I don't recognize. Off and on, a deep voice can be heard. I attempt to knock, hesitate, my hand inches from the doorframe. Twice I turn away, twice I approach.

Swallowing hard, I bang a fist against the door. Nothing happens and I'm already three stairs down when a voice stops me.

"It's the heartbreaker." Greg fills out the doorframe, grinning from ear to ear, while he ogles at my chest. "If I didn't know better, I'd say you're worse for wear."

Trying to look aloof, I say, "I'd like to speak with Mitch, please."

Half of me hopes he isn't home, but already Greg has turned and calls, "Mitchy, your former sweetheart must've forgotten something."

A moment later, Mitch appears, wearing his uniform. He looks even taller than usual and very formal. There is no smile, just a tight nod. "Yes?" When he notices Greg is still standing there, he closes the door behind him and approaches.

I step closer as well, my throat too tight for words. All I can do is look at the man I've fallen in love with, who saved me in many ways. But all the softness is gone from his face. He just stands there, kind of stiff and reluctant.

"I should've told you," I stumble. "Please, I thought he was dead."

"You're married."

"Engaged." I heave a sigh. "It was a last-minute thing, he was on leave from the war. We were… friends. It seemed the right thing to do at the time."

"Which you conveniently forgot to tell me."

My gaze clings to his face. "I love you."

Mitch scoffs. "You've got a strange way of showing it."

"You could leave any day, too. I made that promise years ago, he's returned from a gulag, I never expected…"

"To hook up with the enemy."

"You're my savior," I whisper.

"What?"

"Nothing."

Mitch half turns to open the door. "If you'll excuse me, I've got to get ready for work."

"I'm sorry, I never meant to hurt you," I call after him and then I fly up the remaining two stairs. As he's closing the door, I grab for him. But he pulls back abruptly, my hands grapple at the front of his uniform, slide away. The "please wait" fizzles out unheard, the door shuts with a bang. I look down at my feet, where one of Mitch's uniform buttons rests against my shoe. I pick it up and stick it in my pocket.

CHAPTER FIFTEEN

I don't know how I get back to Tilly's place nor how long it takes. I wander around busy streets, my eyes blind with tears, my heart so heavy I hardly have the strength to breathe.

All I see is Mitch's expression of hurt and fury. His slumped shoulders and pressed-together lips. Those lips I loved to kiss, those lips which had known how to explore my body and bring me such pleasure.

"No luck?" Tilly asks when I enter.

I look at her, try to make out the meaning of her words. My mind is as empty as my stomach and incapable of thought. I slump on the sofa next to Mama, who is playing parcheesi with Margo.

"What happened?" Tilly moves next to me, hands on hips, her expression worried.

A lump clogs my throat, makes it impossible to speak. I swallow and shake my head, swallow again. Tilly takes my hand and pulls me to the kitchen table, where I proceed to tell her about Mitch.

"He sounds like a kind man," she says at last.

"He is."

"What about Fritz?"

"He is so different… or maybe I just don't remember him well."

"Those men have seen a lot."

We look at each other, the old woman and the young one—new friends over a botched love affair. "I suppose I'll try to help Fritz as best I can."

"Perhaps you should give it time. After all, you're not married yet. Let him settle in a bit." When I nod, she gets up and resolutely grabs the pot. "You better wipe your face and help me with dinner. He'll likely show up any time."

I'm glad the bathroom's wall mirror hasn't survived the bombing. This way I can't see my blotchy skin. Washing my face with cold water from the bucket, I take deep breaths and return to the kitchen, resigned to bury Mitch deep in my heart.

By November, the temperatures drop and everybody capable of walking swarms the city in search of firewood. The farther we walk, the deeper we dig for the precious resource to keep our places bearable, cook a watery soup. We only spend time in the kitchen and sleep in our clothes because the rest of the apartment, the rest of Berlin, is freezing.

Fritz comes and goes. After he was unsuccessful finding his parents, he and three other returned soldiers are sharing a basement space. He's away all day, usually to help remove rubble, which pays 0.72 Reichsmarks an hour. The money is nearly useless because of the Reichsmark's runaway inflation; worse, he smokes any cigarettes he manages to trade. Just ten cigarettes would get us 1.5 kilos of bread on the black market. Luckily, one of his vet friends helps organize bread and sometimes vodka. Oma Tilly says it's a good thing he doesn't drink, so at least we've got the alcohol to trade.

I'm relieved Fritz doesn't care to have much physical contact. After losing Mitch, I'm having trouble even kissing another man. Twice when Oma Tilly and Mama were away with Margo, he's tried to embrace me. He feels so unyielding and reminds me of a wooden board, even his lips feel hard. I ended up pushing him away, saying that I needed more time. I thought he'd be angry, but he just nodded and took off on one of his walks. Nothing about him reminds me of the young man I knew. Worse is how tired I feel. At first, I blame my heartache that feels like a full-blown depression. When the war had ended, I'd been elated, most of us had been. Now all that hope has evaporated.

But that's not all. My body feels different, my breasts ache and in the mornings, my stomach bucks or feels queasy. At first, I tell myself it is because of the hunger. But when I rush to the bathroom several mornings in a row, gagging and throwing up a few sips of tea, I know: I'm pregnant.

How could I not have taken precautions? Of course, I'm aware of what can happen and yet, with Mitch, it hadn't mattered. Nothing had. Heat rises up my throat so suddenly, I pull off my heavy sweater. Luckily, I'm alone. What will I do? Pass off Mitch's baby for Fritz's—we haven't even slept together. Besides, I don't feel much like lying and right now, I can't imagine marrying Fritz at all.

I think about telling Tilly, not sure Mama could comprehend it in her current state. But doesn't she have enough on her plate with us and her granddaughter? Worrying about the whereabouts of her son, Walter? I need more time, need to think about my options.

You could tell Mitch. If he is even still living there.

No way. This is my problem, mine alone.

Two weeks before Christmas, I visit Meg. It's been two months since I saw her, and I'm shocked at the dark shadows beneath her eyes. She's lost more weight, her clothes hang on her in folds.

"What's going on?" I ask as soon as we're on the street. Despite the frigid dry wind, I suggested a walk, not wanting to talk in front of her husband, who brooded in the corner of their room.

At first, Meg doesn't want to answer. She just stares straight ahead.

"I'd like to help if I can," I add, patting her back.

A sigh rises from Meg's lips. "Hans has changed. I hardly recognize him. His arm hurts, he says, though it isn't even there anymore. He says he's feeling useless. I leave for hours and when I return, he still sits there fretting. Only when Fritz visits does he perk up."

"Fritz?"

Meg glances at me. "Didn't you know? He comes a lot, they sit in front of the house for hours. Likely grumble about the Americans coming and going. Fritz also talks to that stocky American… Greg. They seemed to hit it off."

"Did Hans know Fritz from the war?" I ask, wondering what Fritz is talking to Greg about and how Fritz can be clearing rubble when he is over here half the time.

"I don't think so."

Worry creeps up inside me. Is Fritz spying on Mitch, thinking I may be continuing the affair? "You think it's because of Mitch?"

"No idea." Meg stops to look at me. "I don't know if I can do this."

"What choice do you have?"

She coughs violently, wipes her mouth with an old rag. "I feel trapped. At least, before, I could take care of myself. Now it feels as if I've got an invalid child."

"Has he told you anything, I mean, what happened to him?"

"Just that it was a grenade."

"Fritz doesn't say much either."

Meg hugs herself, obviously freezing. "At least he still has his limbs."

"To me he feels as broken as this town."

Meg huffs. "Are we just thankless? Shouldn't we be glad our men returned? So many women out there are widows or still waiting." I say nothing. Meg is right. What could be worse than not knowing? But what if you know that the life you dreamed of will never happen?

"On top of that, Hugo is missing. I can't find him anywhere. He must've slipped out when I was taking care of Hans."

"What? Let's search for him." I may be tired, but I know how much Meg loves her dog.

Tears shine in Meg's eyes. "It happened last week. He's gone."

"How do you know?" I cry. "He could just be lost. Or maybe somebody took him in."

Giving me a watery smile, Meg sinks on a stack of bricks. "You know what happens with animals, somebody snatched him."

It's true. Berlin is devoid of pigeons, even songbirds, cats, dogs and anything else that could be eaten. On the black market, I've seen meat sold as rabbit that was undoubtedly from a dog.

I pat Meg's shoulder, but she shakes me off and covers her face with her hands. I stare at the upper window across the street, where Mitch has his room. In my mind, I go to him, tell him about the baby.

"What's going on with you?" Meg asks, bringing me back. "You look different somehow, kind of pale and yet…" She tips a forefinger on her lower lip, studies me.

"Nothing is the matter," I lie. "I'm not feeling too well these days, worry about winter and how to continue with Fritz. He's acting all weird, is gone all day, smokes a lot. Let's get together more often. We could help each other."

Meg frowns, then nods. "Let's meet every other day. We can scrounge together, like in the old times."

Together, we roam the streets and explore new neighborhoods all the way to the edges of the American sector. Meg seems to have perked up a bit, though the cough that rattles around in her chest makes her wheeze. She seems to tire much more easily, which I welcome because I'm always feeling exhausted these days.

"We could try it over there," she says one day as we near the checkpoint that leads to the Russian sector.

"Remember what happened to Mama?"

"That was a while ago. I heard the Russian military is cracking down on their men."

I think about Greg, Mitch's roommate. If you're unlucky, it can happen anywhere. "All right, let's take a look."

We cross without incident and soon hurry down one street, then another. As in the American sector, people are searching the rubble like we are. A couple of women are just leaving with pieces of a roof beam, so we decide to stay. Meg carries an old hatchet while I've got Tilly's saw. Together, we attack the remaining beams, cut them into three-foot pieces and tie a rope around them. Considering our return trip, we each can only manage two pieces.

Progress is slow. My arms and shoulders burn with fatigue. Meg's cough seems worse, so we stop every hundred yards to massage our aching limbs.

"Maybe you should go to the doctor, you may have pneumonia."

"Don't have money and those doctors are hard to find."

"You could ask Mitch for help."

Meg smiles weakly. "You're still in love."

Immediately, I'm teary-eyed. "We'd better get home."

Around the corner, Russian trucks park along the street, men in Red Army uniforms stand watching at the fenced-in entrance to a large square building.

"I think that's the Russian commandant's quarters," Meg huffs. "Let's walk around, I don't care to be harassed."

We are about to turn into the side street, when I see a familiar figure hurrying toward us. Head low against the wind, Fritz hasn't seen us. On impulse, I pull Meg behind a wall.

She's about to speak, when I place a finger on my lips.

By the time I peek around the corner, Fritz has disappeared.

"Why didn't you stop him?" Meg asks. "He could've helped us carry."

"Don't you think it's weird that he's running around here?"

Meg coughs, an ugly, hollow sound that echoes through the

empty streets. "He's likely looking for stuff just like us." She looks at me. "Though I wonder why they released him from the gulag so fast, especially since he's not injured. He was an officer, right?"

"Corporal." I pick up my load again. "Why would he visit the Russians?" Fritz had always been honest, a straight shooter. In fact, I'd always appreciated his sense of right and wrong. There has to be a good explanation. Maybe they stopped him when he crossed into the sector, maybe it was coincidence.

I'm chopping pieces of wood into small pieces to feed them into our stove when Fritz enters. I know it even before I see him because the room fills with the stench of stale smoke.

"Got some bread for you," he says without preamble. The next moment he grabs the hatchet from my hand. "Let me do that."

He works silently as I cut up potatoes and two shriveled onions for soup. Tilly, Mama and Margo aren't home yet. The two loaves of bread on the table smell heavenly. To distract myself, I say, "Saw you today."

Fritz hesitates the tiniest bit before he resumes cutting.

"Meg and I found this wood in the Russian sector."

Fritz looks up. "I'm surprised they let you pass."

"What were you doing over there?"

Fritz produces a smile. "One of them had asked me about the gulag near Krasnoyarsk. He wanted to know if I knew his friend who is working there."

"Did you?"

Fritz's gaze has returned to the hatchet in his hand. "What?"

"Did you know the Russian's friend?"

"There were thousands of us and hundreds of guards, my Russian isn't that good anyway." In a quick move he rises and wraps his arms around me. "Why don't we take advantage while the others are out?" Fritz tries to kiss me, which I barely prevent by moving my head to the side. The nicotine odor makes me gag and, in this moment, I realize I can never be Fritz's lover again. *You could do it to have a father for your baby*, the little voice in my head comments. *You know how scandalous it'll be to have a child out of wedlock. People will stare, point and talk, they will despise you. German Fräulein raises American bastard.*

"I can't," I whisper, push Fritz away with all my might. He lets go, more out of surprise than because he's too weak.

He looks at me with that strange distant expression he's been carrying ever since his return. "Still in love with the Yank, aren't you?"

I straighten my shoulders, eye him firmly. "I'm expecting." Taking a deep breath, I continue. "I cannot marry you."

Fritz lights a cigarette, blows the smoke into my face. "I suppose I should be grateful, eh?" He turns on his heel, heads for the door, then stops and faces me again. "You know, the funny thing is, I would've married you anyway."

Even from across the room, I feel his resentment, his anger like scorching tentacles. Behind him the door opens, and Tilly, Mama and Margo enter. They're chatting, Margo asking Mama to play a game while Tilly talks about making soup.

Without another word, Fritz pushes past them.

"What was that?" Tilly closes the door, hurries to my side. "Did you fight?"

I shrug, force a smile. "Something like that." Letting out a sigh, I point at Tilly's bag. "Are those our rations?"

The little voice in my head is back. *When are you going to tell them about the baby?*

CHAPTER SIXTEEN

On New Year's Eve morning, it's pouring buckets. Rumor has it that some trees are being cut for firewood in the British sector and I am determined to collect enough wood for a decent fire, even if there is a chance the border guards may confiscate it.

The relationship with Fritz is on rocky ground, but he insists on coming along. Together we cross the Herkules bridge or what is left of it. The bridge has collapsed and disintegrated, leaving an oversized iron pipe as a foot path. The Wehrmacht bombed and destroyed most Berlin bridges, forcing us to make huge detours and in many cases cutting off access altogether. People still cross the Herkules bridge, but one wrong step and you could break your neck in the debris below.

By the time we arrive in the area where the trees are being cut, there is nothing left except for a few wood chips I scrape together in my canvas bag. Inside, I am fuming for having trudged this far. These days, I am tired all the time and the prospect of another freezing night with hardly a piece of bread for dinner puts me over the edge.

"Maybe we could look in Tiergarten," I say, the harsh air taking my breath. I am soaked, the icy rain doing the rest, but I can't give up, not like this. It is New Year's Eve, after all, when people open sparkling wine and nibble delicacies. When they dance in elegant dresses and throw confetti. I am going to get something to celebrate, even if it is just a bit of warmth.

Fritz eyes his pocket watch, a newer-model Omega I don't

recognize. "It's late, we should turn back."

Indeed, the afternoon has taken on a gray hue, the sky laden with unshed snow. My lungs ache as we hurry the way we have come.

"I've got a bottle of vodka," Fritz says after a while. We are approaching the bridge or what is left of it a second time. "It'll warm us up from the inside."

I cringe. I am not about to drink alcohol, no matter how cold I feel. "Where did you get it?" I ask, intent on distracting him.

"Traded it for some metal I found."

I don't know why I believe him. Maybe I'm too distracted or maybe it is easier than to assume he is involved in something suspicious.

Fritz takes a couple of steps onto the bridge before he turns around and extends an arm.

Ignoring him, I huff, "Hurry up, I'm cold and hungry."

The next moment my left foot slips, making me lose my balance. The bag flies as I crash onto the metal pipe, arms flailing as I tumble onto a piece of the remaining bridge platform beneath. As my body begins to scream, accompanied by a dull ache in my lower abdomen, I lie there for a moment, dazed and in so much pain, I believe I've broken my legs and back.

Fritz's face swims in the gray sky above like some strange balloon with a face. He is saying things, odd words I can't make out. It is surreal in a funny way. I think I chuckle, which sends angry waves of pain through my back. Maybe I pass out for a moment, but when I look again, there is a stranger next to Fritz, waving his arms.

Both of them yell, "Don't move!" while Fritz climbs down. Balancing on the edge of the stone platform, he pokes my legs, moves my arms, then pulls me up to a stand, strains to lift me over his head, so the man above can pull me up. Something warm trickles down my legs, turns immediately cold.

I am too dazed to say anything, even when the man asks me my name. I just lie there on the frozen ground, staring into the sky, until Fritz appears again and throws me over his shoulder to balance across the frozen pipe. He grunts and huffs, keeping one hand on the shoulder of the other man in front of him, one arm around me.

On the other side, we rest again. The man leaves as Fritz sets me down. "Can you walk?"

I'm leaning against him, test my feet, move my arms and legs this way and that. Everything hurts and yet nothing appears broken. "I think so."

Fritz wraps an arm around my waist and drags me along as the dull ache in my lower belly turns into sharp cramps. It's as if a set of knives is circling through me, scraping and cutting. I think I'm moaning, want to lie down, make it go away, because I realize what is happening.

In that moment I understand that Mitch's baby is gone. The shock of the fall and this new truth takes the last strength. My legs don't want to hold me any longer and Fritz has trouble keeping me upright.

We struggle along, often stop to lean against a wall or rest on a rock while Fritz is catching his breath. For once he isn't smoking. By the time we arrive at Tilly's place, the only decent pair of wool hose I own is soaked crimson.

Of course, Fritz notices and cries, "I need to find a doctor."

I wipe my forehead that is damp despite the cold. "No doctor, just let me rest."

"You're bleeding, you…" His eyes narrow. "The fall… you lost the baby."

I just look at him, my eyes pleading.

"Good!" Anger swings in his voice. "One less bastard entering the world."

I just stare at the man who was once gentle and sweet and who has turned cruel. I've got no energy to fire back a retort. Little Rose has died before having a chance to live. My eyes burn with unshed tears.

"I'm going inside. Thank you for helping me."

"What? That's it?" Fritz cries. "You dismiss me like an unruly child."

I am so tired, kind of dead. Wordlessly, I open the door and climb the stairs, only half registering that Fritz hasn't followed. Nothing matters anyway. Thankfully, nobody is home yet. Tilly, Mama and Margo are visiting the black market, hoping to find something for tonight's dinner.

I strip down and wash myself and my underthings in a bucket of cold water, grab my pajamas and crawl into bed.

When the others arrive a bit later, chatting excitedly about the meal they're going to make with their finds, I pretend to be sick.

All evening I lie there, unable to move, just listening to Mama playing with Margo, and Tilly interjecting little comments, all of it otherworldly, as if their voices are drifting through thick fog.

The pain in my belly has subsided, replaced by an ache in my legs and back. Fritz said something about bad bruises that will hurt for a while. I welcome the pain, open my arms to it, because it distracts me from the terrible emptiness inside of me. I don't know how I would've raised a child amidst the chaos of post-war Berlin, but I would've loved her, the only part I retained of Mitch.

The hole opens and I slide into it, deeper I go, until I know nothing.

For days, I lie in bed, watching the activities from a distance. I no longer belong in this room, am only present as a ghost. Tilly brings me food, wipes down my face. I know I should get up, but I don't—can't.

I think about Meg and that she doesn't even know. But then, why isn't she stopping by? Anger and sadness take turns. I drag myself to the bathroom, to the kitchen to peruse the near empty shelves, back to bed.

Two weeks go by, a third.

"I need your help," Tilly says one day. She sits at the table, watches me intently. "Your mother is not well, and I'd rather not make her carry heavy loads. Besides, it's so cold, I worry about her getting sick."

She scrapes a forefinger along the wax tablecloth. "We need to stock up on wood." She rises, stretches her back and begins to rummage through the bag she always carries.

"I found something for you." She hands me a book. "Isn't healthy for a young woman to sit around."

I study the title: *English for 10th Grade.* English… Mitch. The pain takes my breath.

Tilly hasn't noticed. "With all the Americans and British living here, it may come in useful."

I read the first page… some little scene about a man buying bread in a bakery. Already, my mouth forms the words… *good morning, I would like to buy bread.* It's something to work on, something to keep my mind occupied.

I'm back on my feet, accompanying Tilly and Mama all over the place, cutting and lugging wood, picking up rations, visiting the black market while Margo is attending school. It's as if by exerting myself more, I can push away the memories. Except it doesn't work that way. You cannot outrun, outwork, or outsmart your pain, it stays with you like a tight fist squeezing your heart.

I should see Meg, but then I'd have to tell her about the baby, about my breakdown. It is too fresh, too painful. Nobody can know, not yet. She's likely too busy to stop by, maybe she is angry about something. That sometimes happens. Meg getting into one of her moods.

At the end of January, I take Mama on an excursion to our old apartment, the one we lived in as a family. The message on the house wall, saying that we're still alive, has faded, our new address all but disappeared. I'm just searching for a colored stone or something to write with when I notice a few scribbles beneath.

Leni and Lotte, have news. Your neighbor, Ursula.

I'm trying to remember Ursula, a woman who lived in the next building. "Ursula is alive." I take Mama's hand and pull her to the adjacent house, wondering if she remembers our neighbor. The roof has been patched with tarpaper, mismatched tiles and linoleum. I study the names in the entry, push open the door. The handle is missing anyway and a hole gapes where the glass inserts once were.

The corridor reeks of urine and burned cabbage, but I pull Mama deeper into the gloom. I've been here before, years ago, returning an iron Mama borrowed after hers had quit.

The woman opening the door has red hair, a brightness too gaudy for this world.

"It's Lotte," I say. "You wrote a message."

Ursula's tired face lights up. "How good to see you alive." She turns toward Mama, who is inspecting the partially missing doorframe. "Leni, how have you been faring?"

"Mama isn't doing well," I explain. "She was attacked by Russians."

Ursula puts a hand on her mouth, shakes her head. Everyone knows what it means, the stories of women having been assaulted are circulating at the water pumps, in front of grocery stores and anywhere we have to wait in lines, which is pretty much all the time. She pats Mama on the shoulder. "Remember me?" she shouts as if Mama were deaf. "I'm your old neighbor. You taught me to knit."

Mama smiles and nods, but I can tell she doesn't remember, even if I'm sure, deep inside her, she recognizes the older woman.

"You have news," I ask again.

Ursula turns her attention back to me. "Of course, wait a moment. Where did I put it?" She hurries back inside. It's so dark in there, I can barely make out the kitchen table.

Mama licks her chapped lips. "I'm thirsty."

"We'll stop by the pump later." I straighten Mama's headscarf, when the door flies open and Ursula waves a card in my face.

"It's from the Red Cross."

Squinting at the yellowish paper, I carry the card to the front door for more light. My heart is hammering so loud, my ears seem to ring. Even before reading, I know it is about Papa.

Mama is saying something behind my back, but my eyes are flying across the lines. I can't talk right now, I've got to see, got to read…

Beneath the red cross and a couple of lines of Russian gibberish stands Mama's address, our old apartment.

Alfred Berger, prisoner of war, it reads. *UDSSR Moscow.*

Red Cross, post office box 53.

It's Papa's card, he sent it. He's alive, he… A sob rises from my throat, tears the stillness of the corridor, rises through the stairwell past the broken roof. Papa lives. With shaking hands, I turn the card.

27 November 1945

Liebe Leni, liebe Lotte,

I'm a prisoner of war in Russia. I'm fine. It is difficult and I hope to return home soon. Please write to me as soon as you can. I love and miss you!

Alfred/Papa

I wipe my face and turn toward Mama, who is watching me curiously. "It's Papa," I cry and pull her into my arms. "He's alive."

Mama leans back, studies my face, then Ursula's. "Where is he?"

"In Russia, Mama, he's in a prison camp."

"Why isn't he coming home?"

"He will as soon as they let him."

Mama clucks her tongue, then shakes her head. "What is he thinking, galivanting around Russia? I'm going to have to tell that man, when he shows up."

Ursula hugs us. "I'm so glad you stopped by. I didn't know what to do with the card. After you moved away… I worried something had happened to you."

The remainder of the day, I carry the card beneath my shirt, close to my heart. The black cloud following me is finally lifting.

Papa is alive. That has got to be enough.

Book II: September 1948 – October 1949

CHAPTER SEVENTEEN

As if possessed, my feet carry me past the house where Mitch used to live. The US flags have long gone, so have jeeps and trucks. They moved into new quarters within a year. For months after Fritz's return, I passed by here, hoping for a glimpse of Mitch. I never dared to stay, not only because I didn't want him to think I was stalking him, I was afraid Fritz would see me and get angry again.

The truth is, I'm feeling lost. All that scraping and surviving for the past three years has left me pinched, kind of thin around the edges, a translucent feeling, as if I'm disappearing. I'm tired of scraping, tired of this endless struggle to survive and to forget at the same time.

A sigh escapes me as I blink away the tears. I haven't noticed where I'm going. Whenever I see women on the streets, I ask myself if they too are mourning. Surely many of them have lost somebody. Does it show somehow on their faces, is there a line around their mouths, a deep crease some place where this special pain has engraved itself?

I remember the flyer on the fence. The Americans are looking for people to help with the airlift. I could earn real money, get a warm meal. Besides, what else do I have to do that is so important? Mama can stay with Tilly and Margo and the chance of meeting

American pilots is slim to none.

The air above Tempelhof is abuzz with planes taking off and landing. Children of all ages watch from behind a wire fence, their expressions a mix of fascination and excitement. Long lines of planes are parked in orderly rows, their bellies revealing loads of cargo. Men are unloading boxes and sacks onto trucks that drive off the moment they're full.

I follow the fence for what seems like an hour—the huge, curved building seems to go on forever—to the main entrance guarded by US soldiers. The same flyer I saw earlier hangs from a post.

"I'm looking for work," I tell the first man in English. After I began to study the book, Tilly gave me more than two and a half years ago, I added a tattered dictionary. I've been studying ever since, refreshing what I learned in school before the war sent away the teachers, as if the foreign words could bring me closer to what I lost. Every day, I memorize new words, write them in my head or in the dust outside. On walks I speak to myself, ask and answer questions, form and repeat the words until they are embedded in my memory.

If the soldier seems surprised, he doesn't let on. "You need to register over there." He points down the fence to a separate entrance, where a line of people, mostly men in ragged clothes, are waiting. I rush forward, no longer sure that this is the right way. The line of men and women seems to grow by the minute and by the time I arrive, there must be more than fifty people waiting. Nobody speaks, everyone watches the man at the door, letting one person at a time enter. As I draw closer, I try to estimate how many more are waiting beyond the door.

I've just made it into the room—at least twenty more people are in front of me—when a man in uniform walks past. "We only need men to unload," he says in broken German. "Everyone else can go home."

My heart sinks. I'd already imagined returning home with good news and a bit of our new money, the Deutsche Mark, or some of the rations the planes are bringing in. On June 20, the day of the currency reform, every German received forty marks. The same day, our previously empty stores were stacked again with goods.

We could buy bread and milk and even chocolate, shoes, dresses and fancy hats. Not that any of us cared about that when we could fill our stomachs instead. I felt like a real human to be able to purchase bread in a bakery with real money. We thought we'd passed a milestone, a giant step toward recovery.

But now, three months later, Berlin's supply line is threatening to break down completely. Stalin wants to take over all of Berlin to keep it for himself. Like an island, Berlin lies in East Germany, which is ruled by the Soviets. In order for goods to pass into Berlin, the western Allies must cross Russian-controlled borders. And roads, rail and rivers to West Berlin are now closed. Hence, the western Allies have decided to supply us through the air. I don't think it can work—not to feed two million Berliners. If you believe the East Berlin radio, the Americans will never succeed. Berlin will starve to death, if it doesn't first freeze. And unlike last time, most Berliners don't have much more to give. They're already skin and bones.

I think about the horror years under Hitler, his dictatorship that robbed us of our loved ones, our homes, everything we held dear, but especially our honor. Most of the world must hate us after what we've done to Jews and minorities, how we've started wars with nearly three dozen countries. And when everything was lost, Hitler wanted to sacrifice us all. No, I'm grateful that the Americans and British are fighting for us. Especially since the Russians are constantly spreading lies. In late June, they insisted that Mongolian troops were about to descend on Berlin with tanks and artillery to kick out the Allies. Every morning, we woke up, half expecting to hear shells hitting Berlin—again.

Now I want to show them, want to help the Americans save Berlin. To my frustration, all the women break from the line and file back outside. I don't want to, no, I can't leave like this.

In the front of the line, yelling ensues. "What is wrong with you? I really need this work," a man cries in German.

The American behind the desk says something, I can't understand, but it is clear to me that they're not communicating.

Rushing forward, I address the American in English. "Excuse me, maybe I could help."

"Tell him he needs two good hands to work. Loads are heavy and it's too dangerous."

I turn toward the German, who appears defeated and red in the face. My gaze travels to the empty sleeve and then back. I know this man.

"Hans?"

Meg's husband doesn't seem to recognize me and remains mute while I try to hide my shock. The sadness comes so suddenly, it feels as if my soul descends into an inky hole. How often I have regretted not visiting Meg, not telling her about the baby. She'd died that spring of tuberculosis, my only real friend who'd stood by me when Mama and I needed help and then after Mitch left me. Turned out that Hans had brought the disease with him from the gulag. He'd been envious of her having all her limbs; in the end, he remained behind, a man who'd killed his wife. I knew he hadn't done it on purpose, but I refused to see him after that… if only to calm my own guilt…

Becoming aware of the stares, I hurry on. "They say the loads are heavy and you've got to be healthy."

Hans scoffs. "I left my health in Stalingrad. Tell them that."

I put a calming hand on his good forearm. "I'm sorry. They won't change their mind. It's too important."

Mumbles are growing louder in the line behind us. "Let's get a move on… come on, man, we've got to feed our families."

Head low, Hans turns away. Some men whistle, others pat him on the back.

I nod at the American behind the desk, whose hair is so short, the skin of his scalp shines pink. "He's upset, lost his arm in Russia." *And made my friend sick.* I watch Hans limp away, his head low, surprised I'm feeling sorry for him. A long time ago, he'd fallen in love with Meg, had made plans for a future together. Now he had neither his health nor a future. And he had to live with the guilt of having infected Meg with tuberculosis. That in itself was punishment enough.

"Thank you," the man says.

I'm about to turn when he calls after me. "Wait, miss." He says something to another soldier and waves me to follow him to an adjacent room, where half a dozen women are hammering on typewriters.

"What's your name?" he asks, introducing himself as Thomas Milner. He is the stark opposite of Mitch, short with narrow shoulders and a pale complexion. But his eyes are the color of hot cocoa and as kind as my mother's.

"Lotte Berger."

"You know English, you could translate for us?"

Mitch's face appears in front of me as he encourages me to try my clumsy English on him. "I would love to," I say aloud.

As one of the women writes down my information, Thomas

returns to the front.

I'm asked to assist with the men being hired. Every so often, I walk along the line to let people know what the Americans need. The line never ends until eight o'clock when I send everybody home. They look at me funny, some squint with disapproval that this German woman gets to tell them what to do.

Thomas appears next to me, smiles and winks as if he's won a prize. "I knew you could do it. Be back here at eight tomorrow morning?"

Every night, I study my books, memorize more words and practice sentences out loud. Every day, I work the line, assist with questions, help German men get hired to unload the round-bellied freighters landing every few minutes. Most are nice and thankful, a few belligerent when they don't fit the requirements.

I feel better about my abilities, learning to concentrate on their words and finding a way to explain them in both languages. What I most love about coming here is the atmosphere. The air is filled with a can-do attitude, each landing plane a snub in Stalin's face, another day Berlin doesn't have to go hungry.

In the background, planes land and take off, unending rows of planes that supply Berlin with lifesaving supplies. Americans are my heroes—as if I didn't already know that.

CHAPTER EIGHTEEN

A week in, we no longer need more men and Thomas sends me to assist on the airfield. At the foot of one of the giant Douglas C-54s they call Skymasters, a man is being held at gunpoint.

"We caught him opening a coal bag." One of the soldiers points at a skinny long sack of burlap with strings at the end lying on the ground, spilling its black contents onto the ground. It looks as if the man had tied his goods around his waist and hidden it under his jacket. The man just stands there, wild-eyed. His clothes are in tatters, coal dust and sweat have transformed his skin into dirty grime.

"What did you do?" I ask in German.

At first, he shrugs, but then he breaks down sobbing. "My wife, she's worried about winter. She's pregnant, you see, and we live in a cellar cold as the grave." He coughs, a deep guttural sound like a barking dog. On close inspection, I'm surprised he is standing up at all. His jacket hangs on him like a scarecrow and his eyes shine sickly.

"But why did you open the coal sack?"

The man looks at me with red-rimmed eyes, then lowers his head, a picture of misery. He reminds me of all these men who are groveling in the ruins of Berlin, rudderless and lost.

I turn to the soldier. "He has a pregnant wife and lives in a freezing basement."

I recognize the conflict on the American's face. But then he shakes his head. "Sorry, no exceptions. He's got to go."

I tell the German man, who quietly cries as they lead him away.

Deep in thought, I return to the administrative building. Desperation makes people do all kinds of things, even commit crimes. How often have I taken things, stolen during the past six years when we didn't have enough to eat? It's the way of life in this godforsaken city. Who could blame the man for trying to support his wife with some warmth?

Down the airfield, a handful of pilots in brown coveralls and their crew are heading my way. I squint and slow my steps. But none of them looks familiar. I'm half-tempted to ask them about Mitch, but as they approach and pass me, I chicken out.

Deep in thought, I enter the main building. I could ask in the office, surely they have the names of all the pilots. But do I really want to know, do I really want to meet Mitch after all this time? What would I say? If I'm honest, it's not that at all. What if he no longer flies? That inkling of hope I feel every time I watch a plane land would disappear.

His face appears in front of my vision, the way he looked at me with such fury and disappointment—hurt. I should've gone back and tried to reason with him, but I never did.

The truth is I'm not sure I could handle his coldness, or worse, indifference. He's probably married and has a child. For a moment, I see nothing as the memory of that icy December day returns, the day I slipped and lost our baby.

Better to leave things in the past.

What difference does it make? It wasn't meant to be, and I need to move on and think of Mama, Tilly and Margo.

On the runway, another Skymaster takes off. I watch it climb into the skies. What I would give to fly away like that and never return.

"Miss Lotte," Thomas cries as I enter. "I need your help." He always seems so pleased to see me and even if he isn't my type, it feels good to have somebody on my side.

A man in the typical shabby outfit of a worker sits bent over in a corner, hugging himself. Though his eyes are dry, small whimpers escape him.

"What happened?" I ask in German.

His eyes, full of pain, find mine. "Something inside is tearing me apart." He points a forefinger at his lower belly, then immediately bends over again and groans.

"He is sick," I tell Thomas. "Could be anything." It's true, the lack of hygiene has caused many people to contract dysentery, some have hunger typhus that causes violent diarrhea. "Should I send him to a doctor, only…" I hesitate.

"What?"

"Doctors cost money and they're hard to find, to get an appointment takes time."

Thomas glances at the man before he turns to me. "Take him to the sick bay."

A few minutes later, I help the man, whose name is Erich, to a narrow room with a desk and three chairs.

"What seems to be the matter?" The man entering wears an American uniform, but I would've recognized him anywhere. It's the doctor who helped me with my leg, his hair as short, just a tad grayer. Thanks to him I healed, even if scars crisscross my calf and it feels a bit weaker at times.

"Dr. Rupert, it's good to see you."

He hesitates, but then he says, "Cameron's girl with the shredded leg. What are you doing here?"

I cringe at the mention of Mitch's name, but force myself to smile. "Translating." I nod at the man who sits with his upper body folded over his knees. "He complains of pain in his lower belly."

Rupert makes the man untie the rope holding up his pants and lie on his back as I keep my gaze on the window.

The doctor quickly returns to my side. "He needs to go to the hospital. Immediately. He's got hernias on both sides which have pushed through. He may die anyway."

I stare at the man, who is scrambling up from the cot, his forehead pale and clammy.

"Can you help?" I ask. "He can hardly walk."

Rupert appears reluctant, but then he nods. "Let me make a phone call."

Meanwhile I try to explain to the man that he is in grave danger. He may have survived the war, but carrying hundred-pound sacks has given his malnourished body the rest.

"I know somebody at Charité. Somebody will drive him."

I return to the office, my mind on the sick man who could hardly breathe and still thanked me profusely. I wonder if he'll live through the day.

"Could it be? The heartbreaker?" Mitch's roommate, Greg, wearing the customary pilot's overall, is rushing up to me; as usual, he's standing way too close. I shrink back two steps and force myself to face him. "Hello, Greg, how are you doing?" I say in English, though he has addressed me in German.

He whistles low before he takes a step closer. "Learned English, I see."

I think about Mitch, who shared quarters with him, and wonder if he realized how creepy Greg is. "I'm translating for the airlift."

"Still fishing for an American, eh?" he chuckles. "Been flying for eighteen hours straight, a few of us are going out tonight. Why don't you join us?"

"Thanks, I've got—"

I half turn away, when his hand lands on my forearm. "Oh, come on, you love a good time. Didn't mind spreading your legs for our good Mitch."

I loved him, my inside screams. But no words leave my mouth as I yank free and hurry down the corridor. My arm feels dirty, as if it's been rolled in filth.

I still hear Greg's laugh echoing on my way home. It's later than usual because I had to assist with a broken-down truck and another injured German worker. They've also asked me to help translate maintenance documents for the Skymasters into German. Apparently, they're hiring a number of German mechanics.

I don't care, I'd do anything to keep Berlin out of Stalin's dirty hands. I lived through one dictatorship; I can't stand the thought of another. And the Americans with their unending optimism and can-do attitude are trying to work miracles, infusing me with renewed hope. Even if my personal life is a disaster, this has to count for something. I even catch myself smiling when I enter our place, nodding a greeting to Albert and Karl.

Mama is playing with Margo while Tilly is darning a sock under the single light bulb dangling from the ceiling—since Stalin turned off power to West Berlin, our electricity allotment is two hours a day, if we're lucky. Sometimes we get up in the middle of the night to iron or cook.

The winter after we'd moved in with Tilly, the building began to crumble. Cracks appeared in the walls, at first small, growing longer by the day. Sometimes at night, you could hear popping as the house slowly fell apart. When it grew too dangerous, Tilly packed a few bags and selected the bare minimum of furniture to move here to this one room we are now sharing with Albert and his son, Karl.

At the time, I didn't care.

Because after that day when Meg and I had seen Fritz leave the Russian quarter, things had gone from worse to disastrous. Had I just known the truth then, maybe Mitch and I would've had a chance.

I drop a bag of flour on the table, special payment from Thomas for me staying late.

"I could make pancakes?" I say, eyeing the hot plate Tilly *found* recently.

"Yes, please," Margo cries. She's thin as a wisp and always hungry. "Oma has two eggs."

Indeed, Tilly points at the cupboard where two eggs lie like precious gems. I hurry to fix the dough with flour, dried milk and one of the eggs—power can go out at any moment—and fry up six pancakes. They're dry and a little dark because we have no oil, but the air is filled with baking smells and we wolf them down nonetheless. Margo gets a second pancake and the last one goes to our neighbors.

"Fritz was here today," Tilly says as I wash our dishes in a zinc tub, the same one we use to take baths and do laundry. The plate glides from my hands and with a low plop returns to the water as something cold crawls up my back.

"What did he want?" Hoping my voice sounds normal, I fish out the plate a second time. Even without looking, I feel Tilly's eyes on me like two warm spots.

"He asked for you." After a pause, Tilly continues. "I didn't know you'd given him our address here."

My mind whirls. I hadn't, but then it wouldn't have been hard for him to find me. I take the drying towel and turn toward her. "Did he say when he'll return?"

"He just tipped his hat and left." Tilly still watches me. "Pretty strange he let you go so easily back then."

I keep my eyes on the plates. "I don't think he liked the fact I'd dated an American."

A "tsk" escapes Tilly's lips. "Thousands did that. And why shouldn't they? God knows, we all could've used a bit of fun."

I say nothing because the lump in my throat is too large to swallow. It was fun, sure, but I know that I loved Mitch. Still do. Even if Fritz hadn't done what he did, I would've left him.

Mama laughs. She's playing cards with Margo. Her face is relaxed, her eyes twinkle. I envy her for the way she has escaped her past and this impossible present. *Don't be selfish*, the voice in my head comments. *Mama has gone through hell, she deserves every happiness she can get.*

Since I don't answer, Tilly continues, "I think the sentiment to see the Allies as enemies has changed. Look what they're attempting. It seems impossible and yet they're flying day and night to get us enough food and coal to defy Stalin. I could kiss them for that."

Coming out of Tilly's mouth, an old lady of nearly seventy, it sounds so ridiculous and comical that I burst out laughing.

"It *is* amazing how they swoop in and out."

Tilly straightens and pulls me into an embrace. "Best of all, they've given us our hope back."

My answer is to hug her. She's become my second mother. "I love you, Tilly. Thank you for being there for me… and Mama."

Tilly squeezes me. "You two are my family now."

I know Tilly is still waiting for word from her son, Walter, Margo's father. Even if she never talks about him, just like we're waiting for Papa. According to the Red Cross, both are supposed to be in Russian camps, though it is hard to know where. Papa's cards arrive sporadically, sometimes two come in a week. Then there is nothing for months. He wrote that he has changed camps, but no specifics are known. Last summer, the German Red Cross started an office in Berlin, where many filled out two cards, one with personal information, one with the information of the missing person. I know we are lucky that Papa is alive and able to write. For many there is just silence, and waiting and wondering, lying awake at night. Recalling a last meeting, a last sentence. Still, the Red Cross has reunited thousands of families. On the radio, a sober voice reads the names of the missing: men, women and children who haven't returned to their families… the voice is sober, halting… Ralf Schmidt, Hubert Steinmann, Udo Schulz… Each name represents a story, a wife waiting for her husband, a daughter searching for her father, a woman looking for her brother, parents waiting for their son. In my mind I add Ruth's name to the list. I know in my heart that she is gone. Killed in one of Hitler's monstrous concentration camps, one of six million Jews ripped from this earth.

Why shouldn't Papa return, I tell myself. Nearly every card mentions his hope to be released soon. Soon, what does that mean? How long will Stalin keep those men? He'll be fifty next year. Fritz returned so much quicker, so did Meg's husband. I scoff, the sound loud in the stillness. Everybody is looking at me, so I smile and unpack my bag.

The light clicks off, the darkness is absolute. Today's power allotment is used up. Even if our window wasn't boarded up, hardly a street lantern works, shops and trams remain dark.

In the flickering shadow of a lit candle stub, we undress and go to bed, each of us in our space, a three-foot wide spot on the floor. Only Margo sleeps on a cot in the very corner.

I'm late to work. First, I couldn't sleep, and then I overslept. Near Tempelhof, the air is abuzz with planes. Thomas said they're flying stacked now, several planes at different heights, so they don't collide. Each plane has just one try to land. If they miss, they have to fly back to Frankfurt and try again.

"Lotte, wait." Fritz hurries to my side, a cigarette dangling from his mouth. The stench of nicotine and unwashed skin hits my nose. He looks pale, his chin covered in grayish stubble, even worse than when he'd returned from the camps.

"I heard you've got a new job," he hurries as I reluctantly come to a stop.

What's it to you? But aloud I say, "What do you want?"

He looks at me, then back to the ground as if he's afraid to hold eye contact. "You look good. New dress?"

Indeed, I wear a new outfit, light blue with a narrow top and a wide skirt, bought from my new income. It's too cool for this morning, fall is on its way, but I couldn't wait to try it.

I half turn to continue when his hand lands on my shoulder. I look at it, the black fingernails, the yellowish stains on fore and middle finger. Apparently, it's enough because Fritz pulls back. "I'm sorry, I miss you. It's… all such a mess. Maybe we could have dinner some time? I've got money." He pulls a wad of cash from his pocket—new Deutsche Mark bills with the letter B for Berlin printed on them.

"Russians paying you well, I see." Fritz flinches and I immediately regret my words, but the truth that Fritz is spying for the Russians shocked me even more than his sudden reappearance three years ago. If I'm honest, I blame him for losing Mitch. Had I known then that the Russians let Fritz leave the gulag early, so he could collect information for them, I would've immediately broken it off.

Fritz looks over his shoulder as if somebody is watching him. "I'm trying to get away, that's what I'm coming to talk to you about."

"Away from what?"

He steps closer and whispers in my ear. "I need your help, can't do this any longer. They will never stop, especially now with the airlift in place. Everyone is on edge over there, waiting to see what Stalin will decide, what the Americans and Brits will do. The mood is angry… frustrated."

"How do I know you aren't lying?" I step back to put space between us again. "You know I'm working at Tempelhof. Maybe you just want to squeeze me for information."

Fritz appears defeated. "I wouldn't do that."

"All right, come to the house at eight, we'll take a walk."

I'd rather rest—it's been a long day with another accident, a disagreement between two workers and numerous paperwork issues—but I know Fritz will just return and I don't want him near my family. Back then, when he admitted that the only reason he'd come home so fast from the gulag was that he'd agreed to spy on his fellow Berliners, he'd also mentioned that the Russians might threaten anybody he cared for.

He'd cried then and begged me to forgive him. In the end, we decided it was best to part ways permanently, especially after I'd lost Mitch's baby. Berlin had broken apart and so had we.

Like this morning, Fritz hurries to my side moments after I leave the building.

"Thanks for meeting me." He points down the street, so we begin to stroll past walls of stacked bricks, ready to be used for new buildings. There's still plenty of rubble, Berlin continues to lie in ruins. Still, there is also plenty of life, the streets full of people hurrying this way and that, women with strollers, men in suits and hats, children with sacks over their shoulders. And through it all, thousands of refugees track past us in slow lines, dragging suitcases, boxes and carts behind them. Stalin is clearing out every German from behind the Iron Curtain.

"Tell me what you want, I'm pretty tired."

Fritz doesn't answer. Has he not heard me? I glance at him, the pallid skin and bluish lips, the unkempt appearance and something tugs at my heart. "You asked me here," I say more softly.

Our eyes meet and, with a deep sigh, he says, "I want to leave

Berlin."

"What does that have to do with me?"

Fritz tries to capture my hand, but I pull away. "Don't you see, I can't go *officially*. Berlin is an island, especially now Russians control all the borders. They'd want my papers, want to know why I'm going to the west."

"Why are you going?"

"I can't do this any longer." The defeated look is back. "Last week, they came in the middle of the night, a black car pulled up. They interrogated me, demanded to know why I hadn't given them much intel lately." He pulls out another cigarette and lights it with trembling fingers.

"I'm sorry, but what can *I* do?"

"Don't you work for the Americans?"

"Yes, but—"

"They fly all these planes back to Frankfurt… surely they take passengers."

"These are cargo planes." I stop abruptly and face him. "Are you seriously suggesting that I get you a seat on an American plane?"

"I know you could, if you wanted to. You always had a thing for them."

"A thing?" The old anger creeps up in me.

"You always liked them, that pilot you slept with." Contempt swings in Fritz's voice, as if what I've done is so much worse than his betrayal.

"I can't, Fritz."

"Why not?"

"It's impossible, I just work there. And… I don't trust you."

"You help them a lot with your translation service and—"

"You may be spying out their planes, the routes, who knows, maybe you're supposed to kill pilots."

"Don't be ridiculous."

"Am I? You're the one who decided to make a deal with the enemy, and you have the gall to accuse me of siding with the Americans? Unlike the Russians, the Americans *helped* me, are now helping two million Berliners."

Fritz grinds the stub of his cigarette under his heel. "That was wrong, I know that. I was jealous, I loved you… still do."

"You have a funny way of showing that."

"It's too dangerous, anyway. I can't be close to people, just in case."

"Why didn't you think about that when they asked you in the gulag?"

Fritz throws up his arms, hugs himself. "I just couldn't take it… the cold, no food. You should've seen us, eyeing each other's rations like animals ready to tear each other apart."

"Millions of men endured… many are still there as we speak. Who knows if your Stalin will ever let them go." My thoughts return to Papa, who is surely suffering, if he isn't gone already.

"He isn't *my* Stalin." Fritz lights another cigarette, sucks on it as if he's drowning. "Don't you think I've regretted it ever since? Not a day goes by…" He spits, "Never mind, I'll look for another way."

"I'm going to bed. Please don't come here again." I turn on my heels and rush back the way we came.

I feel horrible. Despite what Fritz did, a part of me understands *why* he did it. He isn't the only one working for the Russians. Likely, there're thousands. Showing an interest in communism, maybe accepting a bribe in prison. They could use anything against a man and wear him down. But I have no way of knowing if Fritz is telling the truth. Maybe all he wants is to infiltrate Tempelhof, one of three airports used to save West Berlin.

Even if I found a willing pilot, I couldn't risk it.

CHAPTER NINETEEN

Fritz hasn't been back, but I can't get his last visit out of my head. Against my will, I'm watching the activities more closely, even if it's ridiculous. This is a huge military operation, there are soldiers and guards everywhere. Everything is tightly controlled, because everything coming into Berlin is lifesaving, whether it's flour or coal or the numerous boxed items like dried potatoes or dried milk. Thanks to my job, I've gotten a few extras, a bit of sugar, some dried potatoes that we mixed with water and enjoyed with a can of meat. I even baked a cake for Margo's birthday with plums Tilly and Mama had organized in the south of Berlin. The dough was chewy—no baking powder—but it felt like a real celebration.

Today Thomas asked me to lead a group of American servicewomen through the airport. I'm supposed to help translate if they have questions for the German workers who tirelessly unload plane after plane.

The women are chatting among themselves as I become aware of a man with a tiny brush who is sweeping bits of flour from the cargo plane's floor into a canvas sack. The white of the flour is mixed with coal dust and who knows what else.

"Did you see that?" one of the women comments.

"I couldn't eat that," another one says.

They look disgusted as they watch the man, who turns crimson when he becomes aware of the stares. He quickly stuffs his sack into the top of his pants and mutters, "I didn't take anything," before climbing down from the plane and hurrying off.

"They're hungry," I say simply. "Many of us have been starving for six years."

The women stare at me. "I thought the war ended in '45."

"There was nothing to eat long before and progress has been slow since."

One of the women nods thoughtfully. "I have seen the town, asked myself how anybody can survive here."

"Hard to believe Stalin is interested," another one says.

We all look at each other, though I'm not concentrating. Out of the corner of my eye, I see a truck arriving at the plane where the man just swept flour and coal dust into his bag.

Two men are filling the plane's belly with empty sacks. There are so many, they stack to the ceiling, fill every crevice. I think of Fritz, who could easily hide among them. Right. I must be insane. He'd be found out, at the latest when the plane lands at the American base in Frankfurt. He'd be arrested, maybe charged, or worse, sent back here.

"Look," one of the women cries. "Pilots!" The chatter grows more animated as they hurry toward a group of three men walking briskly toward the main building. I follow reluctantly, not sure what my role is supposed to be while these women flirt.

That's when I see him. Tall, handsome, he looks just the same as three years ago. Only his eyes appear more serious, kind of brooding. I am in the back of the group, wishing myself away. And at first, it works. The women surround the men, chat excitedly about the airport and the mission to keep Berlin alive and out of Stalin's hands.

"Lotte?"

A shadow falls over me as I look up and straight into Mitch's eyes. I'm shocked at the storm raging inside of me, the clogged throat and racing heartbeat. I heave a deep breath and try for a smile as the servicewomen crowd us. The chatter dies, everyone senses that there's something strange and highly entertaining going on here.

"Hello, Mitch." How often have I imagined seeing him again? Each time the circumstances were different, sometimes I'd run into him on the street, sometimes he'd be standing at the door to my apartment. I'd quite often thought about seeing him here at Tempelhof, but not today, not now. I'd imagined saying something witty or funny, our conversation light and flowing.

None of these scenarios prepared me for the actual situation, him standing in front of me, strangers watching our every move.

"I didn't know you were here," he says, so quietly, I lean forward to pick up his voice.

"I'm a translator," I say. "English and German." *Duh, what else would I speak here?*

But Mitch doesn't seem to notice. A small smile plays around his mouth. "You learned more English."

I nod. "After… I wanted to do something useful." Standing close now, I notice new lines around his eyes and nose. I want to touch them, smooth them out. "You're flying missions again," I say aloud.

"Almost daily, I rarely leave the plane during the unload. Just today, one of my old roommates is celebrating his birthday here. Got leave for a few hours."

I hear his words, but they aren't half as important as just looking at him. I could stand here for an eternity, just watching his face, the broad shoulders now hidden beneath a leather jacket. I want to tell him about Fritz, want to ask him about his life. But then, I'm afraid to ask anything, afraid he is happily married. I can't even muster the strength to search for a ring on his hand.

The crew member by his side says something and Mitch answers, "Sure, of course."

Turning to me, he says, "I've got to go, car is waiting."

I nod enthusiastically to cover my disappointment. "Of course, have fun."

He seems to hesitate, but then he follows the other two down the path while the servicewomen are chatting to each other. I just stand there, unable to move or think. All I do is stare at the receding figures. At the door, Mitch turns briefly. Our eyes meet. Is he nodding at me, smiling? I can't tell for sure.

One of the women takes me aside. "You know them?"

"Just one… from the end of the war."

The woman remains silent, only looks at me knowingly, as if my heartache is written all over my face.

"He helped me with an injury," I hurry. *Why don't I just shut up and forget about him?* Straightening my shoulders, I address the group. "Ladies, I think we should return to the building for some lunch."

Once I lead them to the cafeteria, I hurry to the bathroom and hide in one of the stalls. Forgetting about Mitch is about as easy as not breathing.

All afternoon I work mechanically, speak with German

administrators visiting from the city, explain things to my supervisors, translate articles from *Der Tag*, a newspaper published in the British sector.

On the way home, I'm writing letters to Mitch in my head, explaining things. The words gush onto the page, eloquent words full of meaning. I imagine him reading, nodding his head, smiling. I'm funny on those pages, drawing him in.

I want to apologize again, explain what happened, confirm that I still love him. I imagine him waiting for me at the airport entrance, appearing at my desk. With all the daydreaming, I'm surprised when I arrive at the apartment. Deep down, I know I won't write anything, let alone something Mitch wants to read. I've got to forget him, once and for all. No more pining, no more fantasizing.

Albert, our neighbor, is red in the face while Tilly is pacing back and forth in front of him as Mama and Margo are watching quietly. Albert's part of the room is a smelly mess. With his one hand he is not as capable of cleaning, but I suspect it's his mind and depression that keep him from doing much. Most of the time, he just sits there, while his son Karl, who is thirteen, takes care of everything, from picking up rations to washing dishes and searching for wood.

"Please talk some sense into him," Tilly cries as soon as she sees me. "He wants to go to the Russian sector."

Before I can say anything, Albert cries, "I'm just signing up for their rations. They've got all sorts of vegetables and fruit while we eat dried and powdered everything." He looks up, his eyes red-rimmed and puffy. "I want Karl to have better food."

Tilly continues as if he isn't in the room. "Russians want to lure us with their goods. You can't possibly support another dictator."

I sink down next to Albert, whose good hand keeps rubbing his thigh. "Please don't go over there. Stalin does this on purpose. He wants to create strife here to disrupt the airlift. Maybe I can help with a few extra things."

Albert looks at me. "I'm just so tired, and poor Karl."

"I don't need their vegetables," Karl says. He is a small boy with narrow shoulders and the typical bony body all kids seem to have in common. Margo runs to his side and drapes an arm around him.

"Don't you see," I say. "They are trying to take away our freedom. You know what that's like. We all lived it for years. We can only do this if we stick together *against* them." Lowering my voice, I add, "They raped Mama, remember."

An abrupt movement makes me look up. Mama stands there with a hand on her mouth as if she's trying to keep herself from screaming. She stares at me with wide eyes, glittering with tears.

"I'd forgotten," she cries. "Oh my God, I'd totally forgotten."

Tilly and I rush to her and hold her close while she mutters and trembles. Mama's outburst has apparently shaken Albert, because he gets up too and awkwardly pats Mama's hand. So, we stand together, bits and pieces of broken families, uniting to mend the cracks in our psyches. It is like that all over Germany. Millions of families are missing loved ones, millions more have confirmation that their husbands, uncles, brothers and sons are dead. That is the price Germany paid for following Hitler, for believing and supporting a monster.

"I'm sorry, Leni, I didn't mean to… I'm just so upset." Albert shakes his head as he glances at his son. "I won't go. I'm not selling out our future. Karl deserves better. We all do." He produces a weak smile and returns to his seat.

Tilly resolutely announces, "I think it's time for some strong tea, come on over, everyone." She pulls open the curtain separating the two sides of the room.

I remember the bottle of bourbon on the kitchen shelf, a gift from Thomas for staying late most nights. I could trade it, but this is more important.

A bit later we all sit together, sipping peppermint tea laced with whiskey. Margo and Karl are sharing a precious piece of American gum I've been keeping for special occasions.

Mama sits next to me quietly, her hands wrapped around her mug. Off and on, a tear rolls down her cheek while she looks at me with a searching expression.

"I'm sorry," I whisper, squeezing her hand. "I shouldn't have said anything."

"Hush," Mama says. "I put you through hell." A tremble goes through her as she continues, "I buried it all inside me."

"It was too much."

Mama makes a tsk sound. "All this time, I've been living on the surface… like a different person." She takes my hand. "How did you bear it? I was supposed to take care of you."

"You did, when I needed it. I'm an adult, I can take care of you and myself."

Mama smiles through her tears as Tilly pours more tea and

whiskey.

So, we sit until it turns dark outside and one of us lights a candle. Tonight, electricity will be on around midnight.

What does it matter? I've got my mother back.

CHAPTER TWENTY

I'm half elated, half worried about Mama's recovery. She's returned from her child-like state, helps Tilly take care of errands, our room, and the laundry, a lengthy, arduous affair of washing a few pieces at a time in the tin tub, rinsing in a bucket of water and draping each piece on a line crisscrossing our room. But I also catch her sitting motionless by herself, just staring into space. She's confided that the events of that afternoon have been returning in detail, at first in shreds, then longer parts, and that seeing the faces of her attackers, hearing their grunts and smelling their stench makes her panic.

"Do you want to tell me about it?" I ask during a quiet minute while Tilly and Margo are on a water run.

Mama looks at me, one hand on her throat as if she wants to keep herself from screaming. Her face glows. "I can't." She abruptly rises and begins sorting our supplies. "Let's make dinner before Tilly returns. She's been doing so much for us, I feel terribly guilty. I have been such a burden," she says with her back to me.

I rush to her and we hug for a full minute.

"You are never a burden," I whisper. Secretly, I'm frustrated that I've got no idea how to help my mother. Of course, I'm relieved to have her back, though I'm afraid what this memory will do to her. I need a therapist, but there aren't any available. So many women have been violated, but there is no cure for it, just a covering up and suffering in silence. They must hurry forward, so they can forget. Except, it's impossible—as impossible as forgetting about the child I lost.

When I leave the house the next morning, Fritz appears at my side. If anything, he looks worse than a few weeks ago. His suit hangs on him in folds, the fabric of his pants coated with dirt. "Have you thought about it?" he says without preamble.

"About what?"

"Helping me escape."

I take a deep breath, try to keep a few feet of space between us. "You told me you'd try something else."

"That didn't work. I'm stuck here."

"I told you, it's impossible. The airlift is a military operation. Only registered personnel and US servicemen are permitted on the grounds."

"Can't you ask somebody, I've got money." He pulls out a wad of Ostmarks, the East German currency introduced by the Russians. It's worth one fifth of the Deutsche Mark, but still good on the black market.

"I don't need your money. Why don't you find a driver to smuggle you out on a truck?"

Fritz makes a face, shakes his head once. "Too risky."

"And making me break all the rules is not?"

"They like you," Fritz cries. "Don't you understand, they'll kill me."

"Surely you aren't the only German spying unsuccessfully. Surely the Russians won't kill you all."

"How do you know?"

"I don't." Against my will, I look at him closely. "How can I trust you not to do anything?"

"What could I possibly do?"

"Tell the Russians about Tempelhof, about the planes or schedules."

"Nonsense, Lotte. I'm finished." Fritz sounds so dejected, I am sure he means it.

I take a deep breath. "I've got to go. Try Tegel Airport in the French sector, they're having 19,000 people build a new runway. You could earn money there, 1.20 West Mark an hour." *Honest money*, I want to say. But all I do is look at the man I was once engaged to and who looks like a breeze could mow him down. With a nod, I turn as guilt tugs at my heart. About what, I don't know.

When I arrive at Tempelhof, I'm immediately pulled into a dozen situations. I don't even have time to think about anything, let alone talk to somebody. I heard Thomas mention how pilots fly sixteen or more hours, sleep in bunks and eat on the fly. Not just Americans, but the British too. Even though it is still unclear if Berlin can survive, I sense the urgency everywhere I go. It's as if the air is electrified with the conviction that we mustn't let Stalin win, that the stakes are too high.

I'm willing to do my part, if I can be a tiny wheel in the machinery to stop the Soviets. In a moment of reprieve, I sink onto a chair and rub my aching ankles.

"Long day?" Thomas asks as he sinks on a chair across from me. A small grin brightens his face, even if his eyelids are purple behind the glasses.

I make a face but can't help returning his smile. "You're always so chipper. You must be exhausted."

He shrugs as his cheeks turn a shade of pink. "That may be your fault." His gaze lingers on my face, searching. He may not be tall and attractive like Mitch, but he appears earnest and, right now, it's obvious, he's interested in me. "Maybe you'd like to go out some time?"

I think about Mitch and Fritz and my luck with men. It's no good and I don't want to get involved anymore. "I've got to take care of my mother," I lie.

Disappointment shows in his expression, but he quickly catches himself. "No worries. We're gearing up for even more planes anyway, none of us will have time."

"What did you hear?" I ask.

"Winter is coming. General Clay has requested planes from across the world, so we can transport enough coal."

I study Thomas's face. "Do you really think we'll have enough to heat our homes?"

Thomas avoids my gaze. "Unlikely, not when Stalin keeps cutting off power. It's taking an ungodly amount of coal to keep the electricity going."

"What if he cuts us off for good?"

"I don't believe he would. But he is crazy, so who knows." I must look worried because he leans forward to pat my hand. "We won't let it happen."

"You could all leave and spare yourself a whole lot of trouble."

Thomas resolutely shakes his head. "That's not what I hear. I think Truman is committed to saving West Berlin."

I chew on my lower lip. *It may not be enough.* But then, Berlin made it through unending bombs, it may just make it through this.

"I've got real coffee," Thomas says, rising from his chair. The smile is back, maybe a bit dimmer than before. He pulls a package of Maxwell House from his desk drawer and hands it to me. "For your mother… I better go, five o'clock in the morning comes fast enough."

"Thank you," I call after him, but he just waves a dismissive arm. To my surprise, I jump up. "I'm going to the assembly at the Reichstag. Would you like to join me?" Thomas turns, the smile is back, though it is a measured one. I hurry on. "You know about it? I want to hear what they say."

"Better hurry then, we'll be late."

I don't know what I expected, but the area in front of the Reichstag is thick with people. There must be hundreds of thousands, a sea of men and women, all listening to the speakers on the steps of the Reichstag, its blackened dome broken into pieces, its walls and columns pockmarked from the firefights that raged here more than three years ago.

It doesn't matter. The air is electric with energy, as if each of us is sending our urgent wish to save Berlin into the universe. The voice of Ernst Reuter, our mayor, echoes over our heads. It feels as if he's speaking directly to me. I sense Thomas at my side, but I can't look over there right now, I'm soaking up each word Reuter fires toward us and the world. Elected a year ago, the Soviets don't accept him, but to me, he is Berlin's leader.

"People of the world, people in America, in England, in France, in Italy!" Reuter shouts into the microphone. "Look at this city and realize that you must not and cannot abandon this city and these people! There is only one possibility for all of us: to stand together until this battle is won, until this battle is finally sealed by the victory over the enemies, by the victory over the power of darkness."

I poke Thomas, I'm so excited, I will Reuter's words to transcend borders and reach the right people far away. In this moment, I feel more hopeful than I have since the day Germany capitulated. Clearly, Reuter intends to remind our Allies to stick with Berlin and help save it.

"What did I tell you?" Thomas says as we hurry past the Brandenburg Gate. "How could we refuse now?"

People are everywhere and I'm distracted because a man is tearing down the Russian flag on top of the sixty-five-foot Brandenburg Gate, marking the border between Soviet Berlin and West Berlin. People are clearly angry and fired up after the speeches.

The banging of gunfire erupts, screams and shouts ring out.

Thomas grabs my forearm and pulls me into a side street. "This way. Who knows what will happen?" We zigzag this way and that as I feel a prickle in my neck, that of something threatening and unknowing happening behind me, lurking and waiting to attack. How often did I feel this way during the war when we expected to be shot at or bombed?

By the time we reach my home in Neukölln, I'm out of breath and convinced there will be more unrest, maybe another war.

"Better get inside," Thomas says, as if he's heard my thoughts. "I'm heading for Tempelhof, just in case." He throws me a tight smile and hurries off before I can thank him for taking me home.

"Where have you been?" Mama cries as soon as I enter. "We were worried." She embraces me until I wiggle free.

"Somebody said there was shooting after the demonstration," Tilly adds.

Obviously, the rumor mill is working faster than any newspaper. "I'm fine, but people are angry. We saw a man remove the Russian flag from the Brandenburg Gate. Shots were fired." I sink onto the couch. "I rushed home as fast as I could."

Mama sits down next to me. "I wish you wouldn't go to these protests, it's too dangerous."

I look at her and Tilly. "Not nearly as dangerous as having the Soviets take over. They should know that we won't tolerate their methods. I can't bear the thought of another dictator telling us how to think."

Tilly hands me a cup of tea. "You are absolutely right. What did Reuter say?"

"That we're calling the world to stand beside us and not to forget."

Mama huffs. "But Lotte—"

"Hush, Leni, we must stand together. Even if it's risky." Tilly pats Mama's shoulder before she guides Margo, who got up when I returned home, back to her bed in the corner.

"The Americans and British are willing to fight for us," I say. "The least we can do is support them."

CHAPTER TWENTY-ONE

If you could measure Berlin's temperature after the protest, you'd find it feverish. Yet, beneath all that excitement over Reuter's speech, I'm anxious. I know that seventy-five percent of all the goods flown in is coal that goes to the power companies. What's left is not enough to feed two million Berliners, it's as simple as that.

Even with some extra goodies like Thomas's coffee, the amount of flour, dried potatoes, milk powder and bits of sugar we're allowed leave us at the edge of hunger. I'm craving vegetables, simple potatoes have become a delicacy. We scrape through every day and only my work at the airport keeps me sane.

Tilly appears nervous and hardly speaks these days. I catch her watching Margo, who has grown into a lanky girl of thirteen whose bony knees appear thicker than her thighs and whose eyes are too large for her face.

"I've decided to send Margo to my cousin Hannelore in Lower Saxony," Tilly announces one evening after Margo has gone to sleep. "General Clay is urging parents to fly Berlin's children out, if they can stay with family in the west." Unshed tears brighten Tilly's eyes. The last months have aged her, the skin around her mouth and nose appears almost translucent. I know Margo is the reason why she has continued to fight with such energy.

Mama covers her mouth with her hand to stifle a shout. "You can't," she finally says.

Tilly resolutely shakes her head. "I must. I'm not going to watch Margo starve any longer." A single tear rolls down her cheek. "The girl has been through too much." She pats a letter on the table. "Hannelore lives next to a farm. There'll be food and animals, she can be a child for once, go to school with a full belly and without freezing."

I pat Tilly's hand. She is right. Every person we can safely take out of Berlin also helps keep the remaining population supplied. And if the Soviets start another war, she'll be far away.

"I will ask at work," I say quietly. "Besides, she'll return as soon as this is over." We look at each other as I secretly wonder how long the Americans will keep flying, before they lose interest. Mayor Reuter's speech was fiery, but in the end, it'll be insanely expensive to continue. Cold creeps up my back as I jump to my feet. The lights have come on, we've got a two-hour window of electricity. "Let's make coffee."

"A friend of mine needs to send her granddaughter with Operation Stork," I say the next morning, as soon as I discover Thomas in the backroom. The chocolatey aroma of cocoa he is fixing makes me salivate.

"Want one? Don't have milk right now, but it's still pretty good."

I nod, my gaze against my will on the delicious brew. Hunger makes it hard to concentrate, it weakens my braincells, makes my thoughts foggy. While Thomas fixes a drink for me, I force myself to think of Margo and Tilly. "Do the Americans fly children west?"

Handing me the scalding hot cup, Thomas shakes his head. "We don't want to get involved, the British are flying kids out. Not sure how they select them."

"But General Clay is American, he asked parents to do it. Why aren't his men helping?" I must look upset because he hurries to my side.

"I'll organize a care package for your friend, all right? Now we better get to work."

All day I think about Margo and how I can help. Nothing comes to mind. Until my hand wanders into the pocket of my jacket. Worn around the sleeves and waist, it has two front pockets and in one of them lies a button, wrapped in Papa's handkerchief. Mitch's button, which I've been carrying with me for three years—Mitch.

I remember our evening at the club when he spoke with several British pilots, one of them in particular, a fellow named Frank, who had an American mother and dropped bombs for a living.

You can't ask Mitch. Not now. He's too busy anyway, back and forth between Frankfurt and Berlin, likely sleeping six hours or less. Why should he help you?

When I get home that evening, Tilly steps in my way. "They said we'll have to wait a while, there isn't room for all the kids." She points at a stack of papers. "I have to fill these out, but my eyes…"

I've noticed Tilly squinting whenever I bring home a newspaper. To find reading glasses in occupied Berlin is about as easy as climbing Mount Everest. Mama and I exchange a glance. "We'll help you," we both say at the same time.

Margo watches us, her little face all worried and hopeful at once. "I want to stay here, Oma."

Tilly smiles. "I know, sweetie, it'll only be for a short time."

But Margo throws herself into Tilly's arms and sobs. "Please don't send me. I'm fine here. The Americans are getting us food. Please."

Tilly gently strokes Margo's hair. "Let's see what happens. It may be a while anyway."

I realize that I'm selfish. *This* is bigger than me. Who cares what Mitch thinks, if I can help get Margo to a safe place with lots of food and a normal school life?

In the morning I head for the administrative office and hand them a note.

"This is for Mitch Cameron, one of the pilots. Could you see that he gets it?"

Dear Mitch,

I hope this letter finds you well. I know I don't have a right to ask you for anything, but this request isn't for me. I made many mistakes and regret them every day. None more than to keep the truth from you. My friend Tilly's thirteen-year-old granddaughter Margo is not doing too well. She is very thin and a bit sickly. Tilly has a cousin in Lower Saxony who has agreed to take Margo, if she finds a flight out of Berlin. The British have told Tilly that it may take a while before they'll have capacity. Do you think you could help? I remember Frank, your friend, the British pilot. Could he help arrange a seat for Margo?

Thank you for reading and thank you for helping to save Berlin from the Soviets. It means everything to me that America is standing by us, especially after what Germany did in the war.

My best to you,

Lotte

Immediately after I drop off the letter, I'm having second thoughts. Mitch will consider me forward… demanding. What right do I have to bother him? I vow to return to the office at the first opportunity, but by the time I get there, it is afternoon.

"Sorry," the woman behind the desk says, "all mail went out this morning."

I just nod and hurry away, suddenly embarrassed. Yes, this is for Margo, but Mitch may think that I'm searching for a way to see him. At all costs.

And what if it were so? Would that be so bad? You still love him, you goose.

I shake my head as I continue on my way to one of the planes, where four men are unloading coal. They're supposed to be done within twenty minutes, but apparently there is a problem with this particular crew. They're too slow and I'm supposed to hand out a warning. If they don't speed up, they'll be fired.

As soon as I arrive, I realize that the fault lies with two of the four men. They're talking loudly, arguing about some black-market deal that went wrong.

"Gentlemen, may I have your attention?" I shout. The noise out here is deafening as planes land, roll across the tarmac, and take off. I have no idea how anybody can keep this whirr of planes organized.

The men, their hands and clothes blackened with coal dust, turn to face me.

"Closer, please."

Reluctantly, they climb over the already loaded sacks and crouch down.

"Listen, I'm to warn you that you're too slow," I say in German. "Pick it up or you'll all get fired. It's messing up logistics. Besides, it's unfair to the others."

"Easy for you to say, Fräulein," says one of the men who argued earlier. Broad-shouldered and tall, he is clearly the strongest of the crew. "You picked yourself an easy job."

"This has nothing to do with me. I suggest you quit arguing and get back to work."

"And if I don't?" The tall man glares at me.

"Then I shall report it and you'll all go."

The man spits and bends low enough, I smell his bad breath. "Hear that, boys, Fräulein Know-it-all wants to rat us out."

All of sudden, I'm afraid. What if he jumps out and attacks me?

Trying to keep a neutral expression, I say coolly, "I'm just the messenger. Take it or leave it."

"Come on, let's get back to work," one of the other three says. "It's not her fault that you love to argue." He tries to make it sound funny, but the tall man rounds on him in a flash. "Shut your mouth, Willi. I do what I want."

Willi nods curtly before he hurries to the plane and grips one of the sacks, which must weigh a hundred pounds or more. The other two follow suit, only the tall man still hovers above me on the truck platform. I feel bad for the three who are quickly and efficiently lifting sacks out of the Skymaster's belly.

"If I were you—"

"You need help over here?" a male voice asks from behind. I'm so shocked, I'm momentarily speechless as Mitch steps next to me. He is at eye level with the tall man and watches him curiously. Though his uniform is rumpled and he looks exhausted, the man on the truck immediately turns to join his crew.

"I thought so," mumbles Mitch.

"What are you doing here?" I ask, having found my voice.

"Come with me," he says, guiding me by the elbow off the tarmac. I hurry to keep up as he rushes down a corridor toward the bathrooms. "I'm on a five-minute break, but when I saw you with that thug, I—"

"Did you get my note?" I pant, out of breath, not just from the brisk walk. My mind is playing tricks on me because I forgot how tall he is.

"What note?"

"I sent a letter this morning, asking for help. I thought you…"

Mitch appears surprised, then shakes his head. "What happened? Are you okay?"

"I'm fine. It's for a friend, a child, who needs a ride west."

"Brits are doing that." Mitch frowns, which makes the shadows under his eyes appear even darker. He must be so tired from the strain of flying with hardly a few hours of sleep. "I wish they'd quit sending goods to the Soviets."

"What do you mean?"

Mitch's frown deepens. "They're still sending coal over there, and a third of what's being produced in the British sector."

"Why would they do that?"

"They don't want things to *escalate*." Mitch's voice is low, yet full of venom. "The only ones who are escalating things are the Russians."

I think about my letter, asking about his British friend. They're likely not even talking these days.

I can tell there is more, but he nervously eyes his watch. "Promise me to be careful. I've got to run." Without another word, he disappears into the bathroom.

"It's all in the note," I call after him, pretty sure he didn't hear me, wishing I'd never sent the letter. By the time I pass by the large windows in the office, he is climbing into a plane, the door closes and, within seconds, the plane rolls down the airfield for another run.

Please, God, if you're there, protect him, I mumble, realizing I haven't said a prayer in years.

CHAPTER TWENTY-TWO

Thomas's care package under one arm, I arrive home late once more. It's dusk and the street has turned murky gray. Most streetlights, those that have survived or been rebuilt, are turned off to save electricity. Making a mental note that I'll have to organize a flashlight for the winter months, I shriek when a shadow rushes up to me.

"It's me," Fritz pants, a cigarette dangling from the corner of his mouth.

I adjust the package and huff, "You scared me." For a moment, I expected the tall man from the truck. Earlier today, he was let go. I'd made sure the others could remain.

"Did you ask?"

"I can't. They're trying to get the children out of Berlin. Russian spies are not a priority." Despite the low light, I see Fritz flinch. "I'm sorry, it's a tightly controlled military operation."

"I thought the Brits fly children."

"True."

"Thousands of men work at Tempelhof every day."

"To work an honest job, not to fly to Frankfurt."

When Fritz remains silent, I continue. "Why don't you apply? One was let go today. There'll be others. We need every man."

"To unload coal?"

"Among other things."

"Not sure I can. My lungs are shot."

I huff. "You could quit smoking."

"You always have an answer, don't you? Always so smart and

above it all." Fritz flips the cigarette butt past my shoulder.

"I'm trying to survive, just like you. Only I make different choices. And I've got other people to worry about, not just myself."

"You mother?" Out of Fritz's mouth, it sounds like an insult.

"What does it matter?" Against my better judgment, I step closer. "I wish you'd find another solution and quit bothering me."

Fritz's chin wobbles. "They threatened to kill me if I try to leave. Said they'd find me, no matter where I go." He runs a hand through his greasy hair. "Why did I ever agree to this?"

Why indeed? It's bad enough to live in this beleaguered city without any certainty there'll be food or coal this winter. I can't imagine being followed and interrogated. Aloud, I say, "Something will come up."

Fritz groans. "I don't want to endanger you. They know about our relationship."

"We are no longer together."

"But they know I care about you despite…"

"Despite?"

"Never mind."

Fury rises into my throat, chokes me. *It was love*, I want to cry. "You have a strange way of showing it. During all this time, when did you ever share your cigarettes with me? You knew Mama and I were struggling."

"I offered you money."

"Eastmarks… to pay for your favors."

"Sorry, I'm just in a bad spot."

We're back where we started. Fritz is trying to find a solution for Fritz, no matter what it costs me. "I'm going inside now. For the last time, leave me be."

"I wonder if your American would like to know about his baby. Surely he's flying in the airlift." His words are spoken low and yet each of them reaches me crystal clear.

I turn to face him, search for the right words. None come to mind as the ache of my loss returns full force.

Fritz eyes me, then nods. "You didn't tell him."

A mix of pain and rage catapults me forward until I stand inches from him. "You wouldn't… that is low even for you."

"You leave me no choice. Who knows, maybe you already picked up where you left off."

"For the last time, leave me alone."

"You know I can find him. I learned quite a bit about him while he lived here."

My throat is clogged now, my eyes threaten to spill over. I hurry for the door, stumble through, lock it behind me. Leaning against it, I let out a sigh as tears begin to stream. The pain of losing my baby is always so fresh, it yanks me off my feet. All I want to do is hide in my corner, but Tilly and Mama mustn't find out. I resolutely wipe my face and climb upstairs.

As soon as I enter our room, Margo rushes up to me. Her cheeks burn and I'm afraid something bad has happened. But Mama and Tilly are both sitting on the sofa, watching us. I take a deep breath and produce a smile.

"Guess who I saw today?" Margo cries.

I drop the care packet on the table and capture Margo's fluttering hands in mine. "Uncle Wiggly Wings. Oma took me to Tempelhof to watch the planes and he flew overhead, wiggling his wings. Look what I caught." Margo holds up a handkerchief and nestled within is a pack of Spearmint gum. "Oma helped me catch it, because the older kids were pretty fast. I waited until you got here to open it."

I suppress a smile. Lieutenant Gail Halvorsen, the chocolate pilot, has been a huge hit with Berlin's children. When he discovered a throng of kids watching the airfield from behind a fence, he shared a couple of gum sticks with them. Realizing there wasn't nearly enough candy to go around, he's been asking his fellow pilots for donations. Umbrellas with Hershey's chocolate and gum have begun to rain down on the kids and as time went on, more and more pilots are participating. Gail's superiors have jumped onboard, and he's become famous.

"I hope to meet him some day," I say. It must've taken all of Margo's willpower to wait to open her treasure. "That looks delicious. You'd better try a piece."

Margo pulls me over to the sofa and, surrounded by us, she opens the little packet of gum. She sniffs the silvery paper, breaks off a quarter of the gum and sticks it into her mouth. Then she hands us the stick and we each take another quarter.

"Remember not to swallow it," Mama says. Chewing with closed eyes, Margo nods.

"You think Karl may like a piece?" Tilly asks. We all look at each other. It is deathly quiet on the other side of the blanket that separates our families.

Margo hesitates only the slightest bit before she carries a precious second stick to the neighbors. As the joyous voices of Karl and his father carry across, I unpack Thomas's gift.

"The Americans aren't flying children out," I say as Mama and Tilly quietly join me at the table. We each take turns inspecting the cans of meat and beans, the packages of dried potatoes, instant coffee and chocolate. "I'm afraid Margo will have to wait her turn."

"I dropped off the paperwork today," Tilly says. "I feel as if I'm cut in two, the one side of me glad she's staying for now, the other anxious for her to leave and live in peace. I'm just so worried we'll freeze again."

During the winter of 1946/1947, many people died of cold. The temperatures remained near zero Fahrenheit for weeks and though we slept next to each other in our coats, our breaths steamed and froze the edges of our blankets in front of us. After three years, Berlin is nearly void of firewood. Two million West Berliners have been combing the rubble, cutting down any bush or tree that is unprotected. Once in a while the city allows the logging of a few trees and thousands of people swarm to collect what they can carry. Whatever we find these days, we use for cooking.

Once I'm in bed, I allow myself to remember the encounter with Mitch. He clearly came to my aid when he could've just ignored me. Especially considering the time pressure he was under, that all pilots are under these days.

Wishful thinking, my mind comments. *Likely, any decent human being would've done the same. Just because he asked me to be careful, doesn't mean he wants to have anything to do with me.*

Despite my thoughts, my heart pounds in my neck. Seeing Mitch in his coveralls, knowing he is out there to help us all, has got to be enough. At least that's what I'm telling myself.

CHAPTER TWENTY-THREE

As wonderful as the care packet is, shared with our neighbors, its contents are gone within two weeks. Every morning and evening, we discuss food rations, the upcoming winter and the uncertainty of the blockade. Mama and Tilly have rings under their eyes from the many trips to scrounge wood and suitable goods to barter with. None of us sleep well. The air is stifling behind the blankets, Albert's side having the only window. Each sound travels; little coughs, sighs, drill into my ears as if they were thunder, setting my teeth on edge. I know I should be glad to be safe in a building, with a good job at Tempelhof, but many nights I just want to scream.

I'm convinced Fritz will make good on his threat. He has nothing to lose. How will Mitch react when he learns that I expected and then lost his baby? Again, I didn't tell him something important. Even if we'd broken up before I found out, he'll consider it another insult, another breach of trust. Or worse. What if he doesn't care?

I can't let Fritz tell him, I must find a way to get Fritz out of Berlin.

"We may be home late tonight. Tilly and I will head east to hunt for food," Mama announces at breakfast. "The sector borders remain open, and I've seen people return with bags of potatoes. Margo will remain here with Karl and Albert."

"Do you know where?" I ask.

Mama shrugs. "We'll ask around. I still have Papa's ring and a gold necklace. Tilly has cash. We'll manage."

"Just be careful."

All day, I think about Mama and Tilly, how they're searching for food in the Soviet-occupied farmlands.

As expected, they haven't returned by the time I get home. Margo is reading a book with Karl while Albert is fixing soup from potato flakes and onion slices.

Unable to sit still, I prepare two slices of bread with the last of the blackcurrant jam Tilly traded this summer for Margo and me. Together we sit, chewing our bread.

"You think they'll be back soon?" Margo asks for the third time.

"I'm sure, it's just a long way and they have to find a good source. That takes time."

"I hope they'll get potatoes." Margo looks dreamy. "Imagine eating real potatoes, not that mushy stuff from the box."

"That mushy stuff from the box is helping us survive."

Margo nods enthusiastically. "I know. The Allies are doing a lot for us."

"Yes, they do." Margo is too young to understand the real threat the Soviets pose.

"They protect our freedom." Margo's little face is earnest as she picks up the last crumbs with her forefinger.

I stare at her. "Exactly. That is the most important part of the airlift." I realize she's a lot smarter than I gave her credit for. "Did you learn that in school?"

"Oma Tilly talks about it all the time, too." She rises and stretches her skinny arms. "You think I'll be able to fly and see Oma's cousin?"

I smile at her, thinking that lying is not an option. "I have asked somebody for help, but it's a difficult time. Lots of kids want to leave, so we have to be patient."

Margo nods. "It's all right. Oma would be very sad."

I pull the girl into my arms. "Yes, she would, but also happy for you."

Margo snuggles close and whispers, "You think Karl could go too? He's awfully hungry all the time."

"We'd have to find him a host family," I whisper back.

"I'd let him share my bed." Margo smiles and suddenly perks up. "The door." Quick as a mouse, she hops to the blanket curtain, which is being pulled aside at the same time.

Mama wears a triumphant grin on her face, followed by Tilly, who smiles from ear to ear. Both pull heavy packs from their shoulder and carefully set them by the table.

"Potatoes," Tilly says, "lots of real potatoes."

Margo claps her hands. "Let's fry some."

During dinner, the second one for me, Mama tells us about their trip. "We took the train toward Eberswalde. There were hundreds of people like us, looking to pick up farm food. One of them told me that she's going every two weeks. Soviets are leaving the border open even though they know about us. Supposedly, there is even a delivery service here in the west. Can you imagine?"

"Doubt we could afford it," Tilly says dryly. "But we now have a way to get extras occasionally. As long as we've got money or goods to trade."

I eye the two bulging sacks of potatoes leaning in the corner. "That's amazing." I pick the last of the potatoes off my plate and chew with my eyes closed.

"Maybe I won't have to go then." Margo is rubbing her belly and yawns. "I can eat potatoes every day."

"Looks like it may be a while anyway," Tilly says. I detect the hope in her voice. "Better get ready for bed. School starts early."

The atmosphere at Tempelhof Airport continues to be high energy and hopeful, but I know they're struggling. Airplane fuel is in short supply—and we need more than 200,000 gallons a day. The air vibrates with the noise of planes landing and starting, in fact, there isn't one quiet moment in the day. It is still unclear if the amount of goods being flown in will be sufficient to keep Berlin alive. Maybe the Soviets will leave the borders between east and west open, especially since many from the west work in the east and vice versa.

We all labor until we can't walk another step—I've never walked that much in my life, the corridors endless—but how long can we do it? Wouldn't it be much easier for the Allies to drop everything and leave?

Yet, every day I report to work, the machinery of the airlift functions at top speed. New planes are being pulled from afar to help, more pilots are being trained, France is building new runways at Tegel. British water planes are landing on the Spree River and at Gatow. The question is, will it be enough?

Since I have access to the mess hall now, I get to have a real meal at lunchtime. In the line in front of me stands a woman with a mop of curly blonde hair who throws me a happy smile.

"Can you believe it, a cooked feast every day?" she says in a heavy Berlin accent, her jaws busy chewing precious gum. She cranks her neck toward the front of the line before she turns to face me again. "Looks like mashed potatoes and meat, maybe green beans. Beans, I haven't had any in years, not since Grandma lost her garden in the bombing." She offers me a hand. "Daniela, call me Danny."

I shake, returning her smile. "Lotte."

It seems natural that we grab seats together. Danny throws a worried glance at the wall clock. "I've got fifteen minutes. My boss is a slave driver, handsome, though." In a split second, she bends over her food and begins to shovel.

I'm also in a hurry, having to join a meeting with a couple of German representatives from the city, but I want to enjoy every bite, chew slowly and sometimes even close my eyes. The gravy is from a box and the meat a bit tough, but oh, glorious warmth filling my stomach.

"What do you do here?" I ask, taking a sip of water.

"Driving a jeep, supplying the pilots," Danny says. She's scraping the plate with her fork in quick movements. "Did you know that they're not allowed to leave their plane any longer? Apparently, Willi the Whip General Tunner thinks it's taking too long to eat here, so he hired us to deliver snacks and drinks to the pilots as soon as they land. He even sends the weathermen to the planes, just to save a few minutes." Danny inspects the dessert, some kind of pudding with a red sauce. "Wonder if that's strawberry."

I imagine taking Fritz on a jeep to the airfield, hurrying him inside to hide under a pile of coal sacks. It'd never work. I must find another way. As Danny's pudding disappears at lightning speed, I ask, "So you get to meet all the pilots?"

Danny pushes the bowl away with a sigh and wipes her mouth, pretty with full lips and a bit pouty. "Not all, of course. There're hundreds and we've got an entire team of snack jeeps to keep 'em fed." She glances at the clock again, nods approvingly, as if she's in a race with herself. "What do you do?"

"Translation."

Danny's light-blue eyes dance. "Wow, that's so great. I wish I could do that." She jumps up, takes her tray. "Some time you should come with me to the planes, meet the pilots. It'd help to know what they're saying." She grins. "You could teach me some words."

"Why not?"

Danny winks at me before she hurries off. I doubt I'd ever have time to visit the pilots *for fun.* Too much is at stake. Resolutely, I rise to return the tray. The afternoon is waiting.

At my desk lies a folded paper, addressed to me.

Lotte, Mitch asked me to help with your young friend. Please send the specifics to the address below. I'll see what I can do.

Frank Evans, Wing Commander RAF

Gatow Airport

My hands shake as I put the paper down. So, Mitch had not only received my note, he'd contacted his British friend. Margo may have a chance to escape after all. In between my next two assignments, I jot down Margo's information, our address and that of Tilly's cousin in Lower Saxony.

Afraid to get everybody excited and so as not to worry Tilly, I say nothing that evening. A part of me regrets what I did because the way Tilly drags herself around the tiny space, she seems to have aged ten years. At the same time, Margo has developed a cough that refuses to go away. She's wearing Karl's old coat and Mama's matted scarf to school. I think of Meg, who began to cough after her husband returned from Russia. The guilt comes with sudden viciousness, a nasty pressure in my middle that borders on nausea. Meg, how I miss her strength, her straightforwardness.

After we go to bed, I lie awake, wondering if Frank will find a spot for Margo and how I will get Fritz onto a plane without being fired. One thing is clear, I won't be able to do this alone. Question is, should I try official channels or secretly ask for help? Only one thing is clear, I can't reveal what Fritz has done or they'll kick me out in a flash.

Deep in thought, I arrive at work. Three days have passed, and I still don't have a clue how to help Fritz. Everything inside me revolts at the thought, yet I also am convinced that he'll die if he stays here. He may not survive anyway, considering how he looks and how many cigarettes he consumes.

On my desk lies a brown envelope addressed to me. Inside is a hastily scribbled note and a cardboard tag with a cord.

Lotte,

Margo is scheduled to fly out of Gatow to Lübeck on October 10, 1948, at 9:45. She needs to wear the enclosed card, filled out, for identification. Somebody will pick her up at 7:30 sharp. The RAF will make sure she gets to her destination address.

 Frank Evans, Wing Commander RAF
 Gatow Airport

My eyes blur. I have no doubt that this is Mitch's doing. In a week, Margo will fly to safety. I want to rush home this instant, but an entire day stretches out in front of me before I can bring the good news to Tilly and Margo.

As I step outside, Danny is arriving with her jeep. When she sees me, she waves and jumps out. "Lotte, over here, come and say hello." I hurry closer and there, between boxes and cartons piled high in the back, sits Greg, Mitch's old roommate. "This is Lieutenant Greg," she giggles. "Oops, forgot your last name."

But Greg ignores her, his gaze on me like two pieces of coal. "I don't believe it. The heartbreaker is at it again. We seem to run into each other a lot." He smiles the cool smile he always displays around women, one that is slightly aloof and likely sexy in his own mind. I know better because he can't hide the cruel line around his mouth, the measured glance that reflects the coldness in his heart. Unfortunately, it seems to work on Danny.

"I thought pilots don't get time away from the plane," I counter.

"You two know each other." Danny sounds irritated. "His plane has been flagged for maintenance."

"Hence, I hitched a ride with this little beauty."

Greg's grin gives me the willies, so I address Danny, hoping I can send her a warning with my words. "Greg was stationed in Berlin in '45."

"No way," Danny cries.

"Sure thing. Little Fräulein Lotte isn't as innocent as she pretends. She was getting it on with a dear friend of mine."

Danny zooms in on me. "I didn't think you'd have it in you."

"What do you mean?"

"Dating an American. I thought you're too serious for that with your translating and all."

Forcing a smile, I nod at them both. "I'd better run, be careful."

I don't hear what else they say, because the noise of the planes snuffs out anything farther away than six feet. Internally, I cringe, hoping that Danny won't fall for Greg's deception and to never see him again.

But that proves to be wishful thinking. As I head out for the night,

I watch Danny climb into Greg's jeep. How he organized the car and got time off, I don't know. Nor do I care. But though I don't know Danny very well, I want to warn her, want to call after her.

They drive off in a cloud of dust—Berlin continues to consist of stone and dust—Danny's mock scream loud in my ears. My thoughts wander to Mitch and how different he acted when we went out. But who am I to talk? I screwed everything up, too serious, too focused and still single. Unlike Danny, who's been at Tempelhof five minutes before she lands a pilot.

It isn't you, the voice in my head comments. True, but sometimes, at night, when I lie brooding in my corner, I think about the moments I had with Mitch. How good it felt to be a couple in every sense of the word. How I felt complete.

My hand wanders into my pocket, my fingers trace the button's cool metal. Some people say that they are better off alone. But I'm not one of them. I know my soul hungers for the companionship of another. So why am I holding out, what am I waiting for? I know the answer, but under the circumstances, it is so ridiculous, I don't even want to think about it.

Thankfully, there are more exciting things happening and I forget everything as soon as I enter our room, waving the envelope.

"I'm going?" Margo cries. Tears burst as she hugs Tilly, who remains so quiet I rush over to rub her back. She just shakes her head. Only her mouth trembles as she presses her granddaughter to her chest.

Mama is wringing her hands, sighing loudly every few minutes. "You must write to us all the time," she laments. "Tell us all about your new place, how you are treated. I want to get a complete list of all the animals you see."

Margo smiles brightly, a bit too brightly. "I will, Aunt Leni, I promise."

Remaining silent, Tilly busies herself dishing up potato soup made with the potatoes she and Mama traded, bits of onion and a shriveled carrot she traded at the black market. While Margo chatters, the three of us are listening and smiling.

"I wonder what your room will look like?" Tilly says at last. "Hannelore mentioned that you'll have your own space."

"I wonder how school will be." Margo scrapes her bowl, then licks the spoon. Not a drop of soup can be wasted. Not when there are no seconds, no dessert or bread. She straightens, a beanpole of a girl, who'll bravely venture into an unknown world, just to have enough to eat. "I'd better pack my bag."

"Let's do it tomorrow," Tilly says. "You get ready for bed." She quickly wipes a tear from the inside of her right eye and reaches for our empty bowls.

The three of us mope around for another hour before we crawl into our beds, secretly glad to get this day over with.

The next morning, I don't see Danny, which isn't surprising, considering that thousands are working here around the clock. I barely notice the buzzing, grinding sounds of the Skymaster planes, the constant coming and going of delivery trucks, gasoline trucks and military vehicles, I just rush from one assignment to the next.

The following day, she is sitting in the cafeteria when I arrive, her blonde curls a bright spot in the dreary room full of clinking dishes and silverware. But unlike last time, she is staring straight ahead and doesn't appear to see me waving.

"Busy day?" I ask, setting my tray across from her.

She flinches before she focuses on me.

"Oh, didn't see you." Apparently, she remembers her food and begins to pick at a burger patty with her fork.

"Are you all right?"

At first, she seems to ignore my question, but then her eyes fill with tears.

I find Danny's hand, squeeze it. "Was it Greg?"

She nods and sniffs at the same time. "In hindsight, I think you tried to warn me. He was a… it was bad." The skin beneath her eyes is puffy, either from crying or lack of sleep.

I look at her, wait.

"I don't know what I was thinking. American pilot, great, a bit of fun, great, going out for a meal, some drinks. All he wanted was…" Our eyes meet. "You know."

I know. "Three years ago, he lived in an apartment upstairs."

"He told me you had an affair with a pilot, that you two were in love and you broke his buddy's heart."

Mitch's hurt expression returns, the way he looked at me when I explained myself. Maybe things would've been different, had I had an opportunity to speak with Mitch *before* Greg spilled the beans on Fritz. "It's true. I'm not proud of it. My fiancé returned from the war. I thought he'd died. Maybe it was premature, but I really loved

Mitch. He—"

Danny is watching me intently. "What?"

"Fulfilled me. I would've married him."

Danny's leaning forward. "Even if he'd taken you to America?"

I nod.

"You loved him."

"Still do." I don't understand why I share my secret with a near stranger, but there it is. Somehow it feels good to get it out.

"Is he flying… in the airlift?"

"I talked to him twice. Asked for help."

A little of the old Danny returns as she claps her hands. "Why don't you tell him?"

I let out a deep breath. "It's too late."

"It's never too late when it comes to love." Danny's eyes are dreamy. "I've never loved anyone like that, but this I'm sure of." Her gaze wanders to the wall clock. "Shucks, I'd better run." She picks up her half-eaten meal with a "Think about it," and hurries off.

I have momentarily forgotten my food, too. Maybe Danny is right. If nothing else, I could get it off my chest. The thought alone raises my blood pressure.

"Not hungry today?" Thomas stands there holding a Coke bottle.

I shake off my thoughts and focus on my boss. "I suppose not."

"Must be hard to see your young friend leave."

I stare. "You mean Margo?"

Thomas grins. "Not much goes on that I don't hear about." He checks his wristwatch. "I've got to run."

Mumbling, "See you," I wonder if Thomas knows about Mitch or what Greg is up to. Maybe it's all right among them to date and bed German girls if they get a chance. I'm glad my food isn't finished, and I've got a reason to stay.

On the way to my desk, I think about what I'd say to Mitch, imagine various scenarios and happy endings. "You're such a chicken," I mumble, as an idea forms in the back of my mind.

CHAPTER TWENTY-FOUR

"Will you do me a favor?" I ask Danny the next time I see her at lunch. She looks better, though her previous happy face is absent. "I thought about what you said, and I think I'll risk it."

Danny lights up. "Really, that's so awesome." She leans forward as if the two of us are sharing a secret, which I guess we do.

"If I give you a note, could you hand it to a certain pilot?"

"Sure thing." She frowns. "But it may take time. I might not even meet him."

"It can wait."

"Maybe you'd better send it in the mail."

"Just ask around. And promise me you'll keep it to yourself?"

Danny signs a cross on her lips and opens her palm. "Where's the note?"

I hold out a folded piece of paper with Mitch's name on it, which Danny snatches from my fingers. "I promise I won't look at it."

I can't bring myself to tell her that it is not a love letter, just a thank you…

Dear Mitch,

Thank you for helping my little friend. I won't forget it. Maybe we could talk again some time?

Lotte

In my head I'd written many versions, most of them pages long. Paper is supposed to be "patient" and you can scribble down anything. But some subjects must be discussed in person, we must see their face and eyes, read their expression, the way they hold their shoulders.

I've got to say these things to Mitch—if I muster the strength. I didn't tell Danny that I'm afraid of Mitch's rejection. At the same time, I crave clarity—a final decision that will get me to move forward, one way or another.

The night before Margo's departure, we mope around the tiny room. Karl and Albert have joined us, the blanket between our sides lifted aside. We share a bottle of wine I received at work. We all sip from our mugs, the only drinking vessels we own. Margo is unwrapping a brown paper package Mama and Tilly have handed her. Inside is a new dress of dark blue wool with a tiny, stitched flower on the skirt. It isn't new, but altered and perfect for the approaching winter.

"Thank you," Margo cries, hugging Tilly and Mama. Her bag is packed, no more than a school pack with a couple of changes of underwear, sweater and pants that are too short, pajamas, a second pair of knitted socks, courtesy of Mama, and a couple of books. We hope that Hannelore has access to additional clothes, so Margo can get through the winter.

"I made you something," Karl says, holding up a lump of wood he has carved into a portly cow. He has grown too, though he looks as pale as Margo and just as bony. "So that you remember me."

Margo spontaneously hugs him. "I could never forget you. Oma says I'll be back soon anyway."

Karl tries a smile but fails. "Just eat some cake and sausages, will you?"

Albert rubs his good hand through his son's hair. "We'll get plenty of tasty food again someday, you'll see."

We clink our cups together and toast. "To Margo and tasty food."

As Margo disappears into her bed for the last time, Tilly frantically scrubs the few dishes. I step next to her and quietly say, "It'll be all right. We'll take care of each other."

Tilly's hands hover over the water bowl before she turns to embrace me with a sob. "I know," she whispers. "Help me keep it together. At least until she leaves."

As an answer, I rub Tilly's back as if she's the little girl, and I'm the mother.

Other than Margo, I don't know if any of us sleep that night. I hear

Tilly crying into her pillow, Mama throwing herself from one side to the other. I'm on my back, staring at the ceiling, my thoughts on Tilly's heartbreak and the note I sent with Danny.

How long will Tilly have to wait to see Margo again? Already it feels as if years have passed, when it has only been four months since the Soviets closed all borders. How long will we survive like this?

And Danny? What if she tells others? Thomas seems to miss nothing. Will they laugh about me, some stupid German damsel who is pining after an American hero?

I close my eyes, open them again. Somewhere a clock ticks, its monotone tick-tick annoyingly loud. Mitch looked amazing the last time we met. I won't have the guts to speak to him about my feelings, not now, not when a piece of me is missing.

With a pang I remember Fritz and his threat. Strange how he hasn't returned to torment me. Either way, I must find a solution for him before he tells Mitch about our baby.

I must've fallen asleep eventually, because the bustling in the tiny space wakes me. It's not even six o'clock, but Tilly is already prepping tea. From my corner, I watch her stuff peppermint leaves into the pot, add water. Her movements are erratic, her hands shake, water spills onto the table. She doesn't seem to notice, smacks the kettle back on the stove. Then she pauses. Her gaze travels to Margo's cot, where the girl sleeps beneath rumpled sheets. Tilly's expression is equally loving and sad.

Having seen enough, I rise, wash and dress quickly.

Our last breakfast is quiet. Margo's eyes shine with excitement. Ours with tears.

Though we expect it, the knock on the door makes us start. Albert opens it, greets the visitor behind the curtain. "Right through there," he says loudly.

We all just stand there as steps echo, the blanket swings aside. A man in a British uniform mumbles a short greeting. "Margo Keller?"

Margo steps forward, not an easy feat in the small space. Momentarily, she seems to have forgotten her voice.

"Ready to go?"

"Yes, sir."

In an instant we all crowd around her, tell her… to be good, to write soon, to not forget us… whatever nonsense we can muster to say not to cry outright and scare her further. Her little heart must be beating staccato as she follows the strange man past Albert and Karl, both of them standing there, uttering greetings and wishes.

The door closes. The five of us look at each other. And into the silence, Karl says, "I bet she'll grow ten inches before she comes back."

The tension breaks and we all laugh… a little too loud and dangerously close to hysterical. Tilly turns away to clear the table, I nod at our neighbors and lower the blanket back in place.

Another day awaits and I don't want to think about Tilly, whose heart is surely breaking.

CHAPTER TWENTY-FIVE

The next days seem to drown in a fog of sadness. Tilly is distraught, her usual energy has drained away with Margo's departure. Now she sits at the table, holds her head, and hardly speaks a word. Mama and I try to encourage her, give her little backrubs, and serve her tea.

"What if she never returns?" Tilly says one evening. "Stalin won't stop, and if the Allies don't go away, he may start a war."

"Doubt it," I say, even if I don't feel convinced. "Today, the first plane landed at Tegel Airport. The people of Berlin built that runway in three months. The Allies aren't giving up on us. They're getting stronger and we'll be able to feed all the people."

"That will make Stalin even angrier," Mama comments.

"Let him," I cry. "I tell you, he'll not wage war because he's afraid of the Americans. He hardly has enough soldiers to battle with the mighty US of A, not after what Hitler did."

Tilly lets out a sigh. "He can still bully us. Who knows how long for? Margo may be all grown up before she gets to return." I know she also thinks of Walter, her son and Margo's father, who is still some place in Russia. At least that's what the Red Cross cards Tilly keeps in a little box, like others keep jewelry, say. Walter's notes are as short and generic as Papa's. They're coping and they hope to return soon.

Other than the good news of Tegel, life grows more difficult again. We do get rations, but there is practically no coal, and the temperatures are dropping with each day. Mama and Tilly are anxious to return to the east sector for potatoes, but we have little to trade. With neither of them working, we only have my income and that isn't going very far.

To save energy, hardly any streetlights burn, in some places every second lantern burns, in others one side of the street or none at all. I pick my way carefully through the inky streets, always expecting that Fritz will materialize again. Strangely, he doesn't. My neck prickles, twice I turn abruptly, thinking I'm hearing steps. Twice, I see nothing. Is Fritz sneaking up on me? He never tells me where he lives, and I suspect that he moves around, sleeping on people's couches.

I should feel good about him leaving me alone. But somehow, I'm not. He's weak and strange but was once an honorable man. The war and the Russian imprisonment have changed him. He is desperate and desperate men do despicable things.

Danny hasn't asked me again about Mitch and I'm not going to press the issue. I certainly won't chase after Mitch to share my secrets. Once again, I vow to bury everything deep inside and press forward.

Only there is Tilly who appears to shrink every day. I dread coming home and listening to Mama's whispers about her efforts to distract Tilly. I worry that she has lost her will to fight on. It happens a lot. During the war, people would just lie down on their beds and grow too weak to get up again. During the winter of 1946/1947, many old people froze to death.

I hurry toward our apartment building, which is actually a joke because only one side of it is habitable, the other has a hole in the roof and its inside is crumbling. I expect sooner or later they'll tear it down, but there are so many that it may take years before we'll live in an intact building again. A shadow rushes toward me and I shriek.

"Fritz, don't scare me like that," I cry.

"It isn't Fritz," a man's voice says. He speaks quietly, almost imperceptibly, but I'm not afraid. "I'm looking for Tilly Keller," he continues. "It's hard to see anything in this blackness."

"I know Tilly," I say carefully, trying to catch a glimpse of the man's face. But all I can tell is that he is tall and doesn't smell very good. Tilly isn't up to receiving visitors. My breath catches, thinking this has to do with Margo.

"I need to speak to her."

"Maybe you could return tomorrow," I say. "She is not feeling well and it's pretty late for a visit."

The man makes a sound, something like a laugh and a cry combined. "I just arrived, it's been difficult to find her. I'm her son... Walter."

My mouth opens as I stare at the hulking figure. How could I have missed the slumped shoulders, the exhaustion in his voice? "I'm very sorry, I apologize. Please come with me. I'm sure she will be so happy."

When I open the door to our shared room, Albert and Karl are sitting at their table, playing checkers Albert made from a piece of cardboard and a stick of wood.

Other than a single oil lamp, there is no light. I slip past with a "Good evening," the stranger in tow.

"We are sharing a room," I say over my shoulder. "It's very hard to live in Berlin right now." Before the man can answer, I pull away the blanket to reveal our living quarters.

Mama is sitting on the settee, darning a sock by the stub of a candle. She smiles mildly when she sees me until her gaze falls on the stranger behind me. "Mama, this is Tilly's son, Walter."

Mama's hand claps over her mouth as she rises and approaches the stranger. "It is so good to have you back. Tilly never thought, she is—"

"Where *is* Mother?" Walter sounds irritated and exhausted as he turns slowly in the small space.

"She is sleeping... over there." Mother points at the dark corner where Margo used to have her bed. Ever since she left, Tilly has been sleeping there.

As the man walks past me, I notice his limp. Beneath the stocking cap, his eyes burn dark in the gaunt face. A strong odor is filling the small space.

"*Mutter?*" Walter slowly lowers himself to his knees. He pats Tilly's shoulder, sighs. "It's me, Walter. I'm home."

A small cry rises from the corner as Tilly wraps both arms around her boy. "I thought I'd lost you, too."

Mama and I look at each other. Then I hurry into her arms and we both cry.

"Just in time," Mama whispers.

Sure enough, as Walter comes to his feet with another grunt, Tilly rises from her bed, pulling Walter into our midst.

"This is Walter," she says, her eyes bright with tears. "Margo's father."

"Where is Margo?" Walter studies us one at a time. He still wears his coat, a padded thing with more holes than fabric. He reminds me of Fritz, the day he returned, when Tilly offered him a clean suit.

Tilly takes Walter's hands in hers. "She's away. Safe… with Cousin Hannelore, so she can eat and go to school like kids do." She looks at us, smiles. "These are my friends, Leni and Lotte Berger. We've been living together for a while now."

Walter just nods, kind of obediently, or maybe resigned. "I need to sit down for a bit."

The overhead light comes on and, after the murkiness of a single candle, bathes our room in glistening light. I almost jump back because now I see how sickly Walter looks. His skin appears paper thin with a yellow tinge, his cheekbones stick out and make his face look like a skull. He barely has any hair. I know he is in his late thirties, but the man in front of us looks like a grandfather. He has nothing in common with the image Tilly keeps in a drawer near her bed.

Tilly must see it too because she immediately jumps into action.

Within an hour, Walter has washed and changed into an old sweater and pants. His clothes, wooden clogs and foot wraps are sitting outside to be disposed of tomorrow. Together, we watch him eat a meal of leftover mashed potato soup, flavored with mystery meat from one of our precious cans.

"I didn't think Stalin would release any prisoners. Not now with the Berlin blockade," Mama says.

Walter grimaces what appears to be a smile. "I'm sick… dysentery. The woman doctor we had at the gulag recommended my release. I didn't think they'd let me go, but I was on the next train." He runs a hand over his scalp. "Lost most of my hair last year, some teeth too." He points at a hole gaping where his front two bottom teeth should be. "I'm disappointed that Margo isn't here but, in a way, it's for the best." A sigh escapes him. "I can spare her seeing me like this."

Tilly wipes away a tear and pats her son's hand, its fingers long and bony. "We'll fix you up in no time, you'll see. Tomorrow, we'll get you registered for rations."

And that's how Tilly comes back to life.

While I'm utterly happy for Tilly, it becomes clear quickly that Walter is too sick to do much. He's so weak, he can hardly walk ten minutes before he is out of breath and needs to rest. Tilly is searching high and low for fresh fruit or vegetables, but even with the airlift in full swing, such delicacies are impossible to find. The airlift is concentrating on maximizing space on the air freighters, bringing in boxed supplies: potato flakes, dried milk and cans, occasionally fresh milk for the children.

Tilly and Mama have been perusing the black market and found onions and white cabbage, but because they don't have much to trade anymore, they're only able to get a small serving that Tilly immediately fixes for Walter. He is so thin, every rib shows on his chest and his upper arms are as thin as my wrists. I'm worried that we won't be able to feed him properly. Ideally, he should be in a sanatorium in the Alps.

I read the worry in Tilly's expression as she fusses around our tiny space. Losing her son a second time will kill her. Even if Margo is doing well—her letter was short but full of energy describing the rich meals she is getting and how she made a friend at school.

Five days after Walter's arrival—he has lost another molar—my mind is made up. As soon as I arrive at work, I write another note.

Dear Mitch,

I hope you're doing well despite the exhausting schedule you must surely have. We are so grateful for your service. You might like to know that my friend Tilly's granddaughter, Margo, is doing well and gaining weight. I wish I didn't have to do this, and I know I have no right, but I've got another urgent request. Tilly's son has returned from a Russian gulag, and he is in bad shape. What he needs are fresh fruits and vegetables. He was only released because he is a walking skeleton, but with the current ration situation, we cannot feed him what he needs to heal. Maybe you have a way to help?

Your friend, Lotte

My hand trembles as I place the paper in an envelope. I feel guilty, all I do is ask Mitch for favors. And yet how can I ignore the suffering of my friends? If it means I embarrass myself, so what? It doesn't matter. What matters are the people I can help by working in the place I do. Let Mitch think I'm a leech, let him despise me.

Deciding against asking Danny again—I've already regretted handing her my last note—I take the letter, addressed to Lieutenant Mitch Cameron, to Thomas's secretary, who scans it and laughs. "We won't have to send it. Mitch is in a meeting with Thomas."

Swallowing my surprise, I say, "I thought pilots were flying nearly around the clock."

"They do, but Lieutenant Cameron's plane had a maintenance issue and he and his crew are waiting for the repairs." She holds out the letter and points to a half-open door. "In the meeting room, just give it to him yourself. They're taking a break."

Just like that, all blood leaves my brain. I'm standing frozen as my heart hammers in my throat. It was all right to pin my request on paper. If I give it to him now, he'll read it in my presence. If I walk off, the secretary will think I'm crazy.

What is wrong with you? Move! Mechanically, I wander toward the door. *It's for Walter*, my mind comments.

Men's laughter trickles through the opening. I knock. My mouth is dry, too dry to speak.

"Hello?" comes from the inside.

"Eh, excuse me," I croak, barging in. Mitch and Thomas are standing at the window, each holding a cup of coffee.

"Lotte, what's up?" Thomas says, the familiar smile on his face.

"I'm looking for Mitch," I say, waving my note.

Out of the corner of my eye, I notice the surprise on Thomas's face. "Didn't realize you knew each other."

Mitch chuckles. "Old friends, right, Lotte?" It sounds so casual, so innocent, an empty phrase. Not like the most significant thing I've ever felt. Not like the earthshattering darkness that followed when I lost him and then our child in a freak accident, the one thing I had left of him.

To hide my distress, I charge toward the men, hand with the letter outstretched. "I was hoping you could help me."

Mitch appears surprised, though he remains silent as he takes the envelope.

"I thought you were flying… that's why the letter." I step back, wish myself far away. But then I focus on him, Walter is more important. "I asked you before, but this is life and death. It's all in there, if you care to read it."

"You might as well open it now," says Thomas. "Looks like we've got time, plane isn't done for a while."

Heat rushes to my face. Thankfully, I kept the note impersonal.

Mitch briefly eyes his wristwatch before he steps forward and says, "In that case, I'll take Lotte to the cafeteria. Might as well talk about it there. You don't mind, do you?"

"Of course not," Thomas says, though I could swear he is upset. "We'll finish after…"

I'm so surprised, I've forgotten my voice again. Dreamlike, I accompany Mitch to the mess hall, try to adjust my steps to his, a futile endeavor because he is tall and limber and I'm walking on heels. Thankfully, he notices and slows down. I feel his glance on my temple but can't bring myself to look at him. Chances are, I'll trip and land on my nose.

As usual it is loud, a mix of clanking plates and silverware, scraping chairs, and voices. The air is thick with the aroma of cabbage and fried sausage. Despite my discomfort, my mouth starts salivating. If I know one thing, it is never to turn away a meal.

While we wait in line, I try to think of something casual to say, something to ask, but nothing comes to mind. Not fifteen feet away I make out Danny, who waves frantically to get my attention.

I ignore her, cannot deal with her curiosity right now. She might say something stupid and give me away.

Mitch waits for me to get my tray and then heads toward the backend corner. "Maybe a little quieter here," he says. When I don't answer, he continues, "Let's eat first, then you can tell me about your problem, okay?"

I nod, eyeing my lunch. How can I possibly eat now? But I can, because my body is far more demanding than my brain. After the first bite, I'm hooked, hardly look up because for once, this is real sausage. Deliciously juicy and flavorful. Greasy, too, but oh, what joy to eat something with fat in it.

I think back at the time we went out together. How easy it was to be around him, how we laughed and enjoyed each other despite the horror of an annihilated Berlin around us.

"…really?" Mitch looks at me expectantly, then laughs. "You are miles away, aren't you?"

"I'm sorry, I was… never mind. What did you say?"

"I want to know how you are doing. How do you enjoy your work? How are you holding up?"

"These are at least three questions," I mock. But then I meet his eyes and all the sarcasm melts away. He is actually sitting across from me and wants to have a real conversation. And out of nowhere, the words bubble over. I tell him about Tilly and Margo, about Mama's recovery and now Walter. I leave out Fritz, cannot bring up the pain he caused Mitch—and myself.

"That's why I wrote the letter. I thought you were flying." I take a sip of Coke—real American Coke—to wet my throat. "Will you tell me about your life? You must be exhausted."

Mitch bites his lower lip, then grins. Shadows lie beneath his eyes and his lids are puffy. "Sleep deprived, for sure. I won't lie, it's been a lot. Most days, we fly three shifts. It's risky business, particularly now when we've got fog and slippery conditions. Russians are still playing tricks, shining lights into our flight path, shooting rockets nearby." He focuses back on me. "We've got one try to get it right. If we miss the landing attempt, we take off and go back to Frankfurt. That's how tight the airspace has gotten. Not to waste a minute, General Tunner is combining all Allied flights into one big plan."

"What you are doing is saving our lives. We Berliners are grateful beyond words."

Abruptly, Mitch leans forward and pats my hand. Again, I'm surprised, I almost forget myself and grab his fingers.

"It's the right thing to do," he says. "Can't let that maniac Stalin swallow you."

Forcing myself to ignore his skin on mine, I ask, "But how long can we fight this?"

"As long as it takes." He glances at his watch, then at me. "I've got to leave soon. But first things first." He pulls my envelope from his jacket pocket, hesitates, pulls out a second paper. "Got this from a blonde girl earlier. Danny?"

"Oh, that one isn't important," I stumble, fighting down my embarrassment. "Just a note to say thank you." I point at the envelope. "This one is important, though."

"Tell me what I need to do."

"I feel utterly guilty about bothering you constantly. Back in the day, you rescued me in the rubble, got me a doctor. You asked your friend for help with Margo and now, I'm asking for extra food for Walter. It's—"

"Hush, let me be the judge of that. You needed help and I was glad to give it." A small grin plays around his lips. "And there for a minute I thought you wanted chocolate."

I sigh. "Chocolate, I haven't had any for years…"

Silence settles as we study each other. "Back then, we had a good thing, right?"

I nod, my throat is suddenly tight. I think about our lost love, our baby. I should tell him, but I can't because tears press.

Time stops. Behind me somebody laughs, silverware clatters to the floor. His eyes shimmer like a summer sky in the harsh light of the cafeteria. All I want is to touch his face, just once.

"You look tired," I blurt. "I wish it weren't so dangerous."

"Bunks aren't exactly like sleeping in your own bed," he says. "You should've seen those barracks, disgusting. A few of us have moved to an old barn. Isn't much, but at least it doesn't smell so bad. Gail Halvorsen is there, too, you've heard of him." How could I not? With his candy drops, he's brought hope and lightness to Berlin's children. Mitch empties his Coke bottle. "But then, I don't suppose your place feels like home. Hasn't for a long time."

"They don't even provide you with decent rooms? After all you do?"

Mitch chuckles. "You've always had a big heart, Lotte. The way you helped your mother, and now your friends." He glances at his watch again. "Got to run." Picking up his dishes, he rises. "I'll organize a care package and some extra things. Have got to see what's available in Frankfurt, all right?"

"I'm sure glad you found each other." Danny stands between us with a wide grin on her face.

Mitch mumbles a greeting before he hurries down the aisle.

"Oops, what did I do?" Danny sinks into the chair Mitch just vacated.

"He's on a tight schedule," I say dryly. "Was that really necessary?"

"What?"

"Your comment about finding each other?"

"You two looked so cozy. I swear he's got feelings for you. He seemed pleased when I handed him your note earlier."

"Nonsense." I jump up and grab my dishes. "I've got work to do."

"Sorry," Danny calls after me.

But all I do is run as quickly as I can from the place that once again has ignited my heart.

CHAPTER TWENTY-SIX

When I arrive the next morning, Thomas hardly looks at me as he points to a cardboard box and a small package on top.

"From Mitch."

"So fast," escapes me. I can't help but smile, running a finger over the cartons, thinking how Mitch must've rushed to organize the food for me.

Thomas huffs. "You know, you could've asked me too."

"I just thought, you're my boss, I don't…"

"Haven't I gotten you a care packet before? Why don't you trust me?"

"It's just, I don't want to burden you with my family worries. Everybody is so busy."

"Mitch isn't?"

It's different, I want to say. But then I know I can't. As I turn, the packets under one arm, Thomas's hand lands on my forearm.

"You can always come to me with your concerns, Lotte. Just ask, okay?"

I've got to smile because Thomas seems so serious and earnest. He reminds me of a brother, trying to keep an eye on me. Except, I realize, he is after something else entirely. And it's something I can't give.

"I'm more than grateful for all you do for me, Thomas," I say and mean it. Still, it feels hollow. And he knows it. Knows I'm in love with Mitch. Heat rises to my cheeks as I grab my schedule. "I'd better get busy."

All day I avoid getting near Thomas, afraid he may comment on what happened. What if he fires me? I'd have no way of seeing Mitch, however rare and unexpected our meetings may be. I should be way more concerned about the money and favors I earn, working at the American base, being able to provide additional supplies for Mama and Tilly than thinking about chance meetings. Without these extras, we'd suffer infinitely more.

After a long day, I hurry outside. It grows darker with every step I move away from the base. Because planes fly all night, the airfield and buildings are always lit. Three fully loaded military trucks rumble past me, protected by armed GIs.

When it grows quieter at last, a cough startles me. But when I turn, I see nothing except shadowy streets. I remember my flashlight, shine it this way and that. Nothing. Trying to ignore the prickling on the back of my head, I hurry on, my ears on high alert. Off and on I slow down, listen. Steps crunch, grow quiet. I turn off my light and quickly slide behind the remnants of a former house wall. After a while, somebody approaches, passes by, his breath wheezy as if he can't get enough air.

After a few minutes, I continue on my way, slower now, watching for movement ahead. Maybe I'm imagining things. Luckily this part of my walk is on wider roads with more pedestrians. Berlin never sleeps, no matter how late it is. I'm about to cross the street, when somebody steps into my way.

"Lotte, it's me."

I immediately recognize Fritz, not just by his voice, but the smell that sticks to him: intense nicotine mixed with unwashed skin. A part of me hoped he'd just move away and leave me alone.

"I'm tired. Can't you leave me be?"

"They took me, Lotte, the Russians." Fritz's trembling voice matches that of his hands lighting a cigarette. "I spent a week locked up. They threatened me to produce information or deport me back to Siberia. I don't know what to do anymore." He bends over, coughing violently. Despite the wheezing, he continues to smoke.

Again, Fritz's desperation tugs at my heart. "You are killing yourself with these cigarettes."

"I don't care anymore. I don't have the energy to fight them."

"What would you do if you could get out?" I ask.

"Work some place simple, like an office. I once studied accounting. It's nice work sitting at a desk." He coughs again, spits.

"I wasn't going to ask you again, but I've got no choice."

"How can I reach you? I mean if I find out something."

"I'll wait in front of Tempelhof every other day."

"Now let me go home."

"Thank you, Lotte, I won't forget it." He melts into the shadows, but then hurries back to me. "I almost forgot, I've got cigarettes to trade. Surely you'll find something on the black market."

And that's how I not only come home with a care packet, but with additional currency to find the right food for Walter.

"Will you look at this?" Mama sits in wonder, going through the contents of the package. "Dried plums, lard, canned meat, flour, my goodness…" She holds up a paper bag. "Sugar and egg powder… we can bake something." She sniffs another package. "Real coffee."

"What is this?" Tilly lifts out another cardboard box. "Raisins, oh my."

Taking turns, the two of them are picking up each item, reading its label: marmalade, honey, chocolate, margarine… soap.

"I could kiss your boss," Mama says as she inspects the small package, still wrapped in paper.

"These came from Mitch," I say quietly.

Mama looks at me, puzzled. "The pilot at Meg's place? I didn't know he was here, too."

Secretly, I'm surprised she remembers much from the time after the rape. "He flies almost around the clock, like all of them, Mama."

Mama's hands play with the heavy wrapping paper. "You liked him a lot."

"He has also helped with Margo."

"Oh, Lotte, why didn't you tell us?" Tilly cries. "We must write a letter at once and thank him."

"I'm sure he'd like that."

"What is that?" Mama has opened the second package and lifts out a card. "This is for you, Lotte." She hands both to me.

Lotte,

I couldn't forget your comment about chocolate. I begged my crew, also had a few things my sister sent me. As you know, most of our sweets are going to Gail for the children's candy drop. The care package has chocolate as well, but I thought you should claim this one for yourself. Enjoy!

Yours, Mitch

Inside I find eight bars of Hershey's chocolate, Whoppers Malted Milk Balls, licorice and two packs of gum. As I sniff each package, move it this way and that on the table, I can't get over the fact that Mitch took time to collect these delicacies for me. Does it mean something? Does the letter signed with "yours" mean anything? Or is he just taking pity on a German woman struggling to support her family?

Tilly opens the dried prunes and hands one to Walter, who is sitting quietly at the table. Even he has a sheen in his eyes.

"I'm going to make pancakes," Mama announces. "Tomorrow, we'll need to search for firewood again. Otherwise, we won't be able to cook." Her gaze falls on the cigarettes, half hidden under the many cans. "Were these in there, too? They're Russian."

"Got them from Fritz," I say. "He says to use them on the black market to buy vegetables."

"I thought you two broke it off years ago?" Mama says.

"He wants my help getting out of Berlin."

Tilly huffs. "Wouldn't we all like to leave. What makes him so special?"

I shrug, not wanting to tell them about Fritz's spy work.

"Does he think a few lousy cigarettes will get him a ticket on an American plane?" Tilly walks over to me and takes my hand. "Are you going to help him?"

Here it is, the issue I've been struggling with for months. I can't tell Tilly and Mama that Fritz is threatening to inform Mitch about the baby. They don't know about my miscarriage, the black hole I'd fallen into. I'd pretended to be sick with a stomach flu, being upset about Fritz and Mitch. Since I couldn't eat for days, they believed me.

"I do feel sorry for him, but I also told him that this is strictly a military operation and not a tourist airline."

Tilly huffs. "Just send him on his way. He has no right to bother you any longer. As far as I see, he never works an honest job. Makes you wonder how he can get all those cigarettes."

Isn't that right? Tilly may be old, but she doesn't miss much.

"He's sick."

"So what, many people are sick. That doesn't give him the right to fly off into the sunset." Tilly opens one of the flour bags and measures out six servings.

"I'd discuss it with your boss." Mama adds egg powder to the flour. "Either way, I'm going to take the cigarettes tomorrow and buy whatever fresh produce I can find."

"I could come along," Walter says, his voice barely audible.

Mama jumps up and wraps an arm around his shoulder. "I'd love that."

While we enjoy real pancakes—Mama has made enough to share with Albert and Karl—my mind is circling around Fritz once again. I'm tired of him pressuring me and I've got to come to a conclusion how to get him off my back.

The next morning, I wait until Thomas is at his desk. "I've got a question."

Thomas appears unusually grumpy and exhausted, and hardly looks up. "Shoot."

"Is it possible to fly people out of Tempelhof, I mean just normal Berliners, not kids?"

Thomas frowns and finally meets my eyes. "Why?"

"To get away, leave Berlin for good."

"Civilians are being flown out now." He attempts a smile, fails. "You want to leave us?"

"Not me, it's just I wondered."

"It's a bit of work to reinstall seats for passenger travel, but it's done more and more. Of course, they take important people, politicians or celebrities, maybe people with a critical profession. Our job is to keep Berlin going and General Tunner is pretty tough on rules."

"Understood, thanks."

Thomas rises from behind his desk, lowers his voice. "You're sure you don't want to leave?"

"Not a chance. I've got my mother here, also an old lady and her son I'm supporting."

This time the smile holds. "Good, I'd hate to lose you. You've become an excellent translator. I'm sure you could transfer to our Frankfurt airbase or one of the British bases."

The smile I give Thomas for his praise of my skills soon fades as I think about what to tell Fritz.

CHAPTER TWENTY-SEVEN

That night I hardly sleep. Fritz will be waiting in the evening, wanting an answer. I imagine turning him in, telling Thomas that Fritz is a spy. He'd be arrested, thrown in jail, where he'd wither away in no time. A sigh rises in the darkness. No matter his betrayal, I won't behave the same and deceive my former fiancé. But then, who knows what damage he's done in those years? Stalin is ruthless and will use any method to hurt us… the west. Fritz may have contributed to Stalin's decision to cut off Berlin.

I roll to my side, open my eyes. Though I can't see them in the darkness, Mama and Tilly are lying right next to me. Will we ever be free again and live a normal life? In an apartment with power and running water, private bedrooms and a shelf full of food? How many more years do we have to struggle for the most basic things? If it weren't for the Americans, I'd lose all hope.

It is way past midnight when I fall asleep.

All morning, I drag myself around from assignment to assignment.

Shortly before lunch, Thomas's secretary comes running. "Lotte, you've got to fill in this afternoon at three o'clock. Our other translator got sick."

I scan my list. "I'm supposed to assist a mayor visiting from Hamburg."

The secretary sighs. "That has got to wait. Lieutenant Gail Halvorsen has an interview scheduled to speak about the candy drop, you know, Uncle Wiggly Wings. It'll be broadcast live."

The paper sinks in my hand. "On TV?"

"Just radio."

In an instant, my head feels hot and my brain empty. I can't translate in front of a microphone. Panic is choking me like a couple of hands on my throat. I'm going to be sick. No wonder that other translator found an excuse. It's stressful enough when important visitors from the US or Germany need my services.

"…else?" The secretary studies me.

"Excuse me?"

"I said, if you have anything else to wear." The woman has a lot of nerve. She gets supplied by her American family, can order what she wants. She is always smartly clothed in a suit or dress.

I look at my scuffed shoes, the only *decent* pair I own. Walking so much and especially through the rough streets of Berlin takes its toll. My gray wool dress has seen better days too, but it is the only one warm enough for the drafty corridors of Tempelhof.

Since I don't answer, the secretary nods curtly and says, "I shall organize a couple of things, also get you a ration card for clothes."

It is almost lunch time, but just the smell of food makes me nauseous. My armpits are sticky as I hide myself in the bathroom. *Get a grip, you'll do this like any other translation.*

But this is Gail Halvorsen, the pilot who shared two sticks of gum with thirty children and got inspired to do more. Now he is famous for having created a regular candy drop, releasing chocolates and gum on mini parachutes during the approach to Tempelhof Airport and recently over parks and gardens. Other pilots have since followed suit and Gail has received recognition from his superiors all the way to the president.

Uncle Wiggly Wings, as the children of Berlin call him, will be talking to a Berlin reporter and since time is of the essence, everything is tightly scheduled, so Gail can return to his plane right after.

I don't know how the next three hours pass, every time I think about the assignment, I suck air and sigh. The clock hands move in slow motion, my hands tremble as I try to concentrate on my other work.

Around two o'clock, I'm back in the area. Thomas's secretary has not been able to find fitting shoes, but she has organized brown shoe polish and left a tube of lipstick, hairspray and some perfume on my desk.

Gail shows forty-five minutes later and immediately the room buzzes with excitement. It's as if he's carrying an imaginary cloak of hopefulness that spills over on anyone near him. Some insist he is preventing World War III. Either way, his kindness and good mood are infectious.

He is even taller than the photos indicate, his uniform immaculate. Without much ado, he extends a hand and introduces himself. As if that is necessary. "Glad to have you by my side," he says with a generous smile.

"My pleasure," I say after introducing myself. "I'll try my very best, Lieutenant."

"I'm sure you will, Lotte. Call me Gail."

"Mr. Halvorsen, if you would sit over here." The interviewer, an American reporter, and a second man in charge of sound, wave us over and make us sit behind a desk. Apparently, the network wants Gail's words spread in Germany.

During the interview, Gail talks about meeting the children and how they changed his heart, how he became determined to help against the odds. He tells how impressed he was that the German kids were not as excited about receiving his gum, but worried about losing their freedom. He emphasizes how important it is to help instead of to hate, surely a direct insult to our neighbors to the east. He finishes by promising to continue his candy drops for the children of Berlin.

My ears are on high alert as I translate his words, his optimism and willingness to bend the rules a bit make it easy. I can't help but smile while I retell Gail's words in German.

"Great job," he says afterwards, a twinkle in his eyes. "Sorry, I don't have any chocolate on me."

I smile at the man whose personal determination has touched so many. We may think that the actions of one man make no difference, that it doesn't matter and that we may as well not try. Gail has shown us that that is not true. One man or woman *can* make a difference. "It was an honor," I say, taking his hand, wishing Margo could've met him.

The buzz subsides and the offices are returning to normal. What impressed me most wasn't Gail's words, it was his personality, the aura of goodness that is infectious and powerful. In our shattered city, it feels like a beautiful gift.

Thomas sends me home early, insisting I've worked enough. Still excited about meeting the Candy Bomber and participating in his campaign, sharing his story with German listeners, I hurry outside. Only then do I remember Fritz.

My heart hammers once more with the dread of meeting him. What am I going to say? I'm worried he'll make a scene, threaten me again. I anxiously scan the street still bustling with pedestrians, trams, buses, and American trucks. He's not there.

Relieved, I rush home, trying to enjoy the afterglow of the interview. "Guess who I met today," I announce, pulling aside the blanket to our section of the room.

Silence greets me, as my gaze falls on Fritz, who sits at the table across from Walter, sipping precious coffee. "Hello, Lotte, it's good to see you. I thought I'd visit." Fritz nods approvingly at Walter, as if they're old friends. "I see you've got a new family member."

"Fritz says you two were engaged," Walter says innocently.

I smack down my bag, trying to remain calm. "We were… a long time ago." I'm so furious, I can hardly get the words out. "You've got no right to be here," I say, hoping that Mama and Tilly will return from whatever errands they're running.

Fritz lights a cigarette, which elicits an immediate cough from Walter. I snatch the cigarette from Fritz's hand and throw it into a bucket. "Can't you see, Walter is sick."

"So am I. In fact, we were just comparing notes about Russian camps." Fritz calmly grabs another cigarette and lights it. He looks worse than ever and smells like an ashtray. "Would you care to join us?"

I glare at him, my anger now red hot. I want to smack the man. How could I have felt sorry for him?

"*You* don't care if I smoke, Walter?"

Walter smiles politely. I know he does, but in his current state, he is no match for Fritz.

"What do you want?" I huff.

"Just to see how you live these days. You never invite me up." He looks around the room before taking another drag.

"Let's take a walk. Walter needs rest."

Fritz reluctantly rises and pats Walter on the shoulder. "See you soon, buddy."

To let off steam, I hurry off at a good clip. Fritz follows slowly, so I'm forced to stop and wait for him. "What are you thinking? This is my home and you've got no right to intrude."

Fritz flips the cigarette butt into the street and says, "Just thought I'd visit a fellow comrade. He looks like he needs male company, being surrounded by you women folk."

"We are taking care of him whilst you only know yourself."

Fritz steps closer and takes hold of my arm. "What did you find out?"

I try to pull free, but his hand clamps down harder. "I spoke with my boss. He says…"

"He says what?"

"He'll look into it, may take a while."

"How long?"

"He didn't say."

Fritz's hand lets go of my arm. "Sorry, I don't want to scare you."

I step back three feet and let out a breath. *Why did I lie? Why didn't I tell him what Thomas said?* "I thought you weren't going to hang around here, Russians may watch and threaten you again. Or us. Besides, Walter needs rest and clean air. He's weak and quite sick."

"So we both are," Fritz mocks.

"In contrast to you, *he* did his time." It's out before I can stop myself.

Fritz throws me a nasty glance. "You should control your mouth. It's ugly and unbecoming."

"I'm going back inside. Tell me where I can send a note once I hear something."

"You can't. I'll stop by occasionally. Make sure good old Walter is doing all right."

"Asshole." I turn on my heels and run back to the house. The happiness of this afternoon has evaporated like water droplets on a sunbaked pavement. One thing is clear, Fritz is getting worse, more desperate, even deranged.

With the time he has, he can always watch for Mama and Tilly to leave and get Walter alone. I must warn Walter, I must warn them all. But how can I without divulging Fritz's secret? I'd promised to keep it to myself.

"Fritz was here?" Tilly asks during dinner.

"I didn't know," I say defensively. "He barged in before I got home."

Tilly gives Walter an extra helping of cabbage and mashed potatoes. "I'd rather he didn't."

"What does he still want with you?" Mama asks.

I shrug. "Can't let go, I suppose. He's lonely."

Walter pushes away his plate. The portions he eats are still quite small. "He was nice enough, spent time in a gulag like me."

He's got nothing in common with you, I want to say. "We are not friends anymore and he shouldn't come here."

Walter smiles mildly. "I hardly have the muscle to throw him out."

"We could ask Albert to help," Mama says.

"A one-armed man and a cripple." Walter's laugh turns into a cough.

Tilly snorts. "The man has the nerve to smoke in here. The air is bad enough, not to mention that Walter's lungs can't take it."

"Fritz is weak himself," I say. "I doubt he is capable of fighting anyone."

Tilly frowns. "Maybe not, but I don't understand why he is showing up like this." I see the wheels turning in her head. She's never liked Fritz, who knows, she may figure it out for herself.

We decide to speak with Albert and enlist his help, should Fritz show up again. But as soon as we go to bed, the worry returns.

Fritz is a loose cannon. For the first time, I'm afraid of him.

Everywhere I go the next day, people congratulate me on the successful interview. At lunch, Danny slides into the chair across from me. "So, first you meet with your pilot and then you interview the famous Candy Bomber?" She grins at me. "I'd say you're one lucky girl."

"He's not *my* pilot," I say weakly.

"Could've fooled me. He likes you a lot, I swear."

"How could you tell from that distance?"

"It's all in the body language." Danny stops chewing for a moment. "I read somewhere that words have very little meaning in comparison to the way we move, our expressions."

I grin. "Now you're an expert in communication?"

Danny wipes her mouth and takes a sip from her Coke. "Never said that." Our eyes meet. "I thought you were mad at me."

"I was… a little, when you came over that day. But it wasn't right. I'm sorry. It's not your fault that this is complicated."

"It wouldn't have to be."

"What do you mean?"

Danny breaks into another smile. "Maybe you should just be honest and tell him."

"I can't."

Danny drains her Coke and gets up. "Suit yourself. Maybe you just love being miserable."

Watching Danny hurry toward the exit, I sit there open-mouthed while a small voice in my head comments that she is probably right. At least, if I did, I'd have clarity.

In my mind, I see Meg shaking her head. She would've said the same or worse, always straightforward, always honest. How I miss her. The old guilt creeps up, gives me a sour taste despite the sweet Coke. After losing the baby, I kept to myself for weeks. Didn't go out, didn't visit Meg, though I knew she wasn't feeling well with that cough. The weather had been forbidding in January and February and when it finally broke and I mustered the strength to stop by Meg's place, she was gone. Extinguished like a small flame in a gust of wind. While I grieved for my baby, Meg lay dying in that basement, wondering why her only friend never showed.

They say regret is a wasted emotion. Yet, when I'm not careful, it grips me in its iron claws. How often have I imagined leaving the house to see her, stand by her, tell her about Mitch's baby?

Tears press and I resolutely drain my Coke. The airlift leaves no time for the past, not for my lost friend nor for romantic feelings. Mitch is far too busy, even if he still likes me. But wouldn't it be heaven to know, just dream about an evening out, just the two of us strolling, talking and maybe exchanging a kiss?

"Goodness, you're far away." Greg Taylor, Mitch's former roommate, hovers above me with the usual grinning sneer. Clad in a coverall and leather jacket, he stands so close, his hip nearly touches me. "Still breaking hearts, deary?"

"Why don't you mind your own business?" I say, pulling my chair back. A whiff of alcohol travels into my nose. Greg always liked whiskey.

Anytime I'd visited Mitch in Meg's old apartment, Greg had a glass sitting in front of him. By the end of the evening, he often slurred his words. Back then, I didn't understand enough English, but I could tell he was drunk a lot. How he was able to fly, is flying now, I don't know. According to Thomas and Mitch, it's nerve-racking to pilot a plane through the narrow corridor with exactly one shot to land it, often in fog and rain. The Skymasters and Skytrains are loaded to capacity, and I heard one pilot joke it felt like steering a pregnant cow half-blind through the eye of a needle.

"Having an attitude today, eh?" Greg's gaze travels down my front and back up. Immediately, I'm feeling repulsed. "And here all I wanted was to invite you to dinner. I happen to be staying overnight."

"They won't let you fly anymore?"

"On the contrary. I'll be flying some folks out tomorrow morning. Heard you on the radio with Gail, nice job. Not that I understood anything. German sounds like sending rocks through a shredder."

"Charming." Eyeing the wall clock, I rise. "Got to return to work. See you later."

Greg doesn't move. "What about that dinner? We can catch up for old time's sake."

"There's nothing to catch up on. Better let me pass."

"Or what?" Greg still grins but there's a challenge in his eyes, a glint of something dark I have no interest in exploring.

"Never mind." I smartly step around him and rush toward the shelves to deposit my tray. If Greg says anything else, I don't hear it in the noisy mess hall. Still, the hairs on my neck are at high alert. I'd not want to meet Greg by myself, not even in the busy airport. There's something unhinged about him. Not like Fritz, who is desperate to escape the Russians, but a kind of evil that lives within Greg. With Mitch I felt safe, not so much anymore.

I wonder what Danny thinks of Greg, now that a few weeks have passed. Would she go out with him again? Unlikely, but it's hard to say when a man promises food, drinks, and gifts and the attention many of us have lived without for so long.

Even if there's a price to pay. I'm pretty sure Danny already paid.

By the time I leave, it is dark. A cold rain pounds the streets, my feet are soaked in minutes. I have no umbrella and hold down my hat to keep it from flying away. Thomas even offered to drive me, but I don't want to owe him anything. Not him, not Greg, and certainly not Fritz.

I imagine I shall remain single for the rest of my life. So be it. I can take care of Mama and help Tilly and her family. One day, Berlin will rebuild, even if it seems to be impossible right now.

CHAPTER TWENTY-EIGHT

Mama and Tilly are heading across the border again. We've saved my money for weeks and want to stockpile for the holidays. Albert has contributed a watch he inherited from his father. December has brought freezing temperatures, so both women wear wool sweaters and coats, hats and gloves, both knitted by Mama from old pullovers, their wool unraveled, dampened and stretched.

"We'll try to hurry," Tilly says. "We'll go the same way as last time and want to be back before dark."

By the time I get home, it is after seven o'clock. Walter is pacing back and forth, looking paler than usual. "They aren't back yet. What if something happened?"

I swallow my worry and say, "Maybe there aren't as many trains. The snow is making it more difficult, too."

Deep in thought, I heat water for tea and yet another soup, while Walter peruses an old copy of the *Tagesspiegel* newspaper.

By eight, we are both pacing. I consider going outside, but the temperatures are dropping and I have no idea which direction the women went this morning. I wash out hose and socks in a bucket and drape them over the dividing line to Albert's side. It's quiet over there, but I know our neighbor is just as worried as we are.

By eight-thirty, I'm convinced something terrible has happened. I feel utterly helpless, because I don't even know where to look or who to ask.

Walter is visibly trembling, so I say, "Maybe they missed the train or the snow is worse out there and they're spending the night."

I pour more peppermint tea and grab the cup with both hands like a life buoy. I see Mama running from the Russian men, blood dripping down her legs, her eyes empty. Nothing like this is being reported these days, but who knows what happens under Soviet rule?

"They're both strong women," I whisper.

Walter rises and begins to pace again.

On the other side of our blanket wall, the door flies open, sending a gust of chilly air our way.

Albert mutters something and then the curtain pulls aside. Mama and Tilly look frozen, their cheeks and noses red as cherries, their eyebrows white with ice crystals. But worse are their expressions, a mix of anger and misery—and utter exhaustion.

They sink onto the sofa, still in their coats. Neither of them carries a bag.

"What happened?" I cry, pulling the gloves from Mama's hands. She winces, her fingers are as icy as the streets outside, red and chapped.

Tilly slowly unbuttons her coat as Walter removes her shoes and brings her wool socks. For a moment, neither of them speaks and so I rush to heat more water for tea. The power is on for once, so I borrow Albert's immersion heater. My hands are shaking as I pour hot water into the pan that serves as tea and coffee pot. Albert and Karl have quietly joined us and are sitting at the table.

Other than taking off their winter coats, both women have not moved when I hand them the steaming cups. Both wrap their hands around them, breathe in the steam.

"We made good progress this morning," Tilly finally says. "Took the tram and then the train back to Brandenburg like last time. We found our farmer, bought potatoes." She glances at Albert. "He even gave us an extra helping of rutabagas and onions for Albert's watch."

"We missed a train, another was so full we didn't feel like fighting the crowds with our bags," Mama adds. "By the time we returned to East Berlin it was after five and getting dark. There were rumors of Soviet razzias, but we saw nothing suspicious."

She looks at Tilly, who continues. "The trouble started at the sector border. Last time, nobody even seemed to watch. I mean this morning we just walked across, no problem. But tonight, there was a line. Russian soldiers with guns at the ready checked everyone's papers. When they got to us, they wanted to know where we'd been. We told them we'd visited friends in the countryside. That's when they pulled us aside. We went to some kind of office, a stinky dank place that reeked of vodka and urine." Tilly's sigh rattles through the tiny room. Walter takes her right hand, rubs it gently.

Mama continues, "They asked us what we did in their sector, why we came. Then they demanded to see our sacks. At first, they poked around in them, then poured everything on the floor. Potatoes and onions rolled every which way. Some Russian picked one up with his knife and cut it apart. They talked among each other, joked. The officer who'd spoken to us made them hush up, told us we were forbidden from stealing from their lands and to stay in the west, that they'd tolerated us decadent westerners long enough." Mama's eyes glint with tears. "They collected our things and disappeared, let us sit there for a while. I was so scared." She grabs her throat and rocks back and forth.

Tilly rubs Mama's back. "They let us go at last, but we never saw our food again."

"My watch," Albert whispers. "It was all I had left."

"I'm so sorry." Tilly smacks her little fist on her thigh. "These bastards. Nothing but common thieves."

"I heard the British no longer supply parts and coal to the east," I say. "That's probably why they're cutting us off."

Walter shakes his head in disbelief. "How can the British supply the Russians after what Stalin did?"

"Nobody knows for sure," I say. "The British government didn't want to irritate Stalin further and thought it was a way to appease him. I heard people talking about it at Tempelhof."

"How could they?" Tilly looks at us. "Either way, it's all gone, and we won't be able to go back."

Albert nods dejectedly and leads Karl back to his side of the room while the rest of us just sit there brooding. The winter months lie before us. Who knows what can happen?

During the days before Christmas, the airlift is ramping up more and more and nearly every day, there seems to be a new record. General Tunner's careful oversight of all Allied flights is making a huge difference. As of December 15, the new airport at Tegel is fully operational and I'm no longer doubting that Berlin can be supplied from the air, well, almost. The winter weather is impossible to predict, ice and fog make flying and landing precarious. During work, I often watch the activity outside, listen to the droning engines.

Since the beginning, there have been crashes every month, sometimes several. In October, a Skymaster slid past the landing path and burst into flames. Luckily, pilot and crew were saved by firefighters. More often than not, people die—brave pilots intent on saving us.

I think of Mitch, who I have not heard from since he sent the care package and chocolate. Please let him be safe.

Around the airport offices, small Christmas decorations appear: a sprig of pine, a shiny ornament, a candle… in the mess hall Frank Sinatra crows "Jingle Bells." On my desk appears an orange, a bar of chocolate and some walnuts. Nobody is coming forward, but I take extra care to sniff the orange and keep it safe to take home. I'll share it with my family, a fruit none of us has tasted or even seen in years. Other than that, the operation is going full speed, Berlin is ever hungry.

The morning of Christmas Eve, two envelopes lie on my desk. One is from Thomas, wishing me Merry Christmas and announcing a bonus for the good work I've been doing. I immediately recognize the writing on the other envelope, addressed to me, and rip it open in a hurry.

Mitch's hastily scribbled words swim in a jumble before they order themselves in front of my eyes.

Dear Lotte,

I'm hoping you may be around this afternoon. I have a few hours' break.

Yours, Mitch

My eyes jump to the wall clock. Eleven… what does afternoon mean? I had planned to return home early and help with dinner. We are having canned meat and potatoes, cabbage and onions, and Mama is baking a cake from some of the ingredients she saved from the care package. No matter how carefully we ration, our shelves are nearly empty again.

Around noon, Thomas appears with two bottles of sparkling wine. "Let's all drink to your amazing work," he addresses the office workers. "May Stalin shrivel with envy."

We holler and toast each other, but my thoughts are on Mitch. I rush this way and that for some last-minute projects, helping three newly hired workers with their paperwork, translating an article in the Berliner *Tagesspiegel,* one of the west's largest newspapers, for Thomas's boss and assisting a C-54 crew with letters and packages they want to deliver to friends in Berlin. In between each job, I rush back to my desk to look for a familiar figure, my head a bit light from the unaccustomed alcohol. *What does afternoon mean? What is he planning?*

By two o'clock the office is growing quiet. Nonessential personnel have left, though most will be back tomorrow. Out of excuses, I retreat to my desk.

"Why don't you go home?" Thomas's soft smile is a far cry from earlier times. I have been keeping my distance, afraid to make him angry or encouraging him.

"Just finishing this," I say.

Thomas places a package in front of me. "Something for your dinner."

Heat rises into my cheeks. I'm embarrassed to take any more gifts, especially because I wonder if Thomas is expecting anything in return. But then, I think about Mama's and Tilly's failed excursion. Who can afford to feel guilty when we are scraping by?

"Don't open it until you get home."

"That's very thoughtful, thank you."

Thomas stands there, nods, then seems to want to say something else, doesn't. He is eyeing me strangely through smudged glasses. Should I say something? Is he waiting for an invitation?

Thomas clears his throat. "Maybe we could—"

"Sorry I'm late." Mitch is rushing toward us with long steps, his face and nose glowing from the cold. He's wearing a lined leather jacket like Greg, carries his cap under his arm.

Thomas swivels around. "Mitch! Didn't know you were coming." He pats Mitch on the back. "Merry Christmas." To me, he says, "See you the day after tomorrow, Lotte." He tips his hat and hurries off.

I feel Thomas's disappointment, am sure he wanted to say something important, but then there is Mitch, the man my thoughts have circled around for three years.

"You ready?" he says without introduction. He looks exhausted, his eyelids puffy, and yet he seems excited.

I abruptly jump from my chair and grab my coat and moments later we are stepping into the cold afternoon. "Got us a car," he says, jingling a set of keys.

The military jeep has seen better days, is dusty, the interior spartan. I don't care. All I think about is Mitch's presence, his body next to mine, his breath throwing white clouds mixing with mine. Somehow, it feels like déjà vu: the jitters are back, my heart is racing, and my head whirls in search of something smart to say.

"Where are we going?" I finally manage.

"Ku'damm." He throws me a quick glance and then concentrates on the road again. It's not that slick, but cars, trucks, buses and trams mingle, tired-looking pedestrians hurry this way and that, some carry heavy packs, others pull wagons. The steady stream of refugees from the east has not let up. "I don't know my way around anymore, but there'll be something open."

I study his hands, slender with long fingers, knowing hands that once traveled across my body and brought me a happiness I'd never known.

He parks and hurries around the car to help me out. I'm feeling less than adequate, wearing my old wool dress and felt hat that is shiny in places. He doesn't seem to notice and pulls my hand under his arm. "Let's see what we can find to eat."

My stomach growls in response. Because of his note and the sparkling wine earlier, I haven't eaten much. I push the thoughts of Mama, Tilly and Walter waiting for me far away.

"I hope this isn't too inconvenient," he says as we enter the restaurant.

"Not at all," I lie. Why can't I be honest and tell him that my family is likely worried? Especially today, on Christmas. But I can't because I'll find any excuse to stay here. After we sit and the waitress takes our order, I study Mitch's face. "I'm glad we're meeting again. It feels like old times, well, a bit."

"I never thought I'd return here," he says. "Not after our breakup… leaving Berlin."

"Why did you ask me here?" It's out before I have time to think. A year ago, I wouldn't have been so forward, but the work at Tempelhof and fighting for Berlin has changed things. Or maybe it is Fritz who is pushing me around.

Mitch looks thoughtful. "To be honest, I'm not sure. Our work has been crazy, our schedules insane. It's hard to formulate a single thought, other than prepping for takeoff, flying and landing, then doing it all over again." He pauses and when I don't answer, he says, "Last night, I thought of you here in that huge airport with those thousands of workers and military personnel. How you've fought hard to make a place for yourself." He hesitates, then looks at me with those sparkling eyes, shiny blue like a summer sky. "I felt this intense pride."

I smile, though I'm confused. "It's been challenging, but I do enjoy the work. It makes me feel as if I'm doing something worthwhile. Not as important as your job, but… You think we'll succeed?"

"Hope so, Tunner has been hiring more pilots, many came out of retirement or are new recruits. Surely Stalin is getting a bit tired of the blockade. Especially because he's not getting coal and other supplies anymore."

The waitress delivers our drinks, a Coke and tea for me. The air is warm and filled with chatting patrons. In the background somebody plinks "Holy Night" on a piano. I sip my tea, thinking of the button I carry. How it comforts me to know that it once belonged to Mitch.

"Whatever happened to your fiancé?"

"Fritz?"

He glances at my ring finger. "You never got married."

I put down my cup, take a breath. "Fritz and I split up shortly after you left. Well, we never got together after his return. He was a stranger, still is."

"You continue to see him?" Mitch appears curious, but there's something else, some kind of disapproval.

"He wants to leave Berlin, badly, and asked me to get him on a flight."

Mitch huffs. "He's got a lot of nerve."

I bite my lip. I've carried Fritz's secret for years, remember his face when I asked him pointblank what he was doing in the Russian sector, smoking Russian cigarettes. But there's this thing again, the feeling I can share anything with Mitch. Except for one. "Remember he returned right after the war ended? Apparently the Soviets pressured him to spy for them."

Mitch lets out a long sigh. "I've heard about them doing this. There're supposed to be thousands like him."

"He's in bad shape, tired of struggling. He wants to escape before they deport him east or worse."

"And he wants *you* to help him?"

"I told him I can't." I look away. This is the crucial moment. I cannot tell Mitch about Fritz's blackmail to divulge my secret.

Mitch frowns. "You realize I've got to report this."

The waitress places two bowls in front of us, pea soup with sausage and potatoes. "*Bitte sehr.*"

I ignore the incredible aroma rising into my nose and stare at him. "But he's not hurting you."

"He is hurting Allied Berlin and the western world."

"Will they arrest him?"

"Likely, he's not very dangerous, low-level. But still." The frown crease between Mitch's brows is back. "I remember him hanging out in front of our place. That other guy was with him, Meg's husband, the invalid." He pauses. "Whatever happened to Meg?"

My throat tightens. "Meg contracted TB from her husband, Hans."

Mitch leans forward, whispers, "She died?"

I nod and swallow hard to make the ball in my throat disappear. It doesn't work, because Mitch's face blurs. Regret is showing its ugly face. I missed the chance to be with my only friend. Hadn't the war taught us that life is precious and can be withdrawn at any moment? And yet, I was selfish, thinking about the loss of my baby, indulging in my depression while Meg... A sigh escapes me. "I miss her terribly. She offered a place for me and Mama when we had nothing." I open my mouth, close it. To tell Mitch about my failure to visit Meg would mean that I have to tell him why.

Thankfully, he misunderstands, a warm hand lands on mine. "I'm sorry."

I wipe my face with the other hand and try a smile. "The soup smells heavenly."

Mitch smiles back. "Then we better eat."

Silence descends as we are spooning soup and chasing it with bread. The warm salty flavors spread in my stomach, fill me with warmth. Mitch has long taken back his hand, but his touch is still lingering on my skin like an imprint. He's taken off his cap and in the light of the overhead lamp his brown hair shimmers like dark chocolate.

"What did you do in the past three years?" I ask as the waitress removes our bowls and places servings of roast meat and potatoes in front of us.

"Flew a lot," Mitch says. "At various bases back home."

"Did you get to see your family? Your girlfriend?"

"Now and then." He hesitates. "Helen and I ... Actually, our parents are friends, I've known her for years."

My insides cringe as if icy crystals have hit them. *Keep it together,* my mind comments. All I muster is an "Oh."

Mitch studies me. "It seemed like a good idea. A lot less complicated than dating a German girl."

What should I say to that? My roast is getting cold as I imagine Mitch and some woman walking hand in hand... kissing... limbs intertwined. Is that why he asked me here, to tell me to leave him alone with my pleading for help? Do I seem desperate? "You didn't marry her?"

He shakes his head, eyes my plate. "We better eat."

Once again, we eat in silence. My stomach fills and then some, but I eat every last bite, though part of me feels nauseous. My thoughts are racing around the fact that Mitch is likely going to marry as soon as the airlift is finished. Does he feel sorry for me, the poor girl from Germany?

Suddenly, fury takes over. I push away my plate and take a deep breath. The restaurant is no longer cozy, the people's happy chatter is getting on my nerves.

"I'd better go home," I say, finishing my tea.

"We still have dessert," Mitch says. I can tell he is surprised.

"I'm stuffed as it is."

Mitch nods, looks flustered. He waves to the waitress, pays an insane amount of Deutsche Mark, printed with a red B.

I say nothing, just stand there, already in my coat and hat, trying to feel nothing, trying to keep a distance between what Mitch told me and my life. This isn't me, this is just a woman waiting for a man to pay the bill.

He remains by my side as we hurry toward the jeep. The air smells of snow and the sky is gray as lead. Please let me get home in one piece, without breaking down or crying. Why did my stupid heart begin to hope again? Why do I do this to myself?

In front of my apartment, Mitch pulls to a stop. He throws me a curious glance, then jumps out and opens the door for me. Takes my forearm and walks me to the house.

"I don't know what to say," he finally mumbles.

"You don't have to say anything. Thank you for the meal, Merry Christmas." I turn abruptly, stick my key in the door.

"Wait. Just wait a moment, Lotte." Behind me, Mitch's voice seems thin, kind of broken.

I turn around and since I stand on the doorstep, we are almost at eye level. He is close now, much closer than I thought. The blue of his eyes has turned cadet gray in the gloomy light.

And then his lips are on mine. Cold lips that still taste a bit of Coke and roast, but more so they are incredibly sweet and soft. I'm so surprised, I nearly lose my balance, but there are his hands around my waist, even through my coat I feel their warmth, comfortable like a hot water bottle on a winter night. I'm shivering now, not from the cold, I don't feel the icy air anymore, I'm trembling from the way his mouth feels against mine, how we meld together like we can never separate again.

Of course we do. Too soon does he pull back, his face still close, his gaze on mine, white clouds rising between us. "I don't know what this is, Lotte," he says hoarsely. "You're an enigma to me."

"I thought I was the woman alone at the airport," I say. His lips draw together, he looks pained, kind of hurt. "I'm sorry, I'm just confused. I thought you had a girlfriend."

The pain in his expression deepens. "I do, but…"

"But what?" The old anger creeps into the open.

"I want to see you again."

Ignoring the warmth in my middle, my pounding heart, I say, "In between flying and seeing your girlfriend?"

Abruptly, he leans in again. "Stop it, Lotte, please. I'm trying to figure this out, will you give me chance? It's complicated enough to be a pilot right now."

I bite my lower lip until it hurts. He is so close again, I could just move a few inches to feel his skin on mine. And then I do, my stupid body moves without me, forward until our lips meet once more. We kiss, passionately this time, two lovers giddy and excited to be near each other.

"I'm sorry," I whisper at some point. Darkness is falling along with a drizzle of snow. I should be freezing, yet I am warm. "We could go upstairs." It is ridiculous really, because upstairs five people are waiting for me.

Mitch huffs. "I've got to get back to the airport. Still need to return tonight for the first morning flight."

"Let's write then, the mail works pretty well."

He breaks into a smile. "Let's." He kisses my frozen hand. "Merry Christmas, promise me you'll be safe."

And then he is gone. I awkwardly work the key with numb fingers, climb the stairs as my heart sings "Silent Night."

CHAPTER TWENTY-NINE

I awake with a smile. Our little room is freezing, white fog rises with every breath. After cooking last night's meal, we have hardly any wood left for today. What does it matter? I will wear all my clothes, drape a blanket over my shoulders, if I have to.

In my mind I go over yesterday's events: Mitch's expression of uncertainty when he told me about the other woman, our lunch conversation. Mostly, I think about the way his body felt against mine: firm, powerful. Through our clothes, I imagine my skin touching his, warm skin smelling of citrus and lavender soap, the kind he used when we first met. I want to return to that moment, when he kissed me, wallow in the feeling of giddy elation. He wants to be with me, the German girl with a mismatched family and a missing father.

Nobody is up yet, not even Tilly. We spent a quiet evening together with Albert and Karl. Everybody contributed something to dinner: potatoes, a small helping of salt and a few sprigs of green from Albert—decorated with paper stars from Karl—carrots from Mama. We used the last two cans of meat and Tilly baked a cake with raisins. We sang "O Tannenbaum" and prayed with Albert, who is a devout Catholic. Every so often, I caught Mama glancing at the stack of Red Cross postcards, tied with a ribbon, as if she could conjure up Papa's spirit.

Early on, it had been a relief to know he was alive. Now, more than three and a half years later, we are growing anxious. Walter hasn't spoken of his life in Russia, but stories of the camps rotate, men sleeping on wooden floors without mattresses, infested with bed bugs and lice, clearing forests in Siberia, or working in mines with hardly enough food to keep them going. I try to imagine Papa among the men, dirty faces in torn clothes, dragging themselves around barracks.

My thoughts return to Mitch, the way he makes me feel lightheaded and worried at the same time, as if I'm walking too far onto a frozen lake. Any moment the ice may break, and I'll sink into a frozen grave. Mitch's decision to kiss me was impulsive, but he had also planned this flight to see me. At the same time, he's got a girlfriend waiting for him in the States. Once he returns there, he'll continue with her. It's easier and makes sense in so many ways. My presence is pleasant… convenient, a nice distraction from his real life.

A sigh rises loudly into the room. I don't want to be heartbroken again. It hurts too much. Three years ago, I lost Mitch, then I lost our baby. How different would life be if she had lived? I know it was a girl. Somehow, deep down, I know—Rose.

Now all I've got is the hope that Mitch will see me again, just as I cling to the hope that the airlift will succeed, that West Berlin will be saved from a ruthless dictator. As they say, hope dies last.

Tilly stirs, and after a few yawns, rises to wash in the bucket. We have rigged up a tiny corner with a curtain for some privacy. It is insane how we can still live like this. It seems that all our efforts are geared toward survival. There are hardly any construction materials to rebuild thousands of apartments. Even under normal circumstances, it's a herculean effort that will take decades to complete. Some politicians have said to abandon Berlin altogether. That the damage is too great to rebuild.

Most Berliners disagree. We are staying to create a free Berlin where we can live in peace—never again another war. It is *the* mantra, what keeps us going day after day.

I for one will fight for a free Berlin as long as it takes.

I get up and help Tilly with breakfast. I feed the little oven with leftover twigs and woodchips and pour water into a kettle, a dented white enamel piece Mama unearthed in the rubble.

"What's going on with you?" Tilly whispers. "I could swear you have changed."

I shrug and get busy with mugs. "Nothing, I'm just enjoying the holidays."

"Right."

I know Tilly doesn't believe me, but I can't share what happened—because it may never happen again.

A knock on the door makes me look up. Albert, who sleeps near the entrance, is in charge of opening the door. Mumbled words are exchanged, then the blanket curtain is yanked aside.

"Morning." Fritz, gray-faced and disheveled as ever, tips his hat.

"Merry Christmas," Tilly and I say at the same time.

That doesn't appear to interest Fritz. He only glares at me, sort of hateful and lurking at once.

"What can we do for you?" Tilly positions herself protectively next to me. "This is not a good time for a visit."

Fritz pulls closed the curtain. "Says who?" Immediately, our space fills with the odor of nicotine and body stench.

"All of us." Mama, hair disheveled, has risen from her bed, yet she appears just as resolute as Tilly and hurries to our side, arms crossed over her chest.

"Me too," comes from Walter's corner.

Fritz eyes our display of strength, apparently realizes that he won't win against the four of us. "I need to speak with Lotte— privately."

"Why don't you return at a decent hour?" Tilly asks. "Lotte is too busy as it is."

"This can't wait."

With a sigh I rise. "Wait for me downstairs, Fritz."

"You sure?" Tilly places a hand on my forearm. "You don't need to go out and freeze on your day off. It's Christmas."

Likely I do. "I won't be long."

Fritz wordlessly swivels on his heels and disappears behind the blanket, the door falls shut with a bang.

Mama sinks onto a chair. "What has gotten into him? Why is he even here?"

"He's got a lot of nerve showing up on Christmas morning." Tilly energetically stirs her tea mug.

Despite the situation, I smile. Mitch had used that expression.

"I don't see what's funny about it." Like Tilly, Mama eyes me curiously, while Walter grabs his tea and sits down next to them.

Remaining silent, I put on my coat and hat. "I'll hurry."

Mama abruptly rises. "Do you want me to come along?"

This time my smile is forced. "No need."

Before I open the front door, I hear Fritz coughing, which reminds me of a barking dog. He is pacing back and forth, another lit cigarette between his fingers. As I approach, he is wiping his mouth with a grubby rust-stained handkerchief and, when he sees me, quickly stuffs it into his pocket.

"About time," he says, indicating that he wants me to walk with him.

I wrap my coat tighter around my body. The sky is gray as dirty snow and an icy wind blows. "What's so urgent that it can't wait? You heard Tilly. This is my only day off."

"Hah, right." Fritz spits. To my horror, the spot on the ground is bloody red. A drop of crimson spittle clings to his lower lip.

When I don't answer, he grabs the lapels of my coat and pulls me to a stop. "Yesterday, I saw you and that… that pilot. Your old lover. Looks like you two are getting it on pretty good."

"You're spying on me?" I cry.

"Comes naturally."

"Obviously." I take a deep breath, which I immediately regret because Fritz's entire appearance seems to emanate a foul odor. "It's none of your business what I do or who I meet."

"What have you found out? Didn't your boss want to work on a spot for me? I heard the Yanks are flying out lots of people."

I look away to hide my guilt. "It's not that easy. He's got his hands full. The airlift is ramping up and—"

"I don't give a shit about what his workload is. I've got no time left. Do you understand?" He leans into me, his face inches from mine. So close, I notice the slack skin, the red-rimmed eyes, realize that Fritz must be seriously ill, likely cancer or advanced tuberculosis.

I want to shrink back, but his grip is holding, his fingers sinewy and surprisingly strong.

"Answer me, what are you going to do?"

"Let me ask again. Maybe he forgot—"

"Forgot?" Another coughing fit makes Fritz release my coat. He turns sideways and coughs into his handkerchief.

"You are sick," I say quietly. "You should be in a hospital."

Fritz wipes his mouth. Huffs. "No shit. I told you I want out."

"They'll ask for papers."

A sly expression crosses Fritz's face. "No problem."

"I'll be back there in the morning. Let me speak with my boss."

Fritz approaches again, though he doesn't touch me. In a calm voice, which strangely feels way more threatening, he says, "Don't make me ask again."

I turn on my heels and hurry home, wondering what he'd do, if he'd harm me or my family. The feeling of happiness has been replaced with a feeling of uneasiness. My belly rumbles and by the time I reach the hall toilet all apartment dwellers share, my stomach revolts, spilling the tea I've just drunk.

With a bitter feeling in my mouth, I return to our room.

CHAPTER THIRTY

Thomas appears to be in a slightly better mood this morning, though he is still not smiling when I approach him.

"I've got somebody who is quite sick and wants to leave Berlin," I say.

"Who is it?"

"An acquaintance," I lie. "Is there a way to allow him to fly out?"

Thomas frowns. Behind the smudged glasses, his eyes appear hooded and puffy this morning, as if he's spent all night working. "Is he visiting family?"

"He's sick and wants to leave Berlin permanently."

"Why doesn't he go to the hospital here?"

I open my mouth and close it again. *Why indeed?*

Thomas looks at me intently. "Does he have a permanent address in the West where he will stay? Otherwise, we're just shifting the problems."

"Not that I know of." I thank Thomas and return to my desk. I'm not going to help Fritz. If Thomas had any idea what Fritz was doing, he'd fire me for even asking.

But that's not all. I'm feeling betrayed, worse, I don't trust him. If the Russians have such a reach, they'll find him wherever he goes. Or he's agreed to send them information about the airlift operation.

Mitch said he'd have to report Fritz. Maybe he forgot, maybe he'll wait a while. I peruse my list of assignments and am about to head off when Danny stops by.

"So?"

I look at her, force a grin. "Good morning to you."

"How is your pilot?"

"I told you he isn't my—"

"He was here Christmas Eve, saw him on the airfield. Don't tell me he didn't visit."

Now my smile is real. "Actually, he did."

"And?"

"Oh, Danny, I've got to run. Why don't we meet for lunch? I'll tell you all about it."

Danny grins. "Deal, twelve o'clock, don't be late."

"He says he's got a woman back home," I say after telling Danny about the afternoon with Mitch. The usual buzz of voices, clinking trays and silverware drowns out the planes' engine noises outside.

"Why is he seeing you, then?" Danny scratches her chin. "I mean, it makes no sense. He flies here as a passenger, comes to see you, takes you out, then flies back to Frankfurt."

"Don't know."

Danny's face brightens. "Whoever this woman is, she can't be that important."

"But you know how it is. As soon as this is over, he'll return home and I'll be forgotten."

"Nonsense."

I lower my voice because a group of office colleagues plunks down next to us. "Tell me how this can possibly end well. He has no reason to remain in Berlin."

Danny leans forward. "Except one."

"Which is?"

"Love."

I say nothing as the word bounces around in my head. It is a lofty feeling, love, makes my stomach queasy, blood pressure and pulse rise. I look at the world in a different way, smile all the time and feel happy. My thoughts revolve around the other person as I long for him. Yet it is a feeling only. I doubt Mitch will change his life for me. His parents expect him back, his girlfriend will be, if not loved, convenient.

Danny pats my hand. "Think about it. True love moves mountains, he'll think of a way, you'll see."

I look at her, the blonde girl who started here a few months ago. I'd considered her lighthearted, maybe a bit simple. I was wrong.

She's by my side like nobody else… like Meg used to be. I realize I want to be there for Danny, be her friend. Noticing the puffy skin under her eyes, I say, "How are you doing?"

Danny's smile doesn't reach her eyes. "Fine."

"Why don't I believe you?"

She abruptly rises and grabs her tray. "I'm late. Maybe see you tomorrow?" Without waiting for my answer, she takes off down the crowded aisle.

Something is definitely up and I vow to get to the bottom of it.

Returning to my desk, I find a letter.

Dear Lotte,

I'll ask for time off on New Year's Day.

Meet you at Tempelhof?

Yours,

Mitch

I press the paper against my chest, then grab a pen to answer, hesitate. I'm scheduled to work that day. Damn.

When I discover Thomas at this desk, I knock. "Excuse me, I've got another question."

Thomas looks up from a stack of papers. "Again?"

"I wonder if I could switch my day off to the first of January."

Thomas frowns, scans a board where some of the staff's schedules are listed. "Your free day is on the third." He looks at the lineup of translators, shakes his head. "Sorry, Lotte, we're short as it is. Martina is ill and likely won't be back for a while. General Tunner is still increasing capacity and we can't spare anybody." He looks at me over the rim of his glasses. "Surely you know that."

Of course I do, but my heart sinks anyway. Back at my desk, I write to Mitch that it's not a good day and that I'm off on the third.

And this is how the impossible juggling of schedules begins. During the day, I'm too busy to think about anything but the work in front of me. The airport is buzzing with thousands of people, it is a madhouse. Yet it is tightly organized, dictated by the stringent timetable of thousands of planes starting and landing in cooperation with the other two airports. There is no room for personal lives, for feelings. We all must function to save West Berlin from the Russians.

In the mornings and at night, I hurry home, worrying about Fritz lurking in the shadows or bothering my family again. Sleep is restless, I'm afraid of what Fritz will do next. I sense a dark cloud descending, some kind of threat I can't define. Only at the airport do I feel safe.

Mitch finally appears one morning, when I'm running to an assignment, translating letters from the city's administration.

"Lotte," he calls, as he strides toward me. He looks like he slept in his clothes, his eyelids droopy with lack of sleep. "I don't have much time, just making a bathroom run." He fishes my fingers from the air and squeezes them with both hands. Pulling me into an empty meeting room, we fall into each other's arms. "I missed you so." Our lips meet and time becomes meaningless. All that counts is feeling his body pressed against mine, his skin touching mine. I breathe in his scent, earthy and with a tiny hint of soap remaining.

"When will you visit?" I ask when we come up for air.

"Not sure." He glances at his watch. Sighs. "I've got to run. Unloading is going faster and faster."

"I'm off on the third."

He grins and pecks a kiss on my cheek, then thinks better of it and finds my mouth a second time. We kiss, harder this time, more urgent. My insides are on fire. He pulls away, puts on his cap. "I'll try."

I remain behind, find a wall to lean against. My knees are wobbly as I get my breath under control. In that moment, I know that this is what love feels like. Breathless, intense love.

CHAPTER THIRTY-ONE

On my day off I'm about to leave for a black market run with Mama when there's a knock on the door.

I cringe. Not again, please. One of these days, Fritz is going to do something drastic. I hear voices, then steps approach, the blanket is pulled aside.

And there stands Mitch, in formal uniform, cap under his left arm. "Excuse me, good morning," he says into the round.

Mama, Tilly and Walter greet the visitor as I fly into his arms. "What happened, why are you here?"

After a quick kiss, Mitch draws away and I remember that we're not alone. "This is Lieutenant Mitch Cameron, one of the airlift pilots," I announce way too loudly.

Mama squints. "Don't I know you?"

"You do, Frau Berger, I was stationed in Neukölln in '45." Mitch rushes forward and shakes Mama's hand. "It's good to see you again. You're much better, I see."

Mama seems surprised and pleased. "What brings you here so early?"

"I've got a little time off, hope to see Lotte for a bit." Mitch's eyes find me across the tiny space. "If she's got time."

As I nod enthusiastically, Tilly asks, "Will you have a cup of tea?"

"Sure, that'd be lovely." Mitch throws me another smile while everyone begins to scramble. Walter shakes Mitch's hand, Tilly is fixing a cup of peppermint tea, and Mama and I take off our coats again. Then we all sit down, squeezed together around the table,

Walter on a footstool because we only own four chairs.

As Mitch tells the others about his flying experience, the Russians' disruptive maneuvers, the tight airspace and landing a fully loaded Skymaster, I just sit there, watching him. Despite the dim light he brightens the room, the energy is palpable, springs from him to us, until finally we all chat. At some point, Albert and Karl join us, too.

"Sorry, we overheard," Albert says, shaking Mitch's hand with his left. Even he appears more put together, while Karl is red in the face with excitement.

"Do you drop candy, too?" he asks. "I've been watching the planes, but I'm always too late. The fast kids get most of it."

Mitch eyes the boy and smiles. "You mean you've never had any chocolate from the airlift?"

"Only when Lotte brought the care packet. It was amazing."

With a wink, Mitch pulls a bar of Nestlé milk chocolate from his pocket and hands it to Karl. "Then consider this your personal candy drop."

Karl cries out as he inspects the bar, sniffs it. The joy on his face makes his eyes sparkle, the freckles on his nose dance. "A whole bar just for me?"

"Unless you want to share with your father." Again, the wink.

As I watch this, my heart warms with pride. He just made Karl's day, likely his week or month. Ever since Margo left, he has grown quieter and paler.

I jump up and step next to Mitch. "Maybe we should take a walk."

"And we need to get to the market," Mama says, following my lead. "Tilly, will you join me?"

"I could, too," Walter says with a look at me. His cheeks glow pink, something I've never seen since his return.

Everyone clambers into their coats, while Mitch and I watch. I feel his warmth, his hand next to mine. Our little fingers are touching, enough to send electrical currents through me.

As Albert and Karl return to their side and the other three leave, Mitch slowly but firmly pulls me into his arms. Our lips find each other, our bodies press together. My heart bangs around in my chest, our kiss warm and sweet.

"I missed you," Mitch murmurs.

"Me, too."

Again, silence as we continue. My body is in flames in a way, I tremble. I can't remember that I felt like this three years ago. Maybe I did and I forgot. But all I want to do is remain in Mitch's arms for the rest of my life.

When we draw apart, he's out of breath, too. "Sorry to drop in like that. It was last-minute and there was no way to let you know."

I smile. "You can drop in at three in the morning, I don't care."

Again, we kiss. Behind the curtain, Albert and Karl are rustling around, then the hall door closes. We're alone.

"Maybe we should stay here," I say. "At least it's a bit warmer."

He sinks onto a chair and pulls me on his lap. "In that case, we better get to work."

I don't know how long we sit together, kiss, talk and hug. At some point, Mitch takes off his coat, his hands get busy, mine too.

We meet once more like we had in Mitch's room years ago. I think briefly of the little life I lost, but then I'm swept away in a hurricane. Maybe it is fast, maybe reckless, but I don't care. Life is too short and too busy to waste time.

"We better take a walk now," Mitch whispers into my ear. "Otherwise, they may wonder what we did all this time." He's straightened his uniform, and looks like nothing happened, except that his ears glow pink and there is a shine in his eyes I haven't seen before.

Holding hands, we wander down the street. I don't feel the cold outside. Like in 1945, people are staring at us, except this time, it is not a hateful look, they smile and nod at Mitch. The Americans have gone from villain to hero. Without them, we'd be sliding into a Russian dictatorship.

We find a restaurant where Mitch orders bean soup and bread. I drink real coffee with milk, the aroma of the hot brew filling my nose and making me giddy all over again.

Mitch tells me about his sister, who sends him treats from the States, the horse he used to ride. Only about the other woman does he remain silent. I'm not asking either, too afraid to shatter the happiness I feel. In a way, it feels like wartime when people lived in the moment. Nobody knew what would happen the next day or even the next hour. If there was joy to be had, you took it. The rest of the time, it was a minute-to-minute struggle to survive.

Mitch grabs my hand across the table. "I don't know when I'll have time again. We've got radar now, but the fog is really bothering us. It's frustrating to fly all this way and be forced to return to Frankfurt with a full load."

"Let's write then, even a line or two will do." I know how little time Mitch has. Most nights, he sleeps no more than five or six hours, sometimes he helps collect sweets for Gail's candy drop.

"That chocolate bar was meant for you," Mitch says. "When I saw that boy's face, I couldn't resist."

"Of course you couldn't. That was amazing. You've got no idea how Karl has been suffering. His dad is mostly depressed, and Karl runs around, organizing things when he should be playing or studying."

Glancing at his watch, Mitch calls the waitress to pay. "I've got to go."

"I know." We look at each other, still high on what we did back in the room. "I will miss you terribly."

In front of our apartment building, he pulls me close. "Promise me to be careful." He pauses, then says, "I did inform my command about Fritz. Had to."

I sigh, the worry about Fritz hitting me. I abruptly scan the street in search of a lurking figure. Knowing him, he may be watching right this minute.

Forcing myself to focus on Mitch, I give him a last kiss. "*You* be careful."

He tips his hat and hurries to his jeep, drives off in a flash. Once again, I scan the street where people are running this way and that. Most stare straight ahead or down, heads low against the wind. Fifty yards away, a building is being demolished. Dust rises as dozens of men and women stack bricks along the street. Despite the mess, I feel glad. We're moving forward, even if it is at a snail's pace.

Five days pass before I hear from Mitch. His note says nothing about another meeting, just that he is busy and misses me. Immediately, doubt creeps up inside of me, a bitter feeling in my throat. I was too fast. Let him have me when I should've made him wait. Isn't that what people say? I was so close to telling him, "I love you." If I had, what would he have said? Maybe nothing or I would've scared him off. No, it's better to keep my mouth shut. My heart may be wasted, but it is at least silent to the outside world. Nobody needs to know, though I can't fool Mama and Tilly.

They poked me with questions after they returned from their

outing. How we'd met again, how we got together. What his family is like, his parents, what they do, where they live. At some point, I told them to stop.

"I don't even know when I'll see him again," I said.

But ever since, I catch them smiling at me or nodding to each other as if what I've done is worthy of admiration. I know they mean well, I know they want the best for me. Or maybe this man from America is making them dream themselves… of a lost time, of happiness with their husbands.

I'm not even sure I can call Mitch my boyfriend.

CHAPTER THIRTY-TWO

Snow drizzles hit me as I rush to work. The sky reminds me of pewter, as if it wants to fall from the sky and snuff me out. Despite my fast walk, I'm freezing and sigh with relief when the airport tower comes into view.

"Lotte!" Fritz materializes in front of me. He looks half frozen himself, but the menacing look is back. He pulls me to a stop and guides me to the entrance of a house. "What have you found out?"

I imagine Fritz sending intel about the airport, his flight, making notes on strips of paper. "I can't, Fritz. My boss said that they've got priorities. Please find another way."

Fritz's face grows even redder. He nods, but then he grabs my throat. Cold, bony fingers begin to squeeze. "You didn't try very hard. I heard they're flying lots of people, thousands. Could've asked your boyfriend. I bet he'd do anything to get into your pants."

I can't breathe, try to grip his hand. But my fingers glide away. Trying to push against his chest doesn't work either. There is no air, my throat explodes in pain. So close, I hear the wheezing in his lungs. My nose fills with nicotine. But worse are his eyes, wide open, kind of crazy. *Scream*, my mind comments. But I can't because there is no air. I open my mouth as the pain in my throat grows. My lungs buck as Fritz's face becomes blurry and the edges of my vision go dark. *He may kill you right here in sight of the airport. Woman found strangled near Tempelhof, it'll read in the paper.*

Car doors slam, then steps, muffled. My hearing is playing tricks. "Fritz Mannheim, you're under arrest," a voice says. The fingers slide from my throat as I sink to the ground and am immediately pulled to a stand. The fuzz clears and the face of a man in military police uniform comes into focus.

"Miss, miss, are you all right?" The man looks concerned.

Air forces its way through my windpipe, as I say with a raspy voice, "I'm fine." I massage my throat, blink rapidly to chase away the tears.

A second man appears. "Lotte Berger?"

I nod, suddenly afraid. The man squints at me as if he's having trouble containing his fury, his lips so thin they appear bloodless.

"Please come with me."

As we step from the entrance, the car with Fritz in it speeds off. I follow the man to his jeep, sit next to him in the back seat while an MP drives. Two minutes later, we stop. We're at the airport and my heart sinks. They're going to accuse me of harboring a spy. Why didn't I tell them earlier?

"We have to ask you some questions. Please follow me." The man points toward a room at the far end of the corridor, a section I've never been to. We pass by more MPs, desks with rattling typewriters.

The door closes. This room has no windows, just a desk, a mirror and two chairs—an interrogation room.

"Please sit." The man is all business. "My name is Roger Clark." He clicks on a recorder. "January 12, 1949, eight-fifteen in the morning, interview with Lotte Berger." He turns to me, offers me a cigarette which I decline. "How do you know Fritz Mannheim?"

"We were neighbors, I sometimes saw him on the street. After he was drafted, he returned on leave and asked me out."

"What did he do before the war?"

"He was studying to become an accountant."

"Did you know his family?"

"Not really, I mean, I went there a couple of times for coffee and cake, but we never stayed long."

Clark's questions pelt me like hail. I lose track of time as I tell him about getting engaged to Fritz, Fritz returning from the war while I was seeing Mitch. Our breakup, Fritz smoking Russian cigarettes, his nervousness.

"We broke up because he had changed so much. I didn't love him."

"Did you know what he was doing, why he'd been released from the gulag?"

"No."

Clark leans back, clucks his tongue. "You weren't the least bit suspicious?"

"Not at first. We were so busy, just surviving."

"Right. When *did* you find out?"

"I saw him near the Russian headquarters once, when I was searching for wood, but I didn't think much of it. We were so busy trying to find enough to eat."

"Did you ask him about it?"

"We didn't see each other much."

"So, you didn't wonder at the time? You never wondered where his cigarettes came from, why he didn't work a regular job?"

"I hardly saw him. Many men didn't work regular jobs. There weren't many…"

"When did you learn about his spy activities?"

"When he told me."

"When was that?"

"A couple of years ago. After that I hardly saw him again."

"What did he say?"

"Just that he was being forced to help the Russians."

"When did he contact you again?"

"A few months ago. He wanted to leave Berlin, said the Russians were pressuring him."

"And you did what?"

"I asked my boss, Thomas, if there are flights leaving Berlin."

"You didn't tell him why."

I shake my head.

"You didn't think it important enough to inform us of spy activities in our sector?" Clark appears incredulous.

"I told Fritz to leave me alone, that I wasn't going to help him."

"Why did you ask your boss then?"

I shrug. I don't know why; in my heart, I knew I wouldn't help him. Or maybe, I did in the beginning, when I had felt sorry for him. My head whirls from all the questions, but Clark isn't finished. He just sits there with his cold stare, watching me like a hawk watches a mouse.

"Did he tell you about his work, any details?"

"Nothing, he never said a word."

"And you never asked."

Again, I shrug. "I didn't want to have anything to do with him."

Clark throws shut the folder and rises abruptly. "Wait here."

I don't have the strength to look after him, just stare straight ahead at my reflection. I know it's a two-way mirror. They're likely watching me. Inside I'm cold, icy as a cave in Antarctica. Yet my forehead and cheeks burn hot. I've messed everything up. They'll fire me for sure. I won't have an income anymore. Winter is still in full swing. Mitch will find out what a disgrace I am. He caused it by telling his superior, maybe he didn't think about the consequences, either way, it's too late.

The door swings open. A woman in a tight black dress says, "Please sign this." She places a document on the desk, hands me a pen. "You cannot tell anybody about this meeting or anything else related to this case. Understand?"

I sign, hand the woman the paper.

"You may leave."

Confused, I hurry back through the corridors. It's after ten o'clock, I'm two hours late.

On my desk, assignments pile into a tidy heap. I hang up my coat and purse and begin to read, only to be interrupted by Thomas.

"Something wrong this morning?" He demonstratively glances at the wall clock. "Trouble at home?"

How do I explain my absence? "I wasn't feeling well." It's true, at least that much I can say. "Women's trouble."

A touch of pink creeps into Thomas's cheeks. "All right. I hope you're better now. We've got a shitload of work."

The secretary shouts Thomas's name, then comes running. "There's been an accident, plane crashed in Frankfurt."

"Who?" Thomas barks.

"Don't know yet. They just called, it's a disaster, plane caught on fire, everybody is presumed dead."

Thomas hurries off. All I want is to run after him to find out who it is. My heart beats so fast, I feel as if I've done a sprint. Please, God, don't let it be Mitch. Please let him be safe.

From the other side of the room, Thomas shouts at me. "Lotte, get going, we're running late."

My head in a whirl, I grab my notepad and assignment list and head off. I can't concentrate, even the faces of passersby blur. Clark's angry eyes dance in front of me, replaced by a broken plane in fiery flames.

The next hours pass in slow motion. I perform my work mechanically, help an American write a German letter, assist in disputes, take down notes from various higher-ups to be translated for German politicians. My hands keep shaking and I have trouble reading my own handwriting.

"Ms. Berger, are you unwell?" The man sitting behind his desk is watching me carefully.

Forcing a smile, I check my last sentence, repeat it and we continue.

Lunchtime comes and my stomach feels as if it's filled with a balloon. Just the thought of food is nauseating. I grab a Coke and hasten along the corridors. There is no quiet place in Tempelhof most of the time, which is precisely what I crave.

I need to think, need time to wrap my head around Fritz's arrest and Clark's accusations. He didn't come right out with it, but working here obligated me to tell someone. I know that now. I'm sure Fritz is some kind of low-level spy, not sophisticated at all, sick and, with his long nose and stinky, smoky appearance, too memorable to blend in well.

I'm convinced it's just a matter of time before I'm fired. I lean against a wall and watch the activities on the airfield, my thoughts swiveling back to Mitch. There are more than a thousand pilots flying, so it could be anybody. But what if it's him, what if—

"Lotte, I missed you at lunch." Danny stands in front of me. "Damn, you look chewed up and spat out."

How right she is. I manage a watery grin. "It's been a tough morning. I'm worried about Mitch."

"The crash?" Danny pats my shoulder. "We're all talking about it."

"Surely they must know who it is."

Danny winks. "Why don't you visit Tunner and ask? I bet he has a name."

Bending closer, she clucks. "What happened here? Your throat."

I touch the skin around my neck that is tender and swollen. Everyone I've been around today has surely seen it.

"Somebody choked you." All color has drained from Danny's face. "What happened?"

I shrug. Suddenly, tears press as the scene in the house entry repeats. Fritz's furious expression, the feeling of life leaving my body. I begin to tremble and lean back against the wall.

"Damn, what did they do to you?" Danny embraces me and I begin to sob against her shoulder. "Bastards."

After a while, she holds me at arm's length. "Tell me who it was, and I'll report it."

"No need, he's been arrested. It was Fritz."

"Good. I hope you'll file charges for attempted murder."

Clark's grimace appears in my mind. I don't want to lie, not to Danny, but I can't talk about anything, so I shake my head and wipe my face. "I should return to my desk. Maybe Thomas knows by now."

"Chin up. It isn't Mitch, I know it." Danny takes off down the hall.

I look after her, drain my Coke and head in the opposite direction. Now that I think about it, I realize that Danny looked terrible herself. Beneath that happy façade, she seemed sad, her eyes kind of dim. What kind of friend am I, not even asking her about her own troubles? I will get to the bottom of it as soon as I see her.

Thomas isn't at his desk, the office nearly empty because of the lunch hour. Fighting down trepidation, I sink onto my chair. What an impossible day. Fresh tears press. First Fritz, then Roger Clark and now Mitch. All I want to do is crawl into bed and sleep for a month.

But there is no rest at Tempelhof, not when Berlin needs food and coal. With trembling fingers, I sort my afternoon tasks and head off.

An hour later, when I return from another assignment, a scarf lies on my desk together with a note.

Borrowed this from a girl, you need it more.
Danny

I wrap the gaudy thing around my neck and vow to send Danny some chocolate the moment I get my fingers on any.

Thomas has somebody in his office, so I wait. I must know—now.

"Did you find out whose plane crashed in Frankfurt?" I ask the secretary, who is polishing her nails.

She looks up, eyes me curiously. "One of ours, I'm afraid."

"I know, but I need a name."

"Sorry, dear, don't have that information."

Frustrated, I return to my work.

It is after five before I'm back. This time Thomas is alone in his office. After a quick knock, I burst in. "Who is it?" I cry.

"Who is what?" The document in Thomas's hand sinks to the desk as he eyes me curiously.

"The pilot. Who crashed. I need a name."

Thomas readjusts his glasses and leans back. "Lieutenant Meiers and his crew. Sadly, they all perished."

I nod as relief washes over me. It's the only movement I'm capable of in that moment because my legs are soft as pudding and my mind blank.

"You thought it was Mitch."

Again, I nod.

"Better go back to it then." Thomas glances at the wall clock. "We've got another hour."

By the time I get home, I'm so exhausted I can hardly climb the stairs to our room. I haven't eaten since breakfast and in my head pounds a sledgehammer.

"Do you have a new scarf?" Mama asks when I take off my coat.

I forgot all about it. "Borrowed." I slip behind the little curtain and look in the tiny mirror we recently acquired. At the base of my throat, the skin is bluish black, each of Fritz's fingers like a print.

With a sigh, I wash my hands in the bucket, wipe my face and join my family at the table.

It takes exactly three seconds before Tilly exclaims, "Oh, Lotte, what happened?"

I shrug. "It was Fritz."

"I knew it," Mama says. "That man is no good."

"He got arrested." Fritz's voice echoes in my head … *I'll kill you if I ever get my hands on you again. You did this. You ratted me out.*

"Good." Tilly hands out precisely cut slices of bread to accompany the soup. With a triumphant smile, she picks up a letter next to her plate. "Margo has written. Let me read to you."

Right after dinner, I crawl into bed. Now that Mitch is safe, Roger Clark returns to my thoughts.

Question is, what is he going to do to me?

CHAPTER THIRTY-THREE

February's weather continues with cold temperatures. There's still hardly any coal, which forces Mama and Tilly to search for wood all day. Walter is accompanying them sometimes now, feeling a bit stronger. His cheeks have filled in, his teeth are no longer loose. He writes long letters in tiny handwriting on shreds of paper to Margo and sometimes cooks.

Except for a few brief meetings during Mitch's stopovers in Tempelhof, we haven't had time together. The flying schedule, the weather and the Russians' interference, shooting rockets along the flight corridors, sending planes to distract the Allied pilots, are taking their toll. If I weren't so busy, I'd scream, but there is no time. Never time for anything personal.

We just function. West Berlin continues with gritted and often chattering teeth.

There hasn't been a word from Fritz or Roger Clark. Every day, I expect to be called in and fired. Nothing happens. I do my work, go home and do it again the next day.

Danny and I meet after work for a cup of tea. She seems weary, her skin pale as unbleached flour beneath the blonde hair.

"What's going on with you?" I ask as soon as we step outside. "We always talk about me, but you've not been yourself."

Danny links arms with me. "I've got to tell you something," she says, her voice is grave and a bit shaky.

Alarmed, I stop and face her. "What is it, tell me?"

"I'm pregnant." Red spots have appeared on her cheeks, tears shimmer.

"Greg?"

She nods. "I first thought I had a stomach flu, feeling nauseated all the time." She lets out a sigh. "I went to the doctor last week."

"How far along are you?"

"Three months."

"Damn."

Danny laughs, which sounds close to a sob. "You've got that right. How can I do my job with a baby? My mother will be livid. After Dad fell in the war, she's become super religious, prays all the time." She huffs. "As if that will solve anything."

"Have you told Greg?"

Another huff. "I did. You know what he said? It wasn't his, I was trying to hang the baby on him, so he'd have to pay. That he wasn't born yesterday and all those German Fräuleins like snatching American pilots."

"That sounds like Greg."

"I hate him." Danny begins to cry. "You warned me. I'm so stupid."

"You aren't stupid. Let's have a drink and talk it through.

"I could speak to him," I say as we sip chamomile tea in our favorite café. It's a bakery, shop and café in one, a tiny space carved out between ruined buildings with three tables in the corner.

Danny nods gratefully. "Would you?" She pauses. "How is Mitch?"

"Fine as far as I know." The scare from the crash in Frankfurt still rattles me. "I receive a note every other day, a line or two scribbled in haste. Twice I saw him on a bathroom break." I swallow my disappointment. I don't know what to wish for. If the airlift ever ends, he'll disappear and it'll be over anyway.

Danny's hand lands on mine. "Would you leave with him? Go to America?"

"In a minute. Not that it'd be easy, but I always wanted to do things, go places."

"And your mother?"

"I think she'd continue living with Tilly and Walter. They're practically family. Mama also has a sister near Munich, though she hasn't seen her in years." I drain my tea and place a few coins on the table. "It's just wishful thinking anyway."

"I'll let you know when I see Greg on the airfield," Danny says as we leave.

"Just tell him I need to talk to him."

Danny envelopes me in a hug, gives me a kiss on the cheek. "I feel better now that I told you."

Deep in thought, I walk home. Danny was careless, just like me. Three years ago, I'd gotten pregnant. Now I'd been with Mitch again. What if I carried his child a second time? What would happen to us, my job? I'd be in the same situation as Danny. The men would leave, forcing us to raise our children alone.

Would Mitch act the same as Greg? Hardly. But it is difficult to say what a man would do, if he is pushed into a corner, if what he is presented with doesn't agree with his own plans. Surely that other woman has plans, too. Is likely waiting for Mitch to return to get married. Sure, he transgressed. He is just a man grasping an opportunity when it so easily presented itself. I open the collar of my coat because suddenly I'm sweating. When was my last period? I try to count backwards, can't remember. With things so hectic, I haven't paid attention.

"You're such a goose," I say aloud, making an elderly woman dragging a cart behind her jump.

Greg shows up at my desk two days later. He's out of breath and appears irritated.

"The heartbreaker," he exclaims. "What do *you* want?"

Despite my plan, I'm surprised to see him this fast. "Can we talk?"

"I'm here, am I not?"

"Call me Lotte," I say, guiding him into an adjacent office that is currently empty. "I need to speak with you about Danny."

Greg lets out a theatrical sigh. "Come on. The broad tells stories."

"She's expecting your child."

"Hardly. Look at her. I bet she's got half a dozen pilots she's servicing."

"You're disgusting, Greg. Danny liked you. That's why she agreed to go out. And from what I hear, you were rather forceful, getting what you wanted."

Greg doesn't meet my eyes, which is confirmation enough. "She was asking for it."

"How would you know? You were drunk."

Greg eyes his watch. "Got to go."

"She needs financial support, so think about what you'll do to help her."

Greg turns on his heels and hurries to the door. "Don't ask me here again."

"If you don't help her, we'll file a complaint. Your behavior is unbecoming for an officer."

Greg rushes back and hovers over me, his nose inches from mine. "You wouldn't."

I hold my ground, glare back at him. "I would, actually Danny would, and I'd support her." *I know exactly what kind of man you are*, I want to add. But even I don't want to press my luck. In this moment, Greg reminds me of Fritz right before he choked me.

As we stare at each other, the room sinks into silence. In the background, typewriters clack, voices chat. In here, a war is on. My heart hammers, but I'm determined to hide my anxiety.

"You put her up to this, didn't you?" Greg's voice is low and full of menace. "Better watch your step." Then he turns and is gone.

I link my shaky fingers, take a deep breath.

I have made an enemy today.

CHAPTER THIRTY-FOUR

On my desk lies a letter from Mitch. I rip it open, fly over the lines. This one is longer than the previous ones and I'm immediately alarmed.

Dear Lotte,

I received ten days' leave and am flying back to the States this afternoon. I wish I'd been able to visit again before, but being stationed in Frankfurt makes it rather complicated. I plan on taking it easy at home, sleep, read and help Dad in the workshop. I will write to you as soon as I'm back in Germany. Miss you!

Mitch

I read the lines, reread. He's home… with the other woman. I know it precisely because he didn't mention anything. Except for that one time, he never has—and I haven't asked.

In my mind I see them walking hand in hand, a blonde, curvy bombshell in a tight dress, Mitch in his uniform, tall, handsome and unattainable. At least for me. I'm the fling on the side, the poor German woman who is taking care of her mother.

The lump in my throat swells, so I swallow repeatedly. *Don't cry.* It's silly… stupid. Desperate.

Ten days. Nine to go.

To distract myself, I scan the *Task Force Times*, the daily paper for airlift personnel, detailing loads flown, and updates about various Allied bases. Yesterday, nearly 6,000 tons of supplies were flown into Berlin. And though winter isn't over, and we've received hardly any coal—most of it is delivered to produce electricity—it looks like Berlin has been provided with sufficient supplies to ward off starvation. The airlift is working, thwarting Stalin's efforts to force out the Allies, stopping him from forcing his tyranny on us.

Air Medal Presented to 495 Vittles Men, a headline reads. I peruse the list of recipients in Frankfurt and sure enough, there's Mitch's name. Not only that, he's been promoted to First Lieutenant. When did that happen?

Anger rises and replaces the lump in my throat. I feel left out. Ignored. What do I really know about him? In a huff, I grab a piece of paper, want to write a scathing note. My fingers tremble above, then sink to the desk. What nonsense. He isn't even there and besides, what am I going to say? How dare you have time off, how dare you receive a medal and not tell me. How much more ridiculous can I sound?

I need to face the fact that I hardly know Mitch and that I likely never will. Stuffing the note into my purse, I get busy.

During lunch break, Danny sits at our usual table. Except she looks like she hasn't slept much, her face appears pale, almost gray, and she looks as if she's been crying.

"What happened?" I say, shoving my own thoughts far into the back of my mind.

Danny dabs her eyes with the napkin, tries a smile and fails. "Greg wrote that he has no intention of helping because this isn't his child. He says we never slept together, that I'm lying to blackmail him. If I report him, he'll deny everything. It'll take years and lots of money for lawyers." Danny blows her nose. "It's hopeless."

The old fury is back, intensified by my own anger about Mitch. "That asshole."

"One of the other women drivers told me he is married and has a kid in Florida."

"I'm not surprised." I take a sip of Coke and pick around in my noodles. "I need time to think about it."

"I don't have time."

"Have you told your mother?"

"Not yet."

I sigh and take Danny's hand in mine. "I could come along, be by your side."

A watery smile brightens Danny's face. "You would do that?"

I follow Danny up the stairs of a house whose façade shows the pockmarks of heavy street fighting. World War II may be over, but all of Berlin continues to show the scars. On the top floor, we enter a room that seems to consist of little more than slanted walls with a single two-foot square window. It is about as cold as outside, so I keep my coat and hat on.

"Mother, I brought somebody," Danny cries, way too loud for the tiny space.

"I can see that." Danny's mother, a bony woman with high cheek bones, her gray-streaked hair forced into a tight bun, looks up from the pot she's been stirring.

"This is Lotte, my friend. Lotte, meet my mother."

I hurry forward to extend a hand, but Danny's mother has turned her attention back to the pot. My arm sinks uselessly to my side as Danny gestures for me to sit at the table, set for two beneath the window. There are only two seats and, by the size of the pot, there is hardly enough for two.

"I'm not eating," I say loudly. "I just wanted to see where you live, Danny."

Danny blinks several times as if she has to shoo away tears. She has taken off her coat and for a moment I notice the swell of her belly. It is small and yet telling, especially because Danny is so thin. If her mother were just the slightest bit observant, she'd know.

From my vantage point, I watch her stare at the wall. Something is definitely wrong with her. In a way, she reminds me of Mama after the attack.

"Lotte works as a translator," Danny announces. "She meets lots of interesting people, even interviewed Gail Halvorsen, the Candy Bomber."

Danny's mother seems to snap out of her stupor. "Chocolate and gum," she says. "He is a nice man."

"Will you join us for a bit?" Danny asks with a bright voice.

"The soup is ready, we should eat."

Danny wiggles on her chair, throws me a glance like an apology. "Can't it wait?"

"I'll get my bible, I've got a new prayer." Danny's mother rummages through the mess on the dresser and approaches, turning pages. "Where was it? I thought—"

I jump from my chair and say, "Why don't you sit down?" which makes Danny rise from her seat.

"Please don't leave yet." She is pleading with her eyes, which shimmer once more with unshed tears.

I move next to my friend and put an arm around her shoulder. "Frau Kaiser, we wanted to speak with you."

Maybe it's the severe tone of my voice or the anxiety that is sounding through. Danny's mother pulls her gaze from the bible and looks at me, then Danny, and back. "What is it? We should eat before the soup gets cold."

"It's important, or I wouldn't be here." I feel Danny tremble under my right hand. "Frau Kaiser, something happened, and it is important that you know."

Danny's mother's hands flutter on top of the now closed bible as she stares at us. "You scare me."

"It's nothing scary, it is a reason for great joy." I force my face into a smile. *Now, tell her.* "Danny is expecting."

A "pff" escapes Frau Kaiser's lips like a balloon deflating. I wait for a response, some other reaction, but there is none. She just sits there and looks at us as if I'd spoken Chinese.

"The baby is due in July." Danny sounds out of breath.

"Who's the father?"

"He is not in the picture," I say, matter-of-fact.

"You are not getting married?" Out of Danny's mother's mouth it sounds like an insult.

"No," Danny cries.

Frau Kaiser crosses herself and begins to mumble. She reopens the bible and has seemingly forgotten us.

I pull Danny into my arms and hold her while she sobs—great big sobs of sorrow and despair fill the room, tear at my heart. I'm not even related and feel a terrible sadness for Danny. How can her mother not be affected? How can she sit there and hide in her bible?

"Frau Kaiser?"

No answer. The familiar anger rises at this woman who with all her bible verses is cold as ice.

"Frau Kaiser," I say, enunciating every syllable. "Danny needs your help. She cannot do this alone."

Danny's mother finally looks up again. She looks at Danny with distaste. "You lay with the devil and now you want my help."

"I didn't, I… the man just…"

"Frau Kaiser, a drunken man assaulted your daughter."

With surprising speed, Danny's mother jumps from her chair and pokes a forefinger into Danny's chest. "That's what you get for working with all those foreigners, it's a disgrace." She returns to her pot and gives it a whirl. "Devil's child," she huffs and crosses herself again.

Danny begins to cry anew, and I've seen enough. "Pack your things," I whisper. "You're going to live with us." I've got no idea how we can all fit in the already too tight space, but this is no place for a pregnant girl.

"Mama?" Danny cries one last time, but Frau Kaiser continues stirring her pot. The silence spreads, fills the room from wall to wall, leaving no space for words or feelings. In that moment, I know this is the right decision.

"Come on, I'll help you."

"I brought somebody," I announce as we step through the curtain.

Mama, Tilly and Walter are sitting at the table, all looking up at once. Walter is repairing the wheel of a wooden truck for Karl, Tilly is knitting and Mama is darning a sock.

Both women jump up to shake Danny's hand, Walter takes the bag from her hand and helps her out of her coat. He offers her his chair and grabs a stool to sit on, while Tilly scrapes her pots to fill two plates. It isn't much, but I am about to cry over the love I feel in this tiny space.

"You've come to stay with us," Tilly says. It's not a question, and once again I admire her ability to make people feel at home, to take life as it is, no matter how crappy.

"Danny is expecting," I say into the round.

Mama puts a hand to her mouth, Tilly nods knowingly. "You're nearly four months along, right?"

Danny nods, lowers her head and whispers, "I'm sorry to disturb you."

Mama pats Danny's forearm. "You aren't bothering, we'll make it work."

I look around the table, try to guess what they're thinking. I for one am worried how we can fit and how a baby will complicate matters. But then, I've learned to live each day and take what comes in stride—most of the time.

I just hope the others feel the same.

CHAPTER THIRTY-FIVE

Danny lost a mother, but she gained two new ones. From day one, Tilly and Mama are fussing over her, Tilly sewing diapers from an old bedsheet, Mama knitting up a storm. We can't afford new yarn, but Karl has outgrown a couple of sweaters and Walter has organized two more with moth holes. Mama pulls apart the knitting, dampens and stretches the wool, and forms new yarn balls.

I accompany Danny to the doctor for a checkup and help her trade for shoes on the black market because her swelling feet don't fit in her boots any longer.

And I notice something else: Walter smiles again. Whenever Danny is around, he jumps from his chair, brings tea or a blanket to keep her comfortable. No longer does he sit on his cot and read or brood. A new energy surrounds him. During the day he is out, looking for food or firewood. At night, he watches Danny, talks to her in his quiet way. And she responds, at first shyly, but within weeks, the two of them are so involved in their discussions, the rest of us may as well be invisible.

One Friday afternoon at the end of February, Mitch appears by my desk. He's half soaked because outside the sky has opened up. I blink twice, take in his appearance. He seems thinner, raindrops drip from his chin.

I wordlessly fly out of my chair and into his arms, ignore the soggy uniform. So much for self-control. I wasn't going to do that, I was going to take my time and keep a straight face. He holds me tight as I breathe in his scent. Luckily the office is rather empty, many colleagues are busy elsewhere and Thomas has a meeting with the higher-ups.

"Finally," Mitch whispers into my ear.

I find my voice. "I missed you so." Where is my restraint, my disdain for his absence, his visit home? "You got promoted."

He pulls back, looks at me with raised eyebrows. "I guess I did." He bends close once more. "Any chance you can slip away?"

I check my list, which is short for the moment. "What do you have in mind?"

We find an empty office and fall into each other's arms. After a while, I lean back. "How much time do you have?"

"I'll have to return tomorrow afternoon."

I think about our cramped room, Danny sharing my bed. There's no way we can go there.

As if he's heard my thoughts, Mitch says, "I've got a place in town with a buddy who is stationed in Berlin."

We exchange a glance. Is he asking me to come along? Should I go?

"When will you be done?" he asks, taking my hands in his.

"By five, unless there's an emergency. It's been quiet today, though."

He checks his watch, nods. "I'll pick you up, got a loaner jeep."

Back at my desk, I try to concentrate on my last assignments, translating a couple of letters and a magazine article for Thomas. The clock's hands crawl in slow motion.

I think about the evening, what may happen. I didn't get pregnant last time, but there's always a chance. In a few months, I may sit there like Danny, desperate and without a job. Except I don't feel desperate. I lost his baby and have been heartbroken ever since. With Tilly and Mama, I know I can take care of a child, even work.

At least Fritz is no longer threatening to tell Mitch. I have not heard a word and wonder if he is lying in some prison hospital. There's been no word from Roger Clark or anybody else I met that morning, who likely are secret service.

I think of Mama, what she's been enduring. Losing our home, waiting for my father without knowing if he'll ever return, rape, and living with four adults in a space that is hardly big enough for one person. Not to mention the constant struggle for enough nourishment. When is it going to end? When will we return to a *normal* life, one with decent living conditions and the ability to shop for groceries, when we want?

Right at five o'clock I rush outside. I left a note for Danny, told her to inform the others and not to wait.

A familiar figure jumps from a car, waves. We end up eating at the same café as last time.

"How was your vacation?" I ask.

Mitch has changed into civilian clothes and looks like a different person. He's sipping whiskey and picking through his food while I snarf down mine, already planning on the chocolate cake for dessert.

"Good… relaxing."

"Did you see… your girlfriend?"

Except for that little hesitation in his breath, Mitch keeps his cool. "Helen is an old friend."

"I thought you were *more* than friends."

He shrugs, avoids my eyes. "I suppose that is what she wants."

"And you haven't told her otherwise."

His gaze lands on me. "I'm always gone."

You're always gone from me, too. "What are you playing at?"

Mitch frowns. "What do you mean?"

"Who am I to you?" There it is. The question burning in my heart and keeping me awake at night.

"Lotte, what is this? I thought you'd be happy to see me."

"I *am* happy to see you. I'm just wondering what happens when the airlift ends."

Again, he avoids my gaze. "I haven't thought it through. Who knows when it ends."

I drain my Coke and clank the bottle on the table. "Do you never think ahead? I don't believe that. You seem too organized not to have thoughts about the future."

"Maybe, but then I'm in the armed forces and I do what I'm told."

"Right."

"You're upset." Mitch leans forward and takes my hand which I pull away.

"I feel you're being evasive. You can't even say it… girlfriend. Maybe you're ashamed of dating me, the poor girl and former enemy."

"Nonsense." A vein on Mitch's forehead is pulsing, something I've never seen before. "I just didn't expect to explain my life, which is complicated enough."

"Aren't they all." I can't keep the bitterness from my voice. I lean back, hunger forgotten. "I was simply interested in knowing what you think of me. It seems like I'm no more than a convenient lover without any strings attached."

"Lotte!" Mitch's fist smacks on the table. Glasses, plates and silverware clink, strangers' eyes focus on us. He leans forward, his cheeks glowing. "I'm not prepared to answer. Not here, either." He snaps a finger, and a waitress appears.

In minutes we're on the street. "Come." He leads me to his car, closes the door behind me.

I expect him to take me home, but he heads toward Kreuzberg. I've angered him, but I'm not the young woman he met in 1945. I have seen and done a lot, and I've got to have clarity.

In front of a four-story building, he stops the car, pulls the keys from the ignition. "I suppose I should've asked you if you wanted to go home." He turns toward me, a small smile on his lips. "I just thought we should talk privately."

I meet his eyes, nod. "You broke my heart once before. I can't do it again."

Mitch opens his mouth, closes it. "I thought I'd been the one with the broken heart."

"You are such an idiot. When will you understand that I never loved Fritz, that I loved you, still do?"

"I want—"

"Let me finish. I may never get it out again." I feel like a volcano erupting without control. "You come and go, weeks go by without notes, planes crash, you go on vacation. I feel so close to you when we're together, but then you leave. And my doubts grow until they seem insurmountable. If I'm just a side dish, I'd like to know. You owe me that." I think about the baby I never carried to term. I should tell him—can't.

"You are anything but a side dish." Mitch grabs my left hand, folds his fingers around it. "I've just been through so much turmoil and this flying business makes it tough to think past the next delivery." His fingers squeeze mine. "I don't want to be distracted with you. It messes with my… my mind." His voice sounds no longer sure, in fact there is a slight tremble. "When your fiancé showed up in '45, I cut myself off. It hurt like hell, but I was willing to run as far and as wide as it takes." He snorts. "I suppose I flew full circle, landing right back here."

I say nothing, just watch the man next to me. He reminds me of a little boy, all vulnerable and yet brave in that vulnerability.

"I don't know where this leads," he continues. "I don't need to remind you that you live in Germany, a divided Germany at that and I'm from the US. I don't know what you want… from life… from me."

"I'm not saying it's easy. All I want is to know that you're seeing me in good faith. That you could… maybe envision us as a couple one day… despite the odds."

"God, Lotte, you're like a drug to me." Mitch takes my fingers to his lips, kisses them. "I'm flying hundreds of miles just to see you. Is that not enough because—"

I feel the heat of his breath on my hand and suddenly I throw myself at him, kiss him wildly on the mouth. It has got to be enough. In this crazy moment, in this crazy upside-down world, it has got to be enough.

He responds to my kiss, pulls me so close I can hardly breathe.

"Maybe we should move?" he says after a while. "Neighbors may enjoy the show."

I smile as I wipe away the rest of my lipstick with a handkerchief.

What follows makes anything I previously experienced pale in comparison. Our skin is on fire as we take each other away. There are no thoughts, no guilt or doubt. I drown in his breath, in his movements, at the same time I feel reborn. I have never known such pleasure, such intensity.

When we finally sink next to each other, it is after ten o'clock. With a start, I remember my family, who will no doubt guess what is going on. I snuggle into Mitch's arm and fall asleep.

I awake as the first light falls into our room. Mitch lies on his back, his mouth relaxed in sleep. I lean on one elbow and study the fine lines around his eyes, the shape of his lips. A shadow of beard darkens his jaw, his breath is even and nearly silent. I realize that what I have here is unique and precious—a moment of utter stillness.

A sigh escapes me, another catches in my throat. Why can't I hold on to this moment, why does time pass, no matter how I cling to it?

"Lotte?" Mitch turns toward me, smiles. "Everything okay?"

I nod, swallow away the emotion. He kisses my nose and pulls me into his arms. Warmth engulfs me, utter contentment as we repeat last night.

The morning trickles away, no matter how I try to hold on to it. We eat breakfast in a café and take a drive through the divided city. If Berliners are good at one thing, it is rolling with the punches. Trams are going, people are hustling to take care of business. If you didn't know better, you'd think it to be normal day in Berlin—except that planes cross the sky in all western sectors. I remember the button I carry in my pocket, the way I used to rub it as if I could magically make Mitch appear like a genie.

In a way, it has worked, the airlift has brought Mitch to me. I no longer wish for it to end, because once it does, Mitch will return to his home.

I'm deep in thought as I climb the stairs to the apartment. Neither Mitch nor I said much when we parted. Arranging another meeting in advance is impossible, discussing what happened unnecessary. I have to accept the uncertainty, accept what is given, however much, even if the longing rips me in two as soon as I close the car door and see him speed off.

Our room is strangely silent when I open the door. Albert and Karl are sitting at the table, eating bread with margarine and sugar. Albert nods a greeting while Karl waves. Maybe my family has gone out to visit the black market.

Pulling aside the curtain, I'm about to jump backwards. Danny sits next to Walter, Mama and Tilly are washing dishes. And in the middle of the room, like a caricature of his former self, stands Fritz. He is cleanly dressed, shaven, his hair is cut short. His skin is still pale and wrinkled, though he looks a tiny bit healthier.

"Hello, Lotte."

"What are you doing here?"

Fritz squints at me and I recognize the old anger. "Visiting."

"We told him to leave," Mama says.

I focus on Fritz, think about our last meeting when he nearly choked me to death. "Unless you tell me right now, I'm going to call the police. You've got no right to disturb my family."

Fritz maneuvers around the table and stops in front of me. "I need to talk to you."

"We've got nothing to talk about."

"We do." Fritz takes my arm and pulls me past an open-mouthed Albert toward the door.

"What is it?" I ask as soon as we're on the street, where a watery sun tries to penetrate the afternoon clouds.

Fritz scans the street before he pulls me behind a wall. "You thought I wouldn't find out."

"Find out what?"

"The Americans have been transporting plenty of passengers out of Berlin—thousands."

"I didn't think you'd pass inspection."

"Nonsense, you were afraid I'd do something crazy, when I only wanted to leave. And on top of that you ratted me out."

"You obviously were set free. And yes, I didn't trust you."

He rubs his chest, his fingers still nicotine stained. "I've got advanced lung cancer. Incurable."

"I'm sorry, Fritz."

"Are you? I'm still stuck in Berlin. Now the Americans *and* the Russians are wanting things." Fritz spits, then coughs and wipes his mouth. In the cold midday light, his lips appear blue.

"You almost choked me to death."

"I was angry."

"What do you want from me? I can't help you."

"Nothing anymore. I won't return. Just thought I'd tell you that I know… about your tricks, your lies." He spits again. "And sleeping around."

I say nothing, just look at the man I was once close to. I know in my heart that he won't have long to live. Do I feel sorry for him or is it guilt?

"That's goodbye then?" I ask. We look at each other, two strangers on different paths. When he doesn't reply, I add, "I hope you'll find peace."

He tips his hat and hurries off while I stand there looking after him, a tragic figure and relic of World War II who will be gone soon. In the meantime, he'll be a double agent. Considering his state, I doubt he'll be much good.

CHAPTER THIRTY-SIX

On April 1, Thomas runs around the office, clapping his hands. "Ladies and gents, we've got a new record: 200,000 tons in March."

We holler and cheer, toast with Cokes and coffee. What a difference a few months make. General Tunner has performed a miracle, combining air traffic control at all three airports and optimizing flights and loads. The hope I felt budding last fall, when I saw the efforts put into saving Berlin, has been growing. We are browbeating Stalin into a corner. His plans are failing and together with Allied help, West Berlin continues to survive.

"Isn't it great?" Danny cries as she picks me up after our shift. Her belly is quite noticeable under the new dress Mama has sewn from a flower-printed bedsheet. To the credit of the Americans, nobody has commented about her state except that she has been reassigned to the cafeteria to avoid the strenuous snack runs and fumes of the airfield.

At home, she spends most of her time with Walter. As the weather grows warmer, they walk a lot or sit somewhere outdoors, heads close together, talking quietly. Danny's exuberance has been replaced by quiet contentment, though our crowded home situation requires a great deal of patience from everyone.

I follow Danny out of the office, when I notice a movement near the exit. Several pilots and crew are leaving Tempelhof. But what gets my attention are the chatter and giggles of the women hanging on their arms. And as we move closer, I blink. It cannot be, it mustn't.

But it is.

Mitch, my Mitch, is one of the men, leading a woman with jet-black hair to a small bus used by visiting groups. I want to call after him, except I can't. My throat is parched as if I'd spent the day in the desert.

All I do is lift an arm, then lower it.

Danny, who's been talking about weekend plans with Walter, suddenly cries out, "Mitch, is that you?"

While I stand there, unable to move one step, Danny charges forward, waving. "Wait, guys."

A couple of uniforms and assorted women turn, one of them Mitch. From a distance I see him say something to the woman by his side and then walk with long steps toward Danny. Before he reaches her, his gaze scans the area and finds me. I know he has excellent eyesight, despite the distance of at least seventy yards.

He calls to Danny and continues walking, this time toward me. I'm still unable to move as feelings of anger and disillusionment curse through me.

"Lotte, good to see you." Mitch comes to a stop, his eyes burning into me.

"What are you doing here?" I croak, my voice that of an old woman. I want to add, *with them* and *why didn't you tell me*, but all I can do is stare at the man who occupies my thoughts most of the day.

"Helen wanted to see Berlin, she flew out with a few others to visit."

Helen, I mouth, though I don't know if there is a sound. Not blonde and cute, but tall and severe in a form-fitting tweed suit, she stands waiting in front of the bus. I wish she wouldn't look this way with those dark eyes and that brightly painted mouth. The rage I feel is making me tremble. All those doubts I'd felt are true. Against my will, my eyes blur.

"Why didn't you tell me?" I mumble, though I'm not sure what I'm referring to… the fact that he is spoken for or that he is here in Berlin doing a sightseeing trip for a bunch of bored wives and girlfriends. After the war, many foreigners visited Berlin to see the ruins and walk around Hitler's bunker, where he'd hidden those last weeks while Berlin was being annihilated. We lost the war, caused misery for millions, killed more millions, I have no right to complain. Yet wasn't it gory entertainment to walk through the city of death, isn't it still today?

Mitch touches my arm, a far cry from embracing and kissing me. "I'm sorry I didn't tell you. I was afraid…"

I meet his eyes, finally. "Of what? That I'd make a scene? Learn the truth?"

"I didn't want to make you angry."

"Ha!" I want to say more, but the thoughts in my head scramble as if a tornado is raging in there.

"Mitch, is everything all right?" Helen is waving, the bus horn sounds.

"You'd better go," I say, turning away.

"I'll write," he calls after me. But I don't want to hear it, don't want to hear anything.

Danny, who is by my side again, slings an arm around me. "Damn men," she whispers. But I say nothing, just start walking. Head high, shoulders straight, I walk without seeing. Without Danny's guidance, I would've run into walls and fences, stumbled over rocks and into holes. I'm blind to the world. My hand wanders into my pocket, touches Mitch's button. I squeeze so hard, the metal digs into my skin until it hurts.

We are nothing but a fun place to visit and gawk at. Surely, for women like Helen, this is a fascinating moonscape, a place where people subsist in cellars and half-crumbled buildings. A novelty. I see them driving through the streets, past the pockmarked remnants of the Brandenburg Gate, the sector border signs, garden plots dividing Berliner Strasse, thousands upon thousands of houses without glass windows, holes like eye patches, black markets milling with desperate people looking for supplies, men, women and children eking out a living in this cacophony of opposites—life and destruction existing, maybe not in harmony, but next to each other.

"How is it possible?" they exclaim. "How can these people live in this hellhole?"

Because it is our home. Because we're fighting for the freedom of Berlin and are willing to do what it takes, no matter how long and painful this fight may be.

Without Danny, I would've wandered in circles, gotten lost in some neighborhood. I see nothing, the faces of passersby are blank and gray, as if somebody had eradicated their expressions with a paintbrush. Thankfully, she is holding on to me, infusing my frozen fingers with her warm ones and guiding me gently toward home.

All that passion I've felt, still feel, is whirling through me, unable to escape and refusing to leave me alone. I want to run from it, make it stop, yet I know it will take a long time to get past.

Somehow, in my mind I'd pushed the presence of Mitch's woman away. Somehow, it hadn't mattered. She was far away, no more than a vague figure. Now she is real, she is a beautiful woman with perfect hair and nails who is firmly holding on to Mitch. Who wouldn't?

Danny explains what happened and my family quietly takes care of me. I'm not crying now, I'm just so cold inside. All night, thoughts come and go, and I cannot hold on to them. Only the images remain, sharp and clear, taken with the best camera. The women laughing as they hang on to the arms of their pilots and crew, the lightheartedness that surrounds them. All is good where they come from. Their homes are lit, their stomachs always full. Nobody surrounds them in a vice. They wander toward the bus, chatting about the weather and how exciting all this is. I see it all, am among them, seeing Berlin as they surely see it.

And yet how can I be anything but thankful for the immense support the Allies have given? Without them, we would be living in a hunger camp. Two million Berliners would slowly be boiled until soft to accept their new master, Stalin, a life of deprivation, control and imprisonment.

No, I'm forever grateful for this momentous accomplishment of the men and women spending their living hours to save us, connecting us to the west.

I doze off in the early hours, only to be awakened by Danny. Work is waiting. I just hope I won't run into Mitch and the group of visitors.

I couldn't bear it.

CHAPTER THIRTY-SEVEN

On April 16, General Tunner announces that we have reached the high point of the airlift. Every thirty-one seconds, a plane lands or starts at one of the three airports for a total of nearly 1,400 flights per day. In the office we celebrate with sparkling wine and Budweiser beer. Happy faces and cheers surround me. Forcing smiles, I toast with Thomas and my coworkers. Danny stops by with a glass of lemonade.

I wonder what Stalin thinks right now. He must be furious that his ruse isn't working, the thumbscrews he applied never fit. What will he dream up next?

At my desk, I sort my last assignments: a couple of articles for a German paper, a thank you letter to an American family, a meeting between a German politician and two Americans. The side of my hand touches a small pile of letters, written in Mitch's handwriting.

Lotte Berger, translator, Tempelhof Airport, they say on the front. I haven't opened them, can't… won't. They seem to call to me, whisper even when I'm far from them. I should throw them away, but every time I look at them, my hand begins to tremble. So, they stay, a new one joining every few days.

Danny has offered to read them, but I refused. I'm unable to engage in normal conversation, function without thoughts, get up mechanically, walk to work with Danny by my side, perform my duties. Until my mind clears, and I can lift my chest enough to breathe normally, I will only concentrate on my job and enjoy the small comforts of the ever-increasing success of the airlift: a bottle of milk for breakfast, a pound of sugar, even half a dozen eggs. Mama and Tilly are outperforming each other with new recipes… a raisin cake, oatmeal cookies… bread.

Margo's letters are full of stories of farm life, newborn twin lambs, tending chickens and ducks, and weeding the garden. Most of all, she is asking to return, but Tilly and Walter remain cautious and ask her to wait.

I pull out Papa's handkerchief with Mitch's button, run a forefinger across the engraving. For three years, that button has carried my hope. Now it is empty, the shiny object of faded love. In a sudden move, I toss it against the wall, then hurl it into the waste basket, only to pick it out five minutes later.

The western Allies are saving Berlin, that has got to be enough.

Deep in thought, I wander toward the bathroom, when someone pulls my sleeve.

When I swivel around, I'm face to face with Mitch. "Lotte, finally." Tension deepens the lines around his eyes and mouth, the mouth I know so well. Now all I want to do is run.

"I'm late for my assignment."

He lets go of my sleeve, doesn't seem to know what to do with his hands. "Did you not get my letters?" Since I don't answer, he pulls a rumpled envelope from inside his jacket. "I received this note from… Fritz."

In an instant a lump appears in my throat. I swallow to clear it, no such luck. Still, I don't say anything. Mitch unfolds the paper. "I don't understand. He writes about a child… you lost a child?"

My head grows too heavy to hold and keep eye contact. So, Fritz made good on his word. He is sick and jealous, is getting even for my deception. What does it matter? Forcing out the words, I say, "I can't…" Mechanically, my feet begin to move faster and faster. *Concentrate on your work*, my mind urges, *not the man who is standing behind you.*

"Lotte?" is the last thing I hear before turning the corner.

I'm doing a lousy job at the meeting, where I'm supposed to translate for a German official who is discussing deliveries of coal to the electricity plant. Several times, I have to ask them to repeat because my focus is on Mitch's confused expression, his shaking fingers. He looked so pale and exhausted.

When I return to my desk, I find a note.

Meet me tomorrow after work! I'm switching shifts. Please. Mitch.

No *dear* and no *love* in sight.

Maybe I'll be sick tomorrow. But I already know that I won't be, that I'll have to face what's coming.

Once and for all.

Mitch appears right when Danny is picking me up. I haven't told her anything, not while she is pregnant, but really, who am I kidding? My secret is too heavy and painful to let it out. Now Mitch wants to force me to talk about it.

"What are you doing here?" Danny says, obviously feeling protective.

Mitch, ever so polite, tips his hat. "Meeting Lotte."

"Lotte is going home with me." Danny grabs my hand. "Let's go."

I find her eyes. "It's all right. You go… I'm fine."

"You sure? I could wait."

How I wish. "I'm fine."

Danny walks away, but not without turning around several times, watching us. Mitch offers me his arm, which I ignore. I grab my purse and follow him to the exit.

As before, he is leading me to one of the jeeps waiting nearby. Again, he offers me a hand to climb in. I shake my head and slide onto the seat. The lump is back, threatening to leak into my eyes before we even drive off.

I keep my focus on the road as Mitch maneuvers the car through the ever-increasing Berlin traffic. Trams rattle and clink, cars, trucks and buses slide past. People are walking, crisscrossing the streets in a wild jangle. I see them, yet my ears are on high alert for any sound coming from the driver. But he doesn't speak. Not a word, in fact, he makes no sound at all. With the car noise, I can't even hear his breathing, which I've so loved to listen to. Laying my head on his naked chest, I'd feel his ribs rise and fall, feel his warmth against my cheek.

Stop it. How long ago it seems, like in another lifetime.

The car halts surprisingly fast. I recognize the public park in Mariendorf. Not much is left of the pastoral landscape with the willows and ponds. Hacked-off tree stumps bear silent witness, like war veterans. People are camping, guarding vegetable gardens.

My door opens. I didn't even notice Mitch getting out.

"Let's walk," he says.

So, we wander next to each other, two people who may as well be on different planets. I'm waiting for him to speak, but like before, he remains silent. Our footsteps crunch, somewhere a man coughs, children scream.

I don't know how long we walk. Words form in my mind… refuse to combine themselves into sentences, refuse to pass my lips. The lump in my throat is so large now that I've got trouble breathing.

"Maybe this isn't working." Frustration swings in Mitch's voice. "I'll take you home." He turns around, hurries the other way.

Seeing his back to me, something inside snaps. "Wait."

As he turns around, I point at a couple of stumps. "Let's sit over there."

He follows me to the pond's edge that is overgrown and muddy.

Taking a deep breath, I say, "Fritz wrote to you."

Again, Mitch pulls the rumpled envelope from his breast pocket. By the looks of it, he must've done so a hundred times. "He writes that you were pregnant with our child and lost it."

"I found out after we broke up."

"Why didn't you tell me?"

I feel Mitch's gaze on me. "I walked past Meg's house many times. Never had the nerve. You'd been so angry, I…"

"I was angry, but don't you think I deserved to know?"

The old anger is back. "What would you have done? Acted like Greg?"

"Greg Taylor? What does he have to do with anything?"

"He left Danny high and dry. She's carrying his child."

Mitch squints, then huffs. "Greg has left the service. I heard he was let go, got caught with alcohol on his breath. But I'm not him!"

I know, I want to say. "Either way, I didn't want to be rejected. It was enough to have your baby."

"How did you lose it?"

The lump in my throat expands. "An accident… I slipped and fell," I sob. "It was still early, so I didn't tell anyone. I couldn't." The old pain I've hidden so long is breaking free. I cry like I've never cried before. Great big heaves run through me in waves.

A finely pressed handkerchief appears in my vision, which I take to wipe my face and blow my nose.

"I'm so sorry." Mitch's voice is soft… forlorn. "I shouldn't have left like that. I know now that it was a mistake." I blink to clear my vision. He is leaning forward on his seat, kneading his hands. "I was angry at the time, hurt. Never thought to see how you fared, never expected you'd separate from Fritz. I envisioned you happily married. Since I couldn't bear that thought, I kept pushing your memory away. Until we met at Tempelhof." A smile brightens Mitch's features, disappears instantly. "I was shocked to see you again because it brought the old pain to the surface I'd thought I'd left behind."

"But things were more complicated," I add. "You were in a relationship."

He nods. "After I returned in '45, Helen began to visit on her own. We didn't see each other that often, but our fathers have known each other for decades. It seemed like an easy choice... comfortable."

"Painless."

He nods again. "Except when I saw you that day at the airport, it all didn't matter. I was hooked like an addict, living for each moment I could spend with you." He looks across the mutilated trees, the neglected pond. "After Helen visited here, I was ready to break it off." His gaze returns to me. "I saw your face, could imagine what you thought: rich American women sightseeing destroyed Berlin. It felt wrong... all of it."

"That's what you wrote to me about, that's what's in the letters?" I stare at Mitch.

"You didn't read them?"

I bite my lower lip, taste blood. "I'm an idiot. I thought you two were all settled in. It sure looked cozy."

"Why didn't you tell me about the baby? You could've written... anything."

"You left and I—"

"But we hooked up again." Mitch sounds exasperated. "Don't you think I deserved to know?"

I swallow. "I wanted to... couldn't. I was devastated, didn't get out of bed for days. I never told anybody."

"Not even your family?"

I shake my head. The lump spills over once more. I'm tired of crying and yet feel powerless to stop. I furiously wipe my eyes, try a smile, fail.

He sighs, his gaze wanders off again, across the pond, then back to me. "I feel betrayed, do you understand that? I don't think I can trust you." His eyes shimmer with unshed tears. "It seems that you keep things from me, the important things. First Fritz, then the baby."

I jump up, whirl around to face Mitch. "Don't you see? I was afraid to lose you… and talking about the baby… the pain of that tears me apart even now. I failed to protect her. It was my fault."

Mitch sits there, watches me silently, his eyes dark as the clouds above.

"You'll return to your old friend." My eyes are dry now as I watch the man I've loved for nearly four years and who is still a mystery to me. My mouth is bitter. Fritz had chosen a terrible path and destroyed my happiness. Except he didn't. I did that all by myself. I'd failed to trust Mitch enough to tell him.

Why do we go to such lengths to keep secrets when it would lift burdens if we told them? I know my family would've helped me in an instant. And yet I couldn't say anything. Like Mama, who never speaks about her assault, who hardly ever mentions my father, even when she reads the stack of Red Cross cards every day. We carry these loads until they destroy us.

I realize that this is the moment I was afraid of, the moment I dreaded the most. It is in some ways worse than losing my daughter, because I could've avoided it. It was in my power to share my loss with Mitch, my baby's father. My failure to tell him is what breaks us up, not Fritz, not Mitch's job or the airlift's demands, not even his girlfriend.

Mitch rubs a forearm across his face, rises from the shredded stump. "I'd rather not talk about it." He holds out a hand. "I'll take you home now."

It sounds so final, a dismissal of sorts. I try a smile, am proud that it holds. "It's all right, I'll walk."

He nods. "Goodbye then. Take care of yourself."

Again, I smile. "And you."

I watch Mitch walk off through the old park, shoulders squared, a proud American pilot who is helping save us from Stalin, the father of my lost baby, the man who helped me find myself.

Except that I feel more lost than I ever have.

CHAPTER THIRTY-EIGHT

When I lie awake at night, I envision Mitch and me walking hand in hand along some American river, our two kids running circles around us. They scream and try to get our attention, which we give them indulgently, happily. In those moments, I feel utterly content, my mind offering a perfect escape from reality.

At the office I have gone from being serious and businesslike to laughing at the slightest joke. I smile at people as if the mask I hide behind can shield me from my heart. I feel Danny's gaze on me as we walk to and from work, but she is not prying. Not this time. This is a new Danny who quietly waits her turn, who leads deep discussions with Walter. It does my heart good to see them together, even if it reminds me of my own pain.

The morning of May 6, the office is filled with chattering, laughing people. Thomas runs my way, waving the newest edition of the *Task Force Times* and on the front, it reads in block letters:

FOUR POWERS AGREE TO LIFT BLOCKADE MAY 12.

As I read, people around us cry, "At last," and "It's about time." The paper quotes several pilots' sentiments. One is worried about keeping his job, others wonder what the Soviets will dream up next.

"Let's hope that it'll really happen," I say to Thomas. "Wouldn't be the first time Stalin lies."

"Everything continues as before." Thomas looks around the office. "At least for a while."

What about my job, I want to ask. *What will happen if the airlift closes indefinitely?* How can I wish for the end if it means the end of my employment, too?

The streets are filled with excited people. Anywhere crowds congregate, there is chatter and laughter in the air. Everybody is waiting for May 12.

After dinner—I returned home late, accepting any additional work I could get—Albert and Karl are hanging by the radio, an old piece they traded last week, which is loud enough to penetrate several walls, certainly a flimsy blanket.

"There are lights shining in all the windows, lanterns illuminate streets, shop windows blaze," the reporter's voice proclaims excitedly. "Trams and metros are lit, adorned with white and red garlands, the colors of Berlin and black, red and gold, Germany's flag." Another reporter calls in, talks about dropping the chains Russia has tried to put on us, the zoo's dead lion cub, starved to death in occupied Berlin. A third reporter at the sector border to Russian-occupied East Germany confirms that the turnpikes have opened and trucks from the west are passing through.

Our little space also shines brightly under the ceiling light. Stalin has turned on West Berlin's electricity. Our worst fears of falling into Stalin's greedy hands have been averted.

"It's happening," Mama cries, her eyes sparkle.

That is nothing compared to Tilly, who is downright shouting. "Margo can come home."

"Margo," Walter exclaims, a man who hasn't seen his daughter in five years. Danny jumps up and doles out whiskey we've been safeguarding for special occasions.

"Let's go outside," I say after we toast to a free Berlin.

We aren't the only ones, everywhere people are congregating, chattering, pointing at the sight of hundreds of lit windows in half-broken houses. Berlin's lights have returned, even if it is dim inside me.

Signs hang on cars and walls: *Hurray, we're still alive.*

The next morning, on the airfield, a banner reads, *Blockade ends, airlift wins.* Maybe Stalin is giving up at last. Maybe this is just a test.

At Tempelhof, work continues unabated. To distract me, Danny invites me to one of the cafés on Ku'damm. As we sit, sipping tea, sharing a piece of chocolate cream cake, several American soldiers enter to loud cheers from the crowd. I think of the hateful comments I heard when Mitch accompanied me in public nearly four years ago. Western Allies have gone from enemy occupiers to liberators. They are our friends now.

Not two weeks later, Danny and I are standing squeezed in a crowd of hundreds of thousands in front of Schöneberg's city hall. Today, Chancellor Adenauer signed the Basic Law, our new constitution, that transforms Germany into a democracy and gives Germans sacrosanct rights. After the horror years of Hitler's reign, we are a country again, one where each citizen can voice his opinion without fear of reprisal, where men, women and children can live in harmony—free.

I don't know what it really means, not yet, but I know in my gut that this is the way forward, this is the right way.

I squeeze Danny's hand as we holler when Fritz Reuter, our mayor, appears. Just nine months ago, he'd called upon the world to help us. Maybe nobody would've come, if Reuter hadn't said those fateful words… "People of the world, look upon this city!"

They heard him and came to our rescue, and now we are becoming a new country. I smile, even if a certain sadness will never leave me. Margo can return home, Mama and Tilly, all of us, can walk the streets without fear of attack, we can feel safe and supported, even if it'll take many more years to dig ourselves out of the rubble of what once was a vibrant Berlin.

The first pilots who've spent thirty-six months away from the States are leaving. Nonetheless, Thomas assures me that we'll continue with the airlift, until it is clear that Stalin keeps his word. How would he know?

On June 1, Governor Dewey from New York visits and I'm assigned to help translate during his meetings with German city officials. He calls the Berliners brave and hopes for a united Germany. In the *Task Force Times*, I discover Mitch's name and a number of airmen being welcomed as veteran airlift pilots in Chicago. I have not heard from him since that afternoon in the park. Now he is done with Germany. He rescued a girl from a hole, fell in love, only to be lied to—twice.

I swallow my sadness and continue my rounds. Everything is going just fine, even when the staff is beginning to thin out. A few desks are empty now, the British are discontinuing the delivery of liquid fuel. Gail Halvorsen, the Candy Bomber, already left in January.

The borders to Berlin have remained open and stores are filling again with items we haven't seen in a year.

I'm utterly exhausted when I return home. Not because the day was so hard, but I feel as if I'm carrying a permanent sack of coal on my shoulders. Danny helps me get out of my jacket, though I should be the one who helps her. She's nearly eight months pregnant and will soon stop working. Already, people are asking what she is still doing at Tempelhof.

Our home situation is dire. Margo is supposed to join us soon and Danny is expecting a baby next month. How can we possibly fit with five adults and two children? Berlin's living situation remains incredibly difficult. Even if some people are now leaving, too many of us need decent apartments and building new homes is taking a long time.

"You've got mail." Mama waves a letter with an official-looking address. "It's a notary here in Berlin."

I frown, instantly worried about some unforeseen disaster. While Tilly serves us chamomile tea, I open the envelope.

Dear Ms. Berger,

I'm writing to you on behalf of Fritz Mannheim, whose testament I'm administering. Let me express my deepest condolences on his untimely passing. I would like to invite you to a meeting at my office on June 10 at nine o'clock to discuss Mr. Mannheim's estate.

Sincerely,

Dr. Daniel Peters, Notary

The paper in my hand sinks. Fritz is dead.

"What is it?" Tilly is watching me intently. She never misses a thing.

"Fritz has died, and I'm mentioned in his will."

I hand Mama the letter. "I didn't think he had anything to bequeath. The way he looked, so haggard and disheveled."

"Why did he leave anything to you when you two always fought?" she says.

I look into the circle of questioning faces. "Only one way to find out."

While I'm curious about Fritz's information, I'm dreading the meeting. Who knows what he left me… some old wardrobe or a piano? Things I can't use.

Now that he is gone, I realize how often I've left the house, expecting him to lurk around the corner, jumping at me from the shadows, or worse, spying on me. What a terrible life he led. Always on the jump, always expecting the Russians to pressure him for useful information. I'm surprised how sad I feel. He used to be a good man, twisted and destroyed by Hitler's Reich and his own weakness.

Notary Peters's office is near downtown in a newly remodeled building. Everything is colored white and gray, the smell of paint still sharp in my nose. To me it speaks of renewal, a fresh beginning. What did Fritz think when he came here? He must've known that he didn't have long.

I'm asked into a meeting room with a desk and several chairs. The secretary carefully checks my ID card and records it in a book.

"*Frau* Berger, I presume?" Peters, dressed in a newish suit, a brown file under his left arm, extends an immaculate hand before he points to one of the chairs. "Please make yourself comfortable." He pulls out several documents and hands me one. "Maybe we should start with this letter."

I stare at the envelope, addressed to me in Fritz's surprisingly neat hand.

"Should I read it now?"

Peters studies me over the rim of his glasses. "That is entirely up to you, though it may shed some light on his final wishes… I'll wait."

I tear open the paper, which emits a faint nicotine smell.

Dear Lotte,

I will be gone when you receive this. I realize I've been a difficult person to endure, but hope that what I tell you will make up for it to some degree. Please know I don't blame you for anything, no matter what I said. I'm sorry for not being the man you wished for, nothing would've given me more pleasure. But my fate led me astray, not least because of the choices I made.

As you know I had no place to call home, just a few holes I'd hide in. As such my expenses were low, and being the accountant I was, I put away a sizable amount. I'm leaving it to you, my parents dead, my brother, too. Maybe it'll make up for some of the heartache I've caused you. I'm not proud of many of the things I did. But it is done now and I'm no longer afraid to leave this world.

Take care of yourself, Lotte, know I always loved you,

Fritz

Fritz's lines wiggle as I dig for a handkerchief. I'm not getting a wardrobe, Fritz left me money.

As I wipe my face, the notary shuffles more papers. I'm sure he is wanting to get on with it. "I'm ready now."

Peters reads something, then says, "I'm officially opening Herr Fritz Mannheim's testament," and hands me a document. "This is a list of Herr Mannheim's legacy. As you can see, he has several accounts as well as a safe deposit box at the Berlin Bank for Trade and Industry, formerly the Dresdner Bank." He hands me two keys. "I've prepared a copy you can take to the bank for identification. You should be able to withdraw funds as you please."

I sign my name a few times and leave the office in a daze, a thick envelope under my arm.

Before I lose my nerve, I head to the bank, a stocky brick building with hundreds of windows. After showing my papers, a man in a gray suit and a permanent frown edged between his brows shows me into a private office.

When I hurry to Tempelhof an hour later, my head is spinning. Fritz left me nearly 11,000 Deutsche Marks, twenty-one gold and eleven silver coins from Russia, the US and Prussia, and a gold brooch with diamonds from his mother. I'm rich.

"Can I talk to you?" Thomas asks as soon as I stow away my purse.

"I told your secretary that I had an important appointment this morning, I'm sorry, it took longer than expected."

"There's something else I need to discuss."

I follow Thomas into his office and, rather untypically, he closes the door behind us. My heart pounds, I'm going to get fired. Clark from the secret service has turned me in.

"You've done really good work, Lotte," Thomas begins. Behind his desk he seems small, almost child-like.

But? My thoughts race ahead to the inevitable.

"We're being careful… though you realize that now that the blockade has been lifted, we're preparing to wind down. While we carefully watch Stalin's moves, we assume, it is a matter of time, but—"

My tongue sticks to the roof of my mouth, so I clear my throat. "You've got to let me go."

Thomas fidgets, leans forward. "Not exactly, well, I thought… maybe you could work at our airbase at Frankfurt-Main." A bit of red has crept into his cheeks. "We always look for good translators."

"Frankfurt?"

"It's just an idea, I could make a recommendation."

I look at my boss as the reality of the successful airlift sinks in. "I… my mother, I need to think about it." How could I leave Mama? She's all I've got left. Danny and Walter will marry, I'm sure of it. "What will *you* do?"

A small smile plays on Thomas's lips. "Likely go home. Haven't seen my family in a while."

I rise. "I appreciate all you've done for me."

The color in Thomas's cheeks deepens. "Don't think too long."

Right. How could I move away when all I know is here? Especially after the oppression seems to have ended. *Chicken! Not so long ago, you were ready to get out into the world.*

July is baking the streets and it is stifling in our room, even if Albert keeps the window open most of the time. We've removed the blankets between our partitions, just to get a bit of air. I tell them about Fritz's legacy, our good fortune.

"We should be able to afford a larger place," I say after the cheers die down.

"It's not necessarily a matter of money," Walter comments. "I've been asking around, you know." He takes Danny's hand in his. "With Margo returning and our new baby, I've got to find a place soon. There's just so little available, actually pretty much nothing at all."

"Any half-way decent place changes hands privately," Danny adds. "By the time you get there, the landlord has already rented it out, even rooms with a shared bath and no heat."

"Margo is arriving tomorrow," Tilly says. "She'll have to share Karl's bed. We just couldn't make her wait any longer."

But when we pick up Margo from Bahnhof Zoo the next morning, we hardly recognize her. She's grown several inches and her hair is long and shiny. She throws herself into Tilly's arms, then faces her father. She's studying him, her expression furtive, before she extends a hand. Walter is visibly trembling as he ignores Margo's hand and wraps his daughter into his arms. "Finally," he utters, "finally."

We stand around the two, tears streaming. Margo's pack is filled with delicacies from the farm. Canned meat, sauerkraut, a five-kilo bag of wheat flour, potatoes and homemade blackberry jam.

On the return walk, Tilly takes me aside. "Margo can't sleep next to Karl," she says. "Look at her, she's a young woman and Karl is a teen boy." She wrings her hands. "What are we going to do?"

My thoughts wander to Thomas's offer. If I left, they'd have one extra spot. But leaving Mama is no option. To distract myself, I take Tilly's arm. "Let's celebrate Margo's return and speak to Albert when we get home."

After dinner, Mama edges up to me. "What's going on?"

"Nothing," I lie.

"Trouble at work?" Mama is no longer so easily misled. Her gaze rests on me, kind, and also anxious.

"It's… my boss suggested I work in Frankfurt. Provided the airlift ends."

Mama claps together her hands. "But that's fabulous."

I look at her, surprised. "I don't think I should leave."

Mama sighs. "Why not?" Then she nods, her expression pensive, as she pulls me into her arms. "You are still feeling guilty about that day," she whispers.

The knot in my chest opens and I burst into tears. "It was my fault. We never should've gone over there. I left you by yourself, looking for stupid briquettes."

Mama holds me to her, rubs my back, until I calm down. Then she leans back and studies me. "You're a smart woman, Lotte, really smart. How come you think such nonsense? It was bad luck. Like that of a hundred thousand women who were in the wrong place at the wrong time."

I stare at her, realize how I've blamed myself ever since Mama got attacked.

"I can take care of myself. You need to do what's right for you. If it means you work in a different town, so be it. I'll be only a train ride away. Besides, I know that your father will return one day, just like Walter did." Her gaze slides to the stack of postcards on the shelf, the only lifeline that connects her to Papa. I don't have the heart to tell her that a lot of men are dying over there, especially the older ones. It takes a seemingly minor illness, a small accident to further weaken their emaciated bodies. Fritz had told me about it, Walter had also mentioned it under his breath, after meeting with other returning prisoners of war.

The weekend has been excruciating. The warm temperatures continue turning our room into a furnace. As cold as it was in winter, now we sweat. On the bright side, our landlord has completed a bathroom with running water and a water closet we share with several neighbors. Of course, it's nearly always occupied, and the wait times and constant knocking are getting on my nerves. Danny and Walter are taking walks, Mama has found a job in a launderette.

But nights are impossible as we lie there like sardines in a can, toss and turn and sigh. I'm up at five on Monday morning, ready to escape.

As soon as Thomas shows up, I knock on his office door.

"Did you decide?" he asks.

"Not yet, but I've got a question." I hurry toward his desk. "I thought with all the men leaving, you may know about empty rooms or apartments."

"Eh, yes. Maybe." Thomas scratches his nose. "Where's my list?" He rummages through a stack of papers. "Some of these men and women indeed live in apartments." He peruses the names, then eyes me curiously. "I'm not sure about the rent, though. May be too high?"

This time I smile. *Thank you, Fritz.* "I've got funds… inherited."

If Thomas is surprised, he doesn't let on. "I'll be in touch."

Three days later, I'm standing in the half-empty apartment of a US administrator who is moving back home. Cartons and boxes are everywhere, but all I'm doing is stare at the kitchen cabinets, the tiled bathroom.

"The place has two separate bedrooms, though no central heating." The man points at the coal stove in the kitchen corner. "Should be a lot quieter, once the airlift traffic subsides." In the distance, a Skymaster takes off, another is lining up to land. I don't care, it's perfect. "I could leave you a bed and my living-room furniture. Isn't worth moving anyway."

"I'd love it," I say. "What's the rent?"

"Three-seventy-five, plus power and water."

"What about your landlord… is he nice?"

"No worries, he's easy going. As long as you've got the deposit. Do you want me to ask him?"

I'm ready to kiss the man. "Please. We can move in as soon as you want."

But the American's landlord is frowning when I meet him in the evening. "I've already promised the place to somebody else. Had I known—"

"Please. Will you reconsider?"

He bites his lip, doesn't meet my eyes. "Sorry, it's a done deal."

I want to yell insults, slap the man, but all I do is turn on my heels and leave. I'm exhausted, wasted the entire evening. I'd already envisioned telling everyone about our new place. Would it have been different if Mitch had been there? Likely, he'd have spoken to the man in measured tones, explained the situation. Mitch. My heart cramps as if somebody is squeezing it with sharp fingernails. He is likely sitting on the porch of his family's farm, black-haired Helen on his lap.

I realize how alone I feel. Lost. Mama and Tilly have each other, Margo has her father, Danny is with Walter and will soon give birth. Only I struggle by myself, a rowboat without oars lost in a storm. I expected that Fritz's money would solve things. It doesn't. I'm just as rudderless as before.

And Thomas's question keeps repeating itself in my head. Should I go to the airbase in Frankfurt? Where is my sense of adventure? I could rent a room all to myself, away from the rubble that is Berlin. Away from all the reminders of my pain. Maybe it would be a good idea after all—a fresh start. I'd work a lot, go home and sleep. Repeat. No distractions, no bad memories, just work.

"Will you look for another name?" I ask Thomas the next morning. "It didn't work out."

"Goodness, Lotte, you look terrible."

"I didn't sleep well."

"I did put out feelers, you know." Thomas studies the list of staff who are moving. "You could easily continue at the base in Frankfurt." When I don't answer, he points at another name on the list. "I know his place. We've got the same landlord." Picking up the phone, he says, "I'll call and find out."

"I'll do it," I say when Thomas puts down the phone. "If the airlift ends, I'll move."

A smile scurries across Thomas's face. "Good girl, I think you'll be glad for a change." I wonder how much Thomas knows, certainly he is aware of Mitch's and my breakup. "What about the apartment? My landlord says he'll meet you at six o'clock tonight."

"Oh, that's for my family. We've got five people, six with Danny's baby, living in half a room."

"No wonder you're losing your mind." Thomas picks up the

phone again. "I'll call human resources about Frankfurt."

I'm moving away. A fresh start, a new life. As if it were so easy. Like the skin on our bodies, our memories accompany us through life. We don't cast them off, no matter how far we run.

Everyone breaks out in cheers when I tell them about the new place I rented for them. The landlord was glad to avoid a crowd of desperate Berliners searching for a place and when I told him about my inheritance, he offered me the apartment outright. It's also in Neukölln and in good shape, considering the destruction around us. Again, we've got coal stoves, but this place is remodeled, has a private bath with a tub and two and a half bedrooms. The half reminds me of an oversized closet, perfect to give Margo some privacy.

"How did you find it?" Tilly cries, hugging me to her chest.

Mama joins in. "You're a miracle worker."

"I've got something else to tell you," I say when the noise dies down. Five pairs of eyes are zooming in on me. "I'll be moving to Frankfurt… provided the airlift comes to an end."

There may be lots of people in the room, but it is so quiet I hear Karl's pencil scraping the paper behind the blanket.

Tilly sinks to a chair. "Why wouldn't you stay? We'll have a lot more room."

I hurry to her side, take her hands. "I've got to start over, in a new place. I'll be working at the American base."

"Won't you miss us?" Margo cries.

Tears press, but I push them away. "Of course I will. You're only a train ride away and I can always return."

Everyone except for Mama starts talking. Danny and Walter discuss moving logistics, Tilly and Margo are talking about the dinner menu.

I remain next to Mama, who's sighing loudly. "If only your father…"

How often have I heard these words? Papa has been gone for four years and six months. As far as we know, he is still waiting for his release. I capture Mama's fluttering hands and press them to my heart. "It'll all work out. You've got Tilly and Margo."

Mama smiles. "I'm proud of you."

Tilly steps next to us. "You're like a daughter to me, Leni. We'll stick together."

A screech rises between us as Danny straightens with difficulty, staring at something on the floor. "My waters have broken."

A flurry of activity starts. Mama and Tilly take care of the puddle, Walter massages Danny's shoulders and I pick up the little case she packed for the hospital.

Baby Annegret is born on July 15 and we're in love.

CHAPTER THIRTY-NINE

By October, it becomes clear that Stalin is keeping his word. At least as far as the blockade is concerned. Roads and railways are open, and all three airports are ceasing airlift operations. Angry about the new West German government with its own democratic constitution, Stalin has been kicking out the last Germans from eastern territories. Every day, more refugees arrive in Berlin, transporting their belongings on backs and carts, aggravating the lack of livable space further.

After saying goodbye to Albert and Karl—they've taken over the remainder of the room—we've moved into our new place, with running water in the kitchen and a bathroom I can lock. The former renter has left us a sofa I'm sleeping on for now, two beds, chairs and a table, and lots of kitchen utensils. It is pure heaven, though I know it is short-lived.

I've got a train ticket for the day after tomorrow, October 7, to Frankfurt.

After work, I head back to our old apartment to pick up two books Albert had borrowed. The divider blanket has gone, the room clean and orderly.

"Why don't you have dinner with us?" Albert asks, pointing at the scrubbed dining table that used to be shoved against the wall.

Karl, who's grown three inches in the last year, and whose voice is doing somersaults, is smiling at me. "We made bean soup."

"I've got to get home," I say, stashing the books in my bag and heading for the door. "You should visit soon, I—" The knock on the door startles me. "Are you expecting anyone?"

Albert and Karl look at each other, shake their heads.

I open the door, shrink back. In the shadows of the hallway looms a man of undeterminable age. "I'm looking for Leni Berger." The figure's voice is soft, halting.

"She no longer lives here." It's the last thing that comes out of my mouth, because in that instant I know who the man in the tattered clothes is. I fly forward into his arms, mumble and sob at the same time. "Papa."

Arms envelop me, formerly strong, muscular arms that now feel like twigs ready to break. "Lotte?" Papa sounds wonderous as he hugs me to his chest.

I draw back and take his hand, pull him into the room. "Albert, Karl, this is my father."

I nearly cry out because in the light of the low sun that shines through the window, I see my father's state, the patched clothes and shoes, the old hat. But worst is his face, the eyes so tired, he looks like he needs to sleep for a year. The skin around his mouth and eyes is saggy, deep lines cross his forehead. He wipes his eyes, shakes hands with Albert and Karl.

I explain that we've moved and, after saying goodbye, lead him gently to the street.

It is a thirty-minute walk to our new place, but with Papa it takes an hour. He walks slowly like an old man, stares in wonder and shock at the streets of Berlin.

"Everything is torn apart," he comments at some point.

I wrap an arm around him, thinking how much worse it had been in '45. "It is a slow process, but at least the blockade has ended."

"Oh, Lotte, how grown you are. A young woman." He coughs and I'm immediately reminded of Meg and Fritz, both of them dying of lung diseases. *Please let him be all right.* "Mama wrote that you're translating for the Americans."

I think of my train ticket that will take me away in two days. I cannot tell Papa, not now.

As I unlock the door to our new apartment, my heart beats in my neck. "Mama," is all I can get out.

Tilly comes running, followed by Mama, who stops in her tracks as if she's seen a ghost. In a way, Papa is a ghost of his former self, a man who has seen too much. Just one of millions of men who has experienced war and imprisonment.

Papa moves forward and slowly takes my mother into his arms. "Leni, I'm home."

Mama begins to cry. There are no sounds, just two trembling people who have found each other.

I follow Tilly into the kitchen, where the others already sit at the table.

"What happened?" Danny asks, her expression full of concern.

Margo cries, "Lotte, why are you crying?"

I wipe my face and produce a watery smile. "Everything is wonderful. Papa is home."

Saying it out loud, it finally sinks in that all the worry, all the waiting has finally come to an end. Mama has a husband again, I a father.

Our family has mended.

Tempelhof has quieted, the hectic urgency is gone. Desks stand empty, air traffic is reduced to a trickle, Thomas's office sits deserted. I'm sorting through a stack of papers, pack up boxes to be shipped to Frankfurt. Everything kept on the airbase remains under lock.

I'm ready for a new chapter, a fresh start, even if I will miss my father once again. Only now he is safe, and I can visit him any time I want.

Thomas mentioned something about a room I can rent from a widow. That will have to do for a while. I doubt Frankfurt has many places to choose from.

"Lotte?"

I look up from my files and am face to face with Mitch. My mind goes blank as I open and close my mouth. Mitch looks extra tall in his formal uniform. Obviously, he didn't fly.

"I was worried I'd miss you."

"Packing up," I say, unable to look away. "I thought you went home."

"I did, but then I came back." He keeps looking at me, which makes me fidget. "Do you have time to talk?"

I wave, encompassing the emptiness around us. "Be my guest, we're alone."

Mitch sits down in front of my desk. Nobody ever sat there because I was mostly gone and didn't have many visitors.

I sink into my chair, trying to breathe normally.

He's taken off his hat, which he balances on his right knee. "I'm sure glad this crazy project is done."

"All of Berlin is grateful. You saved us, you and the other Allies." I look toward the window with the nearly empty tarmac outside. "I don't know what I would've done if Stalin had gotten his way."

"He didn't and he won't in the future."

I shrug. "Not so sure, he always seems to have some surprise up his sleeve." I think about my father, who endured four years in a Siberian gulag. I think about Fritz, whose guilt about caving to the Russians destroyed him.

Mitch appears tense, even nervous. "What are you going to do now that your job here ends?"

"You didn't hear?"

"Hear what?"

"I'm moving to Frankfurt to assist there. I'm thinking of going to school to become a certified translator, maybe start my own office. With all those Americans, there'll be lots of demand."

Mitch looks perplexed, the line between his brows deepens. "You've got it all figured out."

I force a smile. *Not really. Not by a long shot.* "You never said why you're here," I say aloud.

"To see you. I wanted… I feel bad about our last meeting."

"That was months ago."

Mitch waves an arm to cut me off. "Please let me finish. I was angry because you lied to me, well, you didn't lie, but you withheld something, just like in '45. I felt betrayed, angry… sad, too." Our eyes meet before he looks away again. "After a while, I realized what a hypocrite I was." Again, he looks at me, this time our eye contact holds. "I lied to you, too, withheld things. I was ashamed, felt guilty."

I say nothing, just hold my breath, as Mitch leans forward. "Do you remember when I told you I had no siblings?"

I nod. It had been that evening when we went to the British club. I'd asked him about his family, where he lived.

"I had a brother… Todd… who died eleven years ago. I was eighteen, he fourteen and I was supposed to take care of him while my parents were visiting family in Ohio. But I was dating this girl from school, trying to get laid before starting college. I let Todd borrow my car because the girl was visiting, and I had big plans. I thought he'd take the car around the property, like we'd practiced. But Todd was in the mood for ice cream and decided to visit town for a root beer float."

Mitch wipes a sleeve across his eyes. Clears his throat. "There's this tight curve not far from our property and around it came this tractor. Todd must've panicked, maybe confused gas and brake pedals. He missed the tractor, but hit a tree at full speed. He died instantly, still had ice cream sticking to his lips." Mitch lets out a long breath. "While I was making out, my little brother died a mile away."

"What did your parents say?"

Mitch gets up, throws his cap on the chair. "Thing is, they never said anything. But I know they blamed me. God, I blamed myself, still do. I had to leave, joined the army instead of college. Turns out I had a knack for flying." He returns to the desk, leans across. "So, you see, I was lying the entire time."

"You were hurt, just like I was." I slowly rise and walk around the desk, take his hand. "Some hurt is too great to let out. It is easier to keep it hidden because you don't know what happens if you allow it to surface. It may tear you to pieces."

Mitch pulls me into his arms. "You've got no reason to forgive me, but I wanted to try… let you know that I'm still thinking about you."

I lean against his chest, feel the fabric of his uniform jacket press into my cheek. I'm feeling warm… protected. "Maybe the third time *is* the charm." I lift my face to his, his eyes so close now, the blue sparkles. Then I see nothing, because my eyes close as we kiss.

My body recognizes him, becomes yielding and pliable. In the corridor, footsteps grow louder, and we pull apart. I hurry around the desk, glad to sit down to give my weak knees a break.

Mitch plops down in his chair once more. "What now?"

I grin and say, "Maybe we can make the third time stick."

Mitch grins back. "Maybe we can."

EPILOGUE

It turns out that the Frankfurt-Main airbase doesn't have nearly enough work for me, so I've signed up for translating classes with the goal of becoming officially certified. I'm also working on a business plan for how to create a language school with a translation service for Frankfurt's growing business world.

After being promoted again, Mitch has requested a move back to Germany, which is pretty easy, because most servicemen are ready to leave. If the war has taught me one thing, it is to be patient and endure. Waiting times for remodeled flats are sometimes years, but Thomas helped Mitch find a two-room apartment we've moved into for now. It only has one coal stove and a tiny bathroom, but what does it matter?

Mitch has proposed and I've accepted, though we will wait until the spring. We want to have our families here to attend and give us time to organize a venue.

Frankfurt is different from Berlin, freer, more dynamic and growing. Construction is everywhere and though the war's footprint of destruction is obvious at nearly every corner, I miss Berlin. Maybe it is the fighting spirit I'm missing. It had been like an invisible band of camaraderie, us against Stalin and his oppression. Frankfurters are edgier, harder, maybe more progressive. In the end, I sense a new freedom, not just for the country, our new western democracy with its own constitution, but also for myself. In paragraph one it proclaims that "the dignity of man is inviolable."

I can't remember a time when we had dignity—until now. Many

Germans played along, admired, and supported Hitler or kept their mouths shut, and that guilt will remain with us as long as we remember history. Hitler had no respect for human beings, not for his perceived enemies, nor for the citizens of his own country. Stalin is no different. A dictator lives for control and represents the opposite of freedom, an ugly combination of power and greed. Many families are still waiting for their men to return from Russian gulags.

Right after Mitch showed up in Berlin, Stalin created the German Democratic Republic or GDR, the socialist counterpart of its democratic neighbor. He may not have succeeded in taking all of Berlin, but he did succeed in splitting Germany. Funny how they call it a *Democratic Republic*, when there's nothing democratic about it, just an extension of Russia.

Thanks to Mitch and all the brave Allies, West Berlin persevered, even if it sits like an island in the middle of East Germany.

"You ready?" Mitch appears in the door to the bathroom, where I've been getting ready. I notice his admiring glance, the smile playing around his lips. "Or maybe we should stay in? You look too good to share."

It's true, I feel amazing in the glittering black dress. It's a simple cut, but my hair is brushed to a shine, not to be outdone by the light in my eyes. I close the drawer where a button rests inside a handkerchief. I no longer carry them, both men have returned to my life.

I embrace Mitch, peck a kiss on his lips. "Not a chance, I've got to see this Christmas party of yours, meet your commander."

As he pulls me close, I feel him chuckle. "But only if you take that off as soon as we return."

I wiggle out of his arms and hand him his hat. "I think that can be arranged, Captain Cameron."

The End

AUTHOR'S NOTE

Gail Halverson

Colonel Gail Halverson (1920-2022) was an American pilot, who rose to fame during the Berlin airlift, when he shared two sticks of gum with a crowd of German children. Inspired by their comments to preserve their freedom, he concocted a way to drop chocolate and gum above Berlin. The candy bomber affixed handkerchiefs to sweets and before a drop, alerted the waiting crowd of kids by wiggling his wings, thus coining the term "Uncle Wiggly Wings." Halverson's efforts soon spread, other pilots chipped in their sweets and at some point, word reached to the highest levels of government. Gail Halverson became the face of the airlift, inspiring the US to help Berlin's starving population, cementing the friendship of two countries. He also demonstrated what was sorely missing in 1948, when Stalin held Berlin in an iron grip: he showed compassion for a beaten-down people, but more importantly, he provided hope. Until his death in 2022, he returned to Berlin to meet with the former children of Berlin, who held him in high honor. To this day, he is celebrated as one of the most influential people of the airlift.

Germany's Basic Law (Grundgesetz)

To this day, the constitution or Grundgesetz of the Federal Republic of Germany is the bedstone of Germany's democracy. It was passed by the parliamentary council of Germany's western states and ratified by the western allies. In nineteen articles, the law spells out the basic rights and responsibilities of citizens, beginning with: *Human dignity is inviolable. It is the duty of all state authorities to respect and protect it.* Other articles describe rights of equality, freedom of speech and religion, protection of marriage and family, school education, the right to assemble peacefully and so on. This law was passed in the face of the Soviet threat from the east, and cemented the cold war that would last until Germany's reunification in 1989/1990. It also highlighted the differences between Germany's east and west. The former German Democratic Republic (GDR), instated on October 7, 1949, was Stalin's answer to the democratic western states. Though it carries "democratic" in its name, the GDR was an autocracy, whose ideology of Marxism/Leninism had been dictated by the Soviets. After experiencing Hitler's dictatorship for thirteen years, the citizens of former East Germany continued to live under strict control until the peaceful resolution and reunification forty years later.

Tempelhof Airport

The old Tempelhof Airport has been turned into a museum and houses refugees in some areas. The former landing areas have been turned into a park, where Berliners can picnic, bike, or roller skate. Here are some images from my visit to Berlin in 2023. In front of the former main entrance (below), an exhibit tells about the airlift. Across the street in a small park, the airlift monument depicts the three air corridors used to supply the western sector of Berlin and memorializes the victims of the airlift. Two more identical monuments stand in Frankfurt/Main and in Celle. Berliners, always keeping a sense of humor, call this monument *Hungerharke*, or hunger rake.

The size of the airport is difficult to capture in a single photo. It took us more than an hour and a half to circle the building. Nearly all images from the time of the airlift depict portions of the building, but mostly concentrate on the activity on the airfield.

Tempelhof Airport, street view, partial view of right hangars

Tempelhof Airport, airfield view of main building

Tempelhof Field, Airlift Monument (with author)

ABOUT THE AUTHOR

Perhaps Annette Oppenlander became a writer of historical novels because she likes to dig in the past. It all started when she asked her parents about their experiences as war children. Over many years, these emotional memories developed into the biographical novel "Surviving the Fatherland." Not only did this story win many awards, it also served as the springboard to a successful writing career.

Ms. Oppenlander likes to shed light on difficult subjects such as World War II from the perspective of civilian Germany, walks alongside ordinary people in the American Civil War or the Middle Ages. To create an authentic historical world, she often uses biographical information, interviews contemporary witnesses and unearths little known facts in the archives.

After studying business administration at the University of Cologne, Germany, Ms. Oppenlander spent 30 years in various parts of the United States. She writes her novels in German and English, and also shares her knowledge – writing workshops, entertaining presentations and author visits to universities and schools, libraries, retirement homes and organizations dedicated to literature – in

German and English. She now lives with her American husband and dog Zelda in the beautiful Münsterland in Germany.

"Nearly every place holds some kind of secret, something that makes history come alive. When we scrutinize people and places closely, history is no longer a date or number, it turns into a story."

From the Author

Thank you for reading 'When the Skies Rained Freedom.' My sincere hope is that you derived as much entertainment from reading this story as I enjoyed in researching and creating it. If you have a few moments, please feel free to add your review of the book at your favorite online site for feedback (Amazon, Apple iTunes Store, Goodreads, etc.). Also, if you would like to connect with previous or upcoming books, please visit my website for information and to sign up for e-news: http://www.annetteoppenlander.com.

Sincerely, Annette

Contact Me

Website: annetteoppenlander.com
Facebook: www.facebook.com/annetteoppenlanderauthor
Email: hello@annetteoppenlander.com
Instagram: @annette.oppenlander
Twitter: @aoppenlander
Pinterest: @annoppenlander

www.ingramcontent.com/pod-product-compliance
Lightning Source LLC
LaVergne TN
LVHW020727200726
843506LV00009B/652